Exploring SOCIAL STUDIES
BOOK 2
GRADES 4–6

Venture into the world of social studies with *The Best Of* The Mailbox® *Exploring Social Studies • Book 2.* This compilation of social studies units—selected from the 1994–98 issues of the Intermediate edition of *The Mailbox*® magazine—will prove to be an invaluable classroom resource.

Senior Editor:
Thad H. McLaurin

Associate Editor:
Rusty Fischer

Art Coordinator:
Teresa R. Davidson

Cover Artist:
Jennifer Tipton Bennett

©1999 by THE EDUCATION CENTER, INC.
All rights reserved.
ISBN# 1-56234-273-8

Except as provided for herein, no part of this publication may be reproduced or transmitted in any form or by any means, electronic or mechanical, including photocopying, recording, or storing in any information storage and retrieval system or electronic on-line bulletin board, without prior written permission from The Education Center, Inc. Permission is given to the original purchaser to reproduce patterns and reproducibles for individual classroom use only and not for resale or distribution. Reproduction for an entire school or school system is prohibited. Please direct written inquiries to The Education Center, Inc., P.O. Box 9753, Greensboro, NC 27429-0753. The Education Center®, *The Mailbox*®, and the mailbox/post/grass logo are registered trademarks of The Education Center, Inc. All other brand or product names are trademarks or registered trademarks of their respective companies.

Manufactured in the United States
10 9 8 7 6 5 4 3 2 1

Table Of Contents

The United States 3
   Colonial America 4–11
   Plymouth 12–13
   The Revolutionary War 14–19
   Westward Movement 20–25
   The Civil War 26–32
   World War II 33–46
   The Presidential Election Process 42–46
   Celebrate Your State 47–50
   Native Americans Of The Pacific Northwest ... 51–54

The World 55
   Latin Americans 56–62
   Voyages, Explorations, And Conquests 63–68
   Ancient Rome 69–73
   European Travelogue 74–79
   The Medieval World 80–86
   Ancient Egypt 87–92
   Writing Research Papers
      On Foreign Countries 93–99
   Africa 100–106
   Peace And Conflict 107–111
   The Inuit 112–117
   World Map 118

Social Studies Specials 119
   Get A Jump On Geography 120–134
   A Nose For News 135–140
   Map Skills 141–145
   Sail Into Social Studies 146–148
   Traveling Travelogs 149–153
   Setting The Stage For Social Studies 154–156

Answer Keys 157–160

The United States

Picturing The Past
Innovative Activities For Studying Colonial America

They came to the New World for different reasons: adventure, an improved life, religious freedom, forced slavery. When settlers and slaves came to North America, they brought traditions native to their homelands. Little did they know that the strange environment they encountered would alter those traditions and lead to a uniquely "American" lifestyle that was a blend of the familiar and the original. Take a closer look at life in colonial America with the following creative activities and reproducibles.

by Nomi J. Waldman and Becky Andrews

Helpful Background Information

The colonial period began in 1607 with the settlement of Jamestown and ended with the start of the Revolutionary War in 1775. It began with a few hardy colonists. By the time it was over, more than two million European settlers called the New World home. Instead of the rough, primitive conditions of the earliest settlers, there was a land of thriving farms and plantations, prosperous towns and small cities, and well-established schools, churches, and institutions of government. No longer solely dependent on foreign shipments of basic goods, these later colonists grew and produced enough to maintain a brisk trade with England and other countries. What began as scattered settlements along the Atlantic coast grew to 13 flourishing colonies and a frontier that stretched westward for hundreds of miles.

Marvelous Map Memos

As curious Native Americans watched the earliest settlers land on their soil, they must have had two burning questions: *who* are these people and *why* are they here? Help your students answer these questions with an engaging map and research activity. Begin by enlarging the map on page 7 (leaving off all labels) and mounting it on a bulletin board. With students' help, label and color the 13 colonies. Follow up by having students complete the reproducible map activity on page 7.

The colonies are often divided into three distinct regions (see the chart). Show these divisions by pinning a different color of yarn around each region. Duplicate the "Marvelous Map Memos" on page 8 on colored paper to match the yarn colors. Next divide the class into three groups: New England Colonies, Middle Colonies, and Southern Colonies. Give each group resource books and a supply of its colored memos. Have groups research to find out *who* came to their regions and *why* they came. Encourage students also to find facts about the Native Americans in their regions and how they responded to the invasion of settlers. Have students write each fact on a map memo, staple the memo to the board, and connect it to the correct region with matching colored yarn. Add to the map throughout your colonial American study.

Scout It Out

Make students aware of geography's role in the development of each region with another fun group activity. Keep the same regional groups used in "Marvelous Map Memos" or form new ones. Tell the groups that they are now official colonial scouting parties, hired by the English monarchy to explore each region and report back on its suitability for colonization. The categories the scouts are to report on include the region's physical features, climate, and resources. Have each group research its region and log its information on copies of the scouting report on page 9. On the day groups are to present their findings, play the role of King James I of England by wearing a paper crown and a large, beach-towel "robe." Ask each group to present its findings and recommendations as to colonization possibilities. After the presentations, discuss the similarities and differences between the regions. How does the growing season in the Southern Colonies compare to New England's? Which area would be most suitable for large farms? Which region is the most mountainous? How will that affect travel?

New England Colonies:
MA, NH, CT, RI

Middle Colonies:
PA, DE, NJ, NY

Southern Colonies:
MD, VA, NC, SC, GA

Nothing Simple About It

For today's young consumers, acquiring food, clothes, and other household items is as easy as a quick drive to the local K-mart. Not so for colonial Americans! When it came to clothing, for example, a colonial family was responsible for the entire process: raising sheep for wool, gathering plants to make dyes, carding and spinning the wool into thread, weaving and dyeing the cloth, and sewing the clothes.

At the beginning of your colonial American unit, give each student a card labeled with an everyday item (see the list below). Ask, "How would your family obtain this item if they lived in colonial times?" During free time, have students use resource books to find out how their items were obtained. Have each student draw a picture or make a model of his item; then have him complete a copy of the reproducible tag on page 8 and attach it to his picture or model. Hold a Simple Things Symposium during which each student shares his item and information. Display the items/pictures at a learning center for lots of free-time browsing.

Items: cooking pot, shirt, rocking chair, pillow, broom, hammer, bucket, bread, apple pie, candle, hat, socks, doll, soap, pair of shoes, ax, table, vegetable soup, blanket, bowl

Different Places, Different Faces

America's diversity began during the colonial period. Colonists came from homelands with different languages, religions, and customs. In the earliest years, most colonists were farmers. As the population grew, many people left the farms for small cities and towns where they became craftsmen, merchants, shopkeepers, manufacturers, and traders. There were also differences in economic status. Some colonists grew wealthy. Others were unskilled laborers, indentured servants, or slaves who lacked the training, skill, or opportunity to lift themselves out of poverty. Somewhere in the middle were those who owned property but were not wealthy.

Acquaint students with the diversity of colonial America by having each child take the role of a colonial youngster. Give each student a copy of the reproducible on page 10. Discuss the information listed on the sheet. Inform students that in addition to parents and siblings, a colonial child was likely to share his home with other relatives, such as a grandparent, an unmarried aunt or uncle, or a cousin whose mother had died. Have students complete their census forms; then let them discuss their choices. At the end of the discussion, have each child cut out his form and glue it to a large index card. Collect the cards; then use the information on them to form cooperative groups for the following activity.

Let Me Introduce Myself

After taking on the personality of an early American child in the preceding activity, it's time for each student to find out what his or her life in colonial America is like. Use the census forms completed in the preceding activity to divide the class into research teams, grouping students according to colonies, places of origin, or economic status. For fun, have each student make a nametag labeled with his colonial identity to wear during research periods. Provide students with construction paper and notebook paper with which to make research logs. As students gather research on family life, education, shelter, recreation, and other aspects of colonial living, have them note the information in their logs. Have students use the information to complete any of the following application activities:

- Keep a journal for several days. Tell about yourself, your family, and your friends. Describe your schooling, your chores, and how you have fun.

- Draw a picture of yourself outside your house. Write a brief description of the rooms and furnishings. Describe your favorite room in detail.

- On a piece of tagboard, draw and cut out a paper doll of yourself that is 12 inches tall. On separate pieces of paper, draw some of the clothes you wear to fit on your paper doll. Don't forget to draw tabs on the clothing so you can attach it to your cut-out. Include other articles that you might carry, such as needlework, tools, etc.

- Use graph paper to draw a diagram of your farm, neighborhood, or frontier settlement. Label the buildings and show such items as roads, rivers, gardens, stables, and fields. If you live on the frontier, show what defenses have been set up to protect settlers. If you live in the city, be sure to label all of the businesses and residences in your neighborhood.

- Write a conversation that your family might have after dinner at the end of a long day. Write the conversation in the form of a short skit. Make simple stick puppets of your family. With a friend, practice the puppet skit and perform it for the class.

School Days

What was school like 250 years ago? Children of wealthy colonists had tutors or were sent to private schools. Colonists established some schools, but most children from poor families were taught by their parents at home. New England had many private "dame schools" held in the homes of women who taught the alphabet, spelling, writing, and simple arithmetic. Many children got their education by becoming apprentices, taught by their masters as they learned a trade such as carpentry or housekeeping.

A famous textbook used in colonial days was *The New England Primer*. It taught the alphabet using two-line rhymes, some of which taught moral values such as "A **dog** will bite a thief at night." Create your own updated version of *The New England Primer* by assigning each pair of students one or two letters of the alphabet. Have each pair write a two-lined rhyme for each letter. Copying the format of the original book (see the illustration below), have students compile their rhymes and illustrations on large pieces of paper to make a giant, class big book. Display the book in your school's library for other classes to enjoy.

C  The cat doth play
And after slay.

D  A dog will bite
A thief at night.

E   An eagle's flight
Is out of sight.

Learning A Trade

A boy (and sometimes a girl) often left home at the age of 14 to become an apprentice to a craftsman. For the next three to seven years, he would become part of his master's household and learn the master's trade. The apprenticeship benefited everyone. The boy's parents had one less mouth to feed, clothe, and house. The master had a helper. And the boy not only learned a trade but was also taught to read and write by his master.

Write the list of craftsmen found on page 10 on the chalkboard. Discuss the various trades and have students add other occupations they learned about in their research activities to the list. Explain that some craftsmen also were shopkeepers who sold their goods to the public. The shops were often identified by wooden signs hanging outside the shops' doors. Have each student choose a trade he would have liked to apprentice had he lived in colonial days. After looking in resource books to learn about the trade, have the student design a sign for the shop, using the reproducible pattern on page 11. Post the cut-out signs on a bulletin board entitled "Signs Of Colonial Times."

The Other Colonial Americans

When studying colonial America, it's easy to romanticize the period and forget two groups of people whose lives were adversely affected by America's colonization. For African-Americans and Native Americans, this period brought oppression and slavery rather than independence and opportunity. Slaves had little hope of improving their lots in life. Native Americans, who were initially friendly and helpful towards colonists, soon learned that the settlers were committed to taking over their lands.

Help students understand the impact of colonization on these two important groups with the help of outstanding children's literature. Jean Fritz's excellent book, *The Double Life Of Pocahontas*, provides a vivid picture of the conflict between Jamestown colonists and the Native Americans whose land they began to colonize. *I Am Regina* by Sally M. Keehn is based on a true account of a young colonial girl who grows to admire her Native American captors and regrets leaving them when returned to her former life. To shed light on the African-American experience, share excerpts from *Many Thousand Gone: African Americans From Slavery To Freedom* by Virginia Hamilton. This outstanding book includes direct quotes from actual slave narratives.

Map skills

THE ENGLISH COLONIES IN 1763

0 100 200 mi.

- Massachusetts
- New Hampshire
- Rhode Island
- Connecticut
- New York
- New Jersey
- Pennsylvania
- Delaware
- Maryland
- Virginia
- North Carolina
- South Carolina
- Georgia

Name _____

The Start Of Something Big!

It all started here—13 small colonies on their way to becoming 50 states! Color in each box with a different color or pattern to make a key. Use your social studies book to help you color each colony. Remember: the solid lines show the state boundaries today.

- ☐ Connecticut
- ☐ Delaware
- ☐ Georgia
- ☐ Maryland
- ☐ Massachusetts
- ☐ New Hampshire
- ☐ New Jersey
- ☐ New York
- ☐ North Carolina
- ☐ Pennsylvania
- ☐ Rhode Island
- ☐ South Carolina
- ☐ Virginia

Check each item that can be found on the map; then label the item on the map. If an item can't be found on the map, write "NOT!" In the blank.

____ Atlantic Ocean
____ Great Salt Lake
____ Boston
____ Charleston
____ Jamestown
____ Pacific Ocean
____ Canada
____ New York City
____ Plymouth
____ Mexico

Note To Teacher: For instructions on how to use this reproducible, see page 4.

Patterns

Use with "Nothing Simple About It" on page 5.

Researcher: _____
Item: _____
How item was made: _____
_____
_____
_____
_____
_____
_____
Who made item: _____
_____
Approximate hours of labor: _____

©1999 The Education Center, Inc. • *The Best Of* The Mailbox® *Social Studies* • *Intermediate* • TEC1474

Use with "Marvelous Map Memos" on page 4.

Marvelous Map Memo
Researcher(s): _____
Region: _____
Fact: _____
Resource used: _____

Marvelous Map Memo
Researcher(s): _____
Region: _____
Fact: _____
Resource used: _____

Name(s) _____   Research, critical thinking

A New World Scouting Report

By order of King James I of England, this scouting party has traveled to the New World and explored the region known as

_____.

Below is a summary of the area.

Physical features (land and water): _____

_____
_____
_____
_____
_____
_____
_____

Climate: _____

_____
_____
_____
_____
_____
_____

Valuable resources: _____

_____
_____
_____
_____
_____

Recommendations concerning colonization:
Should this area be colonized? _____ Why or why not? _____

_____
_____

What predictions can you make about life in this colony? _____

_____
_____
_____

Note To Teacher: Use with "Scout It Out" on page 4. Have each student/group fill in the blank at the top of the page with the name of the colonial American region (New England Colonies, Middle Colonies, Southern Colonies) or colony to be researched.

A Colonial American Identity

What would your life be like if you lived in colonial America? Pretend that you are a colonial American boy or girl by filling out the census form. (A *census* is a count of a place's population.) Use the information below to help you complete the form.

PLACES OF ORIGIN:
England *(largest numbers in the New England Colonies)*
Africa *(homeland of slaves who were brought against their will to the New World)*
Germany *(Middle Colonies, Virginia, Carolinas)*
Ireland *(Middle Colonies, Virginia, Carolinas)*
Netherlands *(Middle Colonies)*
France *(several colonies from Massachusetts to South Carolina)*

COLONIES:
New England Colonies: *Massachusetts, Connecticut, New Hampshire, Rhode Island*
Middle Colonies: *New Jersey, Pennsylvania, New York, Delaware*
Southern Colonies: *Maryland, Virginia, North Carolina, South Carolina, Georgia*

My father is a/an...

Farmer	**Craftsmen:** lived in cities and towns
Merchant	Shoemaker — Wig maker
Blacksmith	Cabinetmaker — Cooper
Planter (Southern Colonies)	Baker — Potter
Shipbuilder	Tailor — Hatter
Fisherman	Bricklayer — Weaver
Miller	Printer — Silversmith
Minister	Clockmaker — Housewright

Other: Slave, Indentured servant

Colonial Census Form

Name: _____

Colonial name: _____

Colony: _____

Place of origin: _____

Father's name: _____ Date: _____ Age: _____

My father is a/an: _____

Other family members (names and ages): _____

Note To Teacher: Have each student cut out his census form and glue it to a large index card. Use the cards with "Different Places, Different Faces" and "Let Me Introduce Myself" on page 5. Use the craftsmen list with "Learning A Trade" on page 6.

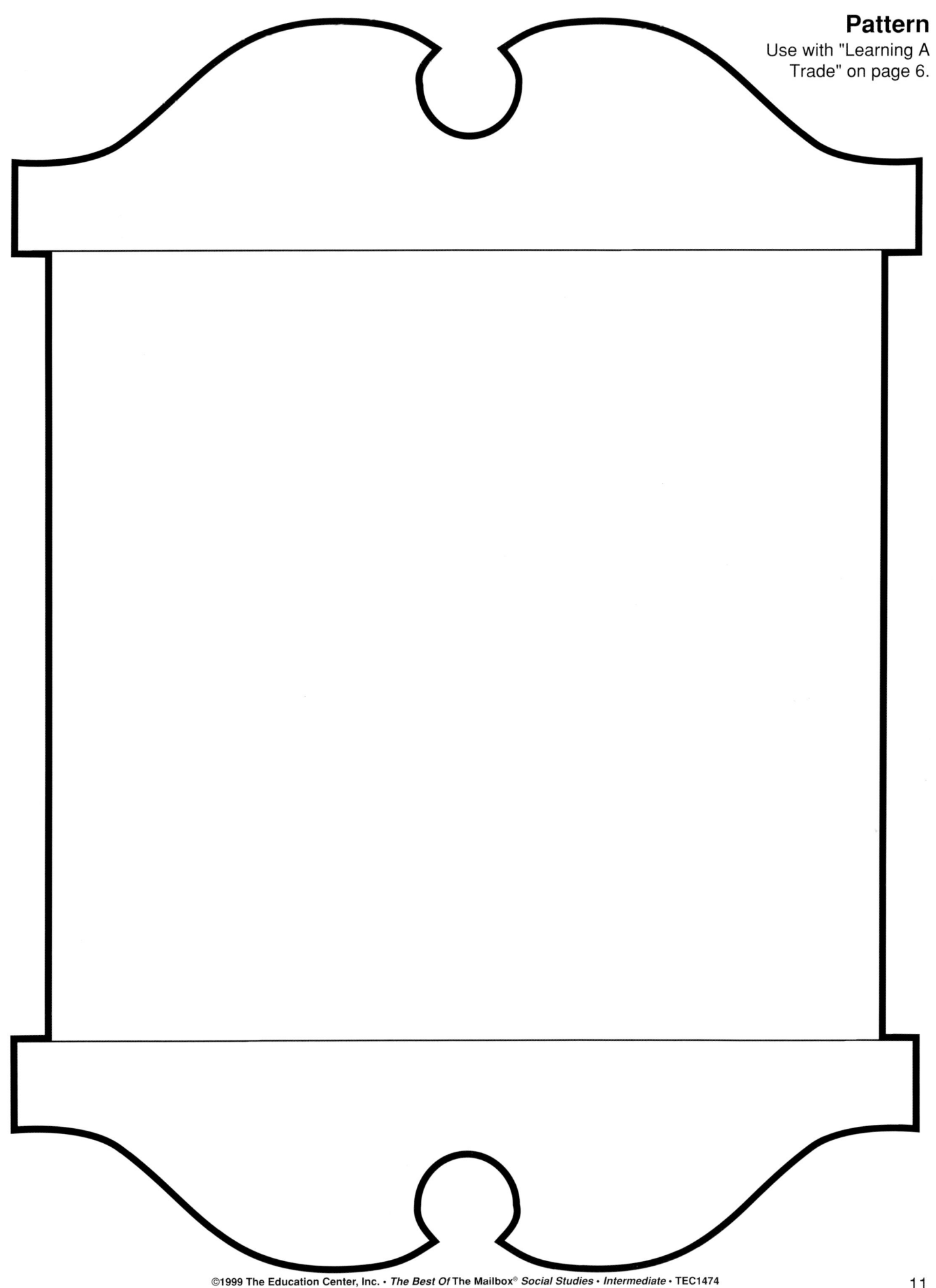

Pattern
Use with "Learning A Trade" on page 6.

Plymouth Revisited

Creative Activities For Studying The Pilgrims

As our nation celebrates Thanksgiving Day this November, visions of a large gathering of happy Pilgrims and Native Americans breaking bread together will likely come to mind. But just how accurate are those images? Help your students fine-tune their knowledge about Thanksgiving's beginnings and the people of Plymouth with the following thought-provoking activities.

with activities by Terry Healy

How To Use These Activities

The approach of Thanksgiving provides a timely opportunity to involve your students in some fascinating investigative research, creative projects, and learning-packed experiences. Ask your media specialist to help you gather plenty of resources about the Pilgrims. As a class, complete one or more activities each week during the month of November. If you prefer a cooperative learning approach, divide students into investigative teams. Assign three to four of the activities to each team. Or form interest groups and let students choose their own activities. Have groups present their finished projects during a "Plymouth Revisited" forum, to which you've invited parents or other classes.

ACTIVITIES

- While legend would have us believe that all Plymouth residents wore dull-colored clothing and tall black hats, the truth is much different. Wills left by citizens of Plymouth show estates that included scarlet-colored capes, yellow skirts, and other bright adornments. Have students research the clothing and other lifestyle elements of Plymouth's citizens. Then have each child pretend to be a Plymouth resident. Instruct the student to write a will listing his possessions and who is to receive them at his death. Remind students that their wills should reflect life as it *really* was in Plymouth.

- Even though they had some information about the New World—including maps from Jamestown and trading expeditions—the Pilgrims did not have an accurate picture of their destination. There were tales of miraculous plants, Indians who worshiped the white man, mountains of gold, and even fountains of youth! Have students research to find out what the Pilgrims thought about the New World before setting sail. Then have each child pretend to be William Bradford, the second governor of the colony. Instruct the student to write a journal entry—dated September 15, 1620 (the day before the *Mayflower* left England)—in which Bradford tells what he expects to find in America.

- Sailing to America on the *Mayflower* was not a thrilling adventure, but a perilous trial for the Pilgrims. Hundreds of pounds of cargo—together with 102 men, women, and children, and a menagerie of dogs, cats, birds, and livestock—were crammed into a very small ship. Challenge students to try this experiment to see what life was like on the *Mayflower*. First, tell students to imagine sitting on a single bed, the approximate amount of space each grown person had on the *Mayflower*. In this space, a Pilgrim adult had to cook all her meals, take care of her children, store her possessions, and spend most of her time. Now have students imagine sitting on their beds for an hour, unable to leave. (To help them envision an hour, have students imagine not leaving their beds until they had watched an entire episode of "Star Trek," including commercials.) Tell them to imagine the terrible odors that would be around because of the lack of sanitation. The *Mayflower* also encountered lots of bad storms. So have students imagine that every few minutes someone throws a bucket of icy water on them, and that the ship is pitching so violently that they have to be tied to their beds. At the end of the session, have each child write in his journal about the experience. How did he feel? How would he feel knowing that he had to live like this for many more weeks? How would he feel when land was finally sighted?

- The Plymouth colony was able to live peaceably with the nearby Native Americans for more than 50 years. The Indians—particularly two English-speaking natives named Samoset and Squanto—taught the Pilgrims many new skills that were vital to their survival. Have students research the relationship between the Plymouth colonists and their Native American neighbors; then have them research the colonist/Indian relationship in Jamestown and the Massachusetts Bay Colony. Finally have students compare the three colonies by making large Venn diagrams.

- In several famous paintings, the Pilgrims—including some women—are shown stepping triumphantly onto Plymouth Rock to begin their new lives. In reality, the *Mayflower* stayed anchored off the New England coast for about six weeks while an appropriate site for the settlement was chosen. When supplies—especially beer—began to run low, the exhausted Pilgrims decided on the Plymouth location. There were no triumphant speeches or celebrations—nor is there any evidence that women or Indians were present. The weary Pilgrims simply got to work unloading provisions and building a shelter from the freezing weather. Share some of the romanticized pictures of the Pilgrims; then have each student draw his own version of the Pilgrims' arrival at Plymouth.

- Many of the early citizens of Plymouth chose names for their children which today seem highly unusual. Share this list with students; then have them guess which individuals were male or female. Have students speculate about the reasons for some of the name choices.

  Oceanus Hopkins (male; born on board the *Mayflower* as it was sailing to America)
  Wrestling Brewster (male; named for "wrestling with the Devil")
  Love Brewster (male)
  Fear Brewster (female)
  Patience Brewster (female)
  Desire Minter (female)
  Humility Cooper (female)
  Peregrine White (male; name means "pilgrim"; lived to be 83 years old)
  Resolved White (male)
  Experience Mitchell (male)
  Remember Allerton (female)
  Constant Southworth (male)

- The first winter in Plymouth was anything but celebratory. Almost everyone got sick. Scarcely 50 people—only six of whom were women—survived that winter. Have students research the winter of 1620–1621. Then have each child pretend to be one of Plymouth's inhabitants and write a letter to a relative back in England. In the letter, have the student describe the conditions under which he/she lived during the winter of 1620–1621.

Fighting For Independence

Creative Ideas For Studying The Revolutionary War

Freedom—it's a gift that we often take for granted. Not so for the early Americans who fought fiercely to gain independence from the British during the Revolutionary War. Help your students catch the spirit of '76 as they study this classic conflict with the following creative ideas and activities!

by Lisa Waller Rogers

How It All Started

War doesn't happen overnight, and this one was 12 years in the making! Use this research project to study the events leading up to the Revolutionary War. Divide your class into six groups. Assign each group one of the events leading up to the war listed below. Instruct each group to research the event, then prepare a short skit about it to teach the rest of the class. Have each group perform its skit for the class in chronological order.

Causes Of The American Revolution

- 1763—Parliament issued the Proclamation of 1763.
- 1765—Parliament passed the Stamp Act.
- 1767—Parliament passed the Townshend Acts.
- 1768—British soldiers moved into Boston, which eventually triggered the Boston Massacre in 1770.
- 1773—Boston colonists took part in the Boston Tea Party.
- 1774—The British passed strict laws that colonists called the Intolerable Acts.

The Midnight Ride

In 1775, British General Thomas Gage ordered Lieutenant Colonel Francis Smith and 700 men to Concord. They were to destroy colonists' military supplies there and arrest Samuel Adams and John Hancock for treason. This secret plan was discovered. On the morning of April 19, 1775, Paul Revere and William Dawes rode to Lexington and neighboring towns warning colonists that the British were coming. When the British arrived, they were met by alert colonists. No one knows who fired the first shot, but eight colonists were killed and the American Revolution had begun.

Paul Revere's feat inspired Henry Wadsworth Longfellow's "Paul Revere's Ride," one of the most popular poems in American literature. Share with your students *Paul Revere's Ride* by Nancy Winslow Parker (William Morrow & Company, Inc.), an illustrated version of Longfellow's famous poem. Point out how Longfellow makes his words almost gallop through the poem, like a horse's hooves. Discuss how history might have been different had news of the secret attack not leaked out.

I Have Rights!

Thomas Jefferson wrote in the Declaration of Independence "that all Men are created equal, that they are endowed by their Creator with certain unalienable [unchangeable] Rights." Do kids also have rights that no one can take away? Challenge each student to make a list of "kids' rights." Then have the student turn his rights into short slogans. For example, if one student thinks that kids have the right to choose the food they eat, then his slogan might be "Our Food, Our Choice!"

After each student has chosen his slogan, give him two 18" x 24" sheets of light-colored construction paper, two 18-inch lengths of yarn, and markers. Instruct him to create the same slogan design on both sheets of paper, then punch two holes at the top of each sheet. Direct the student to use yarn to connect the two sides, making a sandwich board (see the illustration). Allow each student to wear his sandwich board as the class holds an impromptu Kids' Rights Parade through the school.

Sign Here, Please!

Not only was John Hancock's signature the first on the Declaration of Independence, it was also the largest and most famous. He said he would sign his name large enough so that King George could read it without his glasses. Familiarize your students with the signing of the Declaration of Independence by reading aloud *Will You Sign Here, John Hancock?* by Jean Fritz (Putnam Publishing Group, 1982). Afterward have each student simulate how tedious writing was at that time by guiding him through the directions at the right for making a quill pen. Then cover a bulletin board with white paper and title it "Colonial-Graffiti Corner." Invite each student to sign his own John Hancock on the board using his quill pen.

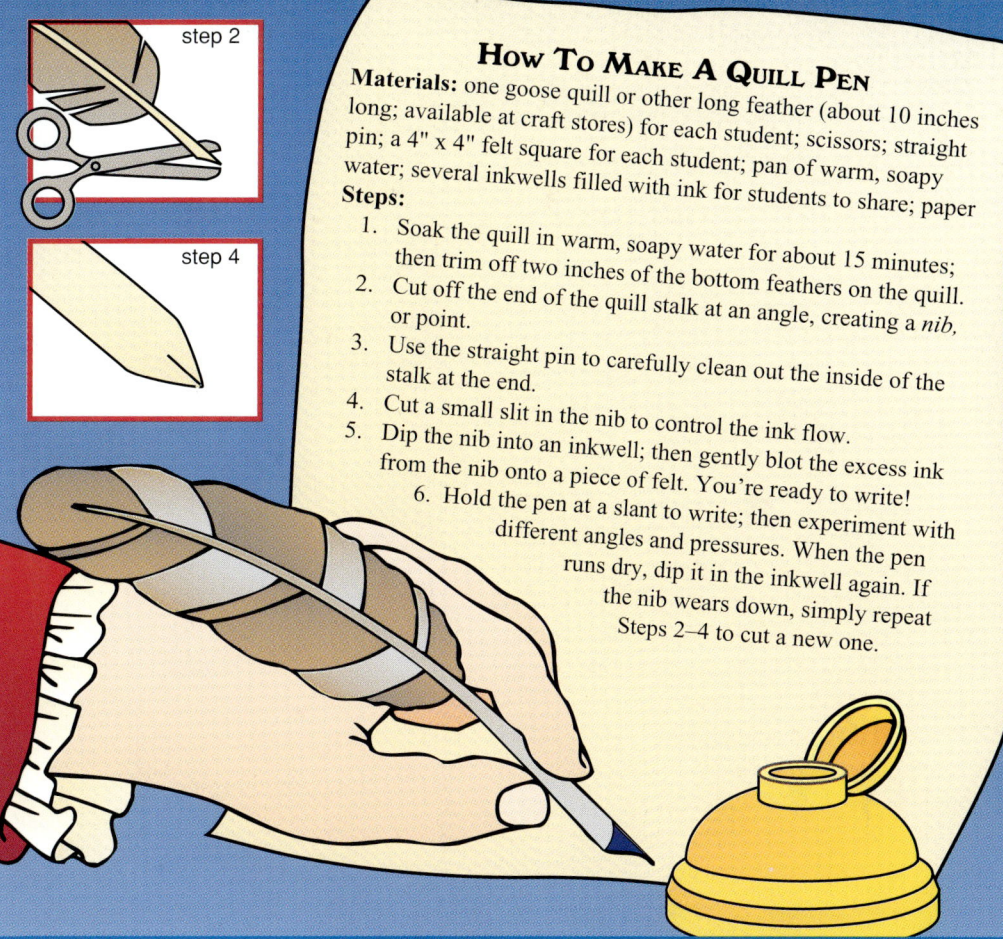

How To Make A Quill Pen

Materials: one goose quill or other long feather (about 10 inches long; available at craft stores) for each student; scissors; straight pin; a 4" x 4" felt square for each student; pan of warm, soapy water; several inkwells filled with ink for students to share; paper

Steps:
1. Soak the quill in warm, soapy water for about 15 minutes; then trim off two inches of the bottom feathers on the quill.
2. Cut off the end of the quill stalk at an angle, creating a *nib*, or point.
3. Use the straight pin to carefully clean out the inside of the stalk at the end.
4. Cut a small slit in the nib to control the ink flow.
5. Dip the nib into an inkwell; then gently blot the excess ink from the nib onto a piece of felt. You're ready to write!
6. Hold the pen at a slant to write; then experiment with different angles and pressures. When the pen runs dry, dip it in the inkwell again. If the nib wears down, simply repeat Steps 2–4 to cut a new one.

The Colonial Cities

Cities were the center of life in the 13 colonies. The largest cities—Boston, Baltimore, Charles Town (Charleston), Newport, New York City, and Philadelphia—lay along the Atlantic coast. Display a map showing the 13 colonies during this time. Point out each of the six cities listed above; then discuss why both the British and the colonists would want control of them. Next duplicate and distribute one copy of page 17 to each student. Divide your students into pairs; then challenge each pair to use reference materials to match the six cities with their descriptions.

Help From The Home Front

Although a few women did fight alongside men in the war, most of them stayed home working in ways they never had before. In addition to their regular work, women ran farms and businesses, sewed uniforms for soldiers, and made gunpowder and cannonballs. When soldiers fought near their homes, women were expected to feed and nurse the wounded. Some women followed the army as cooks and laundresses, while others acted as spies.

Divide your class into pairs. Assign each pair to research one of the women listed at the right. Then give each pair a 9" x 24" sheet of white construction paper, a ruler, and colored pencils or crayons. Direct the pair to create a comic strip illustrating how its assigned woman aided the war effort. Display the completed strips on a bulletin board titled "Heroines Of The American Revolution."

Women To Research

Abigail Adams
Anne Bailey
Margaret Corbin
Lydia Darragh
Mary Katherine Goddard
Sybil Ludington
Mary Pickersgill
Mary "Molly Pitcher" Hays
Deborah Sampson
Phillis Wheatley
Betsy Ross

THE HARSH WINTER

It was next to impossible to get food to the Continental Army camped at Valley Forge during the winter of 1777. When food did arrive, either there wasn't enough to go around or the meat was already rotten. The men ate dried peas, moldy bread, hardtack (a dry biscuit), and sometimes the corn meant for their horses.

Give students a taste of life as a colonial soldier by following the recipe on the right to make hardtack. Then give each student one biscuit to sample while you read aloud *Valley Forge* by R. Conrad Stein (Childrens Press®, Inc.; 1994). This picture book gives firsthand accounts of what it was like for those soldiers during the winter of 1777. Afterward direct each student to write a journal entry as if he were a soldier at Valley Forge. Invite students to share their entries with the class; then bind all the entries into one class journal.

HARDTACK

Add enough water to flour to make a soft but sticky dough. Knead the dough for about ten minutes or until it becomes elastic like bubble gum. Roll the dough out to a 1/2-inch thickness; then cut the dough into circles. Prick each biscuit with a fork and bake at 450° for seven minutes. Reduce the temperature to 350° and bake for another 7–10 minutes. The biscuits should be rock hard, so warn students before they take a bite.

WHO'S WHO IN THE REVOLUTION?

Familiarize students with some important people involved in the American Revolution with this activity. Duplicate and distribute one copy of page 18 to each student. After each student has completed the reproducible, assign him one of the names on the list. Give each student a 4" x 4" square of poster board. Instruct the student to illustrate his assigned person or that person's contribution on the square; then have him add the patriot's name and a one-sentence biography from the reproducible to the square. Post the squares in rows on a bulletin board, adding stitch lines as shown to make the display resemble a quilt. Label the completed display "Who's Who In The Revolution?" *(For a game using this reproducible, see "History Maker!" below.)*

HISTORY MAKER!

Use the information from the reproducible on page 18 in this variation of bingo. As a class, review the answers to the reproducible to ensure that students have similar responses. Instruct each student to keep this page on her desktop for reference while playing History Maker!

Direct each student to make a bingo card by drawing a large 5 x 5 grid on a sheet of paper. Have her write one different person's name from the reproducible in each space on her card. Give each student a handful of markers such as dried beans. Begin the game by calling out one of the lines of information that describes a person from the reproducible. Direct each student who has that person's name on her card to cover the space with a bean. Have the first person to cover five spaces in a row call out, "History Maker!" If that student can correctly read off the five names *and* tell a fact about each person without using her reference page, allow her to be the caller in the next round.

Name _____ The Revolutionary War: research

Who Am I?

In 1776, cities were the center of life in the 13 colonies. The big cities were the places to see a play or catch up on the latest fashions, news, or gossip. However each city was also different in its own way.

Read each of the clues below. Then use these clues along with reference materials to match each of the six cities listed with its correct description.

Cities
Boston
Charleston
Philadelphia
New York City
Newport
Baltimore

1. I am called the "City Of Brotherly Love."
I was home to the first incorporated hospital in the colonies.
Benjamin Franklin founded the first subscription library in the United States [or colonies] here.
Who am I? _____

2. I have one of the world's largest natural harbors.
I was founded by a man as a safe place for Catholics.
I served as the national capital in 1776 for over two months during the Revolutionary War.
Who am I? _____

3. I am home to a college that is the country's oldest.
I am home to the nation's oldest public park.
My capture was the first major American victory in the Revolution.
Who am I? _____

4. I lie on Narragansett Bay.
I was founded in 1639.
I am home to the Touro Synagogue, the oldest Jewish house of worship in the United States.
Who am I? _____

5. I was the wealthiest colonial city in the South.
Enslaved men and women farmed the rice on my land.
I lie on a peninsula between two rivers.
Who am I? _____

6. The first Europeans to live on my land were Dutch.
I was captured by the British in 1776 and held until the war ended in 1783.
I was the site of George Washington's inauguration as the nation's first president.
Who am I? _____

Bonus Box: Create a travel poster for one of these six cities on a sheet of drawing paper.

©1999 The Education Center, Inc. • *The Best Of The Mailbox® Social Studies • Intermediate* • TEC1474 • Key p. 158

Note To The Teacher: Use with "The Colonial Cities" on page 15.

Name _____

Revolutionary War: research

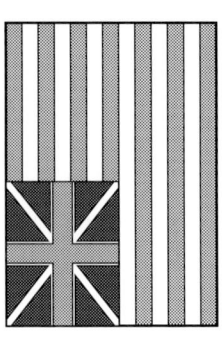

WHO'S WHO IN THE REVOLUTION?

A *biography* is "a story of a person's life written by another person." The information below is a copy of a page from an imaginary encyclopedia of biographies. Your job is to write a one-sentence biography for each person listed. In the sentence, explain the major part he/she played in the American Revolution. Use reference materials to help you. The first one is done for you.

1. Abigail Adams, *the wife of John Adams, influenced her husband to consider the rights of women.*
2. John Adams _____
3. Samuel Adams _____
4. Ethan Allen _____
5. Crispus Attucks _____
6. George Rogers Clark _____
7. Margaret Corbin _____
8. William Dawes _____
9. James Forten _____
10. Benjamin Franklin _____
11. Nathanael Greene _____
12. Nathan Hale _____
13. John Hancock _____
14. Mary "Molly Pitcher" Hays _____
15. Patrick Henry _____
16. Thomas Jefferson _____
17. John Paul Jones _____
18. Marquis de Lafayette _____
19. Richard Henry Lee _____
20. Francis Marion _____
21. Thomas Paine _____
22. Samuel Prescott _____
23. Paul Revere _____
24. Deborah Sampson _____
25. Roger Sherman _____
26. Friedrich von Steuben _____
27. George Washington _____
28. Phillis Wheatley _____

Bonus Box: Why is Benedict Arnold a well-known person of the American Revolution?

©1999 The Education Center, Inc. • *The Best Of The Mailbox*® *Social Studies* • *Intermediate* • TEC1474 • Key p. 158

Note To The Teacher: Use with "Who's Who In The Revolution?" and "History Maker!" on page 16.

Name _____   Revolutionary War: letter writing

LETTERS TO HOME

Some colonists still had relatives living in England during the American Revolution. Pretend that you are one of these colonists in 1776. On another sheet of paper, write a draft of a letter to a relative who still lives in England. In the letter, explain your point of view on the Revolution. Then edit your draft and neatly copy it onto this page.

_____
(date)

Dear _____,

_____
_____
_____
_____
_____
_____
_____
_____
_____
_____
_____
_____
_____
_____
_____

Sincerely,

_____

Bonus Box: On the first draft of your letter, underline the sentence containing the statement that would be the most difficult for your relative to understand.

Note To The Teacher: After each student completes this page, have him cut out the letter along the bold line. Collect and post the completed letters on a bulletin board titled "Letters To Home."

HEADIN' WEST!
CREATIVE IDEAS FOR STUDYING AMERICA'S WESTWARD MOVEMENT

Restlessness, a desire for land, and an itch for adventure—sounds like Oregon Fever! For people in the mid- to late-1800s, the most common cure for this condition was to gather their belongings and head west. Use the following ideas and activities to get the wheels turning on your study of America's westward expansion.

by Wanda Helmuth and Debra Liverman

PACK YOUR WAGON

Imagine cramming your possessions and the necessary supplies for a six-month, 2,000-mile trek aboard a 10' x 4' wooden wagon! Obviously, selecting what to bring along on a westward trip was difficult. Travelers not only needed to be prepared for the trip, but also for life as settlers once they arrived.

Divide your class into groups of four or five students. Challenge each group to make a list of supplies—including food, clothing, tools, and cooking gear—that might have been taken on the trip west. Then have the group rank its list in order of importance. Next share the list below containing items that were typically taken on the trip west. Enlarge the pattern on page 23 to make a large wagon outline to mount on a bulletin board titled "Pack Your Wagon!" Invite each student to use a colorful marker to write a sentence on the display explaining one personal possession she would bring along (besides the necessary supplies).

CALIFORNIA
Land Of Beauty
And
Unlimited WEALTH
For ALL!

Land For Everyone!
GOLD
For The Taking!

TOO GOOD TO BE TRUE?

Was the West too good to be true? Those who encouraged others to move west often made it sound better than it really was. Stories were spread of abundant land, plentiful gold, mild winters, and no disease. With your class, brainstorm a list of words and phrases, such as "thousands of acres" and "rivers filled with fish," that may have been used to lure people westward. Write students' responses on the chalkboard. Then instruct each student to use items from the list to design an advertisement that might have been seen in an 1800s newspaper. Give the student a sheet of newsprint on which to re-create his final design. Hang the completed ads around the classroom. Have the class vote on the most persuasive ad.

- flour
- yeast
- crackers
- cornmeal
- bacon
- eggs
- dried meat and fruit
- potatoes
- rice
- beans
- coffee
- sugar
- salt
- water
- cows for milk and meat
- cloth
- needles
- thread
- pins
- scissors
- leather
- saws
- hammers
- axes
- nails
- string
- knives
- soap
- wax (for making candles)
- lanterns
- washbowls
- tents
- medicines
- cooking supplies
- eating utensils and cups
- pots and pans
- weapons

Landmarks Along The Oregon Trail

Scotts Bluff, Nebraska
Register Cliff, Wyoming
Independence Rock, Wyoming
Devil's Backbone, Oregon
Chimney Rock, Nebraska
Soda Springs, Idaho
Steamboat Springs, Idaho
Fort Laramie, Wyoming
Courthouse Rock, Nebraska

PIONEER LANDMARKS

The early trails that the pioneers traveled were just that—trails. There were no road signs or mile markers to help the travelers along. Instead the pioneers relied on landmarks. Assign each student to research one of the Oregon Trail landmarks listed above. Then give the student an index card on which to design a postcard illustrating that location. On the back of the card, have him write a message that might have been sent from a pioneer on the trail to a friend or relative back east. Display the postcards in a plastic-sleeved photo album for easy viewing or on a bulletin board.

HANG ON TO YOUR HAT!

Tip your hat to the history-making men and women of the westward movement with this research activity! Duplicate several copies of the hat and bonnet patterns on page 23. Assign each student to research one of the people listed at the right. Then give the student the appropriate pattern—a hat if his assigned person is male or a bonnet if the person is female. Instruct the student to write on his pattern a few sentences explaining his assigned person's contribution to the westward movement. Next direct the student to lightly color and cut out the pattern. Finally post the completed hats on a bulletin board titled "Hats Off To These History Makers!"

People To Research
Mary Achey
Antonio Armijo
William Becknell
Catharine Beecher
Daniel Boone
James Bowie
Jim Bridger
Evelyn Jephson Cameron
Kit Carson
William Clark
Davy Crockett
Marie Dorion
William George Fargo
John Charles Frémont
James Gadsden
Mary Anna Hallock
Sam Houston
Thomas Jefferson
Mary Jemison
Meriwether Lewis
Abraham Lincoln
James Marshall
Biddy Mason
John McLoughlin
Esther Morris
Carrie Roach
Sacajewea
Jedediah S. Smith
Eliza Spalding
Robert Stuart
Tecumseh
Marcus Whitman
Narcissa Prentiss Whitman
Sarah Winnemucca

James Marshall He discovered gold while clearing out the stream near Sutter's sawmill where he worked. About one year later, news of his discovery reached the East Coast.
Name Sammy

NOW WHAT DO WE DO?

Traveling such a great distance was an exciting, but challenging experience. The pioneers were aware that they would face many problems and obstacles along their six-month journey, but being aware didn't make it any easier! Divide your class into groups of four or five students. Give each group one copy of page 24 and challenge its members to think like pioneers to answer each question. Afterward allow a few groups to share their answers. Next refer to the answer key on page 158 to explain to the class what the pioneers actually did in each situation. After this brain-boostin' activity, your students will feel ready to hit the trail!

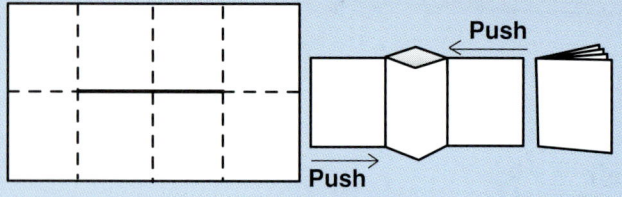

Begin with the basic eight-section fold. Cut along the boldface line as shown. Refold lengthwise. Push in the outer sides toward the center. Fold and close the book.

TRAVELING TIPS

Just as more Americans were hurrying west, publishers were rushing to print trail guides and manuals for these novice travelers. Many books proved very helpful. Unfortunately some of the printed guides were written by men who had never traveled west, and hence offered incorrect advice.

Give each student a 12" x 18" sheet of white construction paper; then guide the student through the steps above to create a blank booklet. Challenge her to use reference materials to create a trail guide filled with tips for traveling west. Each page of her guide should be on one of the following topics: Food, How To Stay Healthy, Landmarks Along The Trail, Crossing Rivers, How To Prevent Boredom, and Tricks Of The Trail. Have each student decorate the cover of her booklet; then post the completed guides on a bulletin board titled "Tips For Trail Travelers."

TRAIL OF TEARS

America's westward expansion led to conflicts over land between Native Americans and the white settlers. Some Native Americans fought for their land, but all of them were eventually forced to sign treaties giving more and more of it to white settlers. In 1830 Congress passed the *Indian Removal Act,* which gave the government the right to relocate the Native Americans. By the time the Cherokees moved the 800 miles to their new home, one-fourth of them had died from starvation, disease, or the cold weather. This journey became known as the *Trail Of Tears.* By 1900 all the remaining Native Americans had been forced from their homes and onto reservations.

Pose a "what if" situation to students. Suppose the Native Americans had won the right to retain their land, some of which contained gold. Have each student write a paragraph about how American history might have been different if Native Americans continued to live without any interference from the settlers. Let volunteers share their paragraphs with the class.

LITERATURE SUGGESTIONS

- *Caddie Woodlawn* by Carol Ryrie Brink (Simon & Schuster Children's Books, 1990)
- *Only The Names Remain: The Cherokees And The Trail Of Tears* by Alex W. Bealer (Little, Brown And Company; 1996)
- *Daily Life In A Covered Wagon* by Paul Erickson (National Trust For Historic Preservation, 1994)
- *Wagon Train: A Family Goes West In 1865* by Courtni C. Wright (Holiday House, Inc.; 1995)

Pattern
Use with "Pack Your Wagon" on page 20.

Patterns
Use with "Hang On To Your Hat!" on page 21.

Name(s) _____   Critical thinking

NOW WHAT DO WE DO?

Traveling west was not easy! Along the way, settlers were faced with many problems and situations that were new to them. Put on your pioneer thinking cap to imagine what you would do in each of the situations below. Write your answers on the lines. Use the back of this page if you need more space.

1. When would be the best time of year to start your trip west? (Remember: the trip will take five to six months.)

2. How can you cross a river with your wagon without a bridge?

3. Pioneers brought along many foods, including eggs. How can you store the eggs so that they won't break on the bumpy trip?

4. A buffalo would provide a large amount of meat for the pioneers. How can you make the meat last a long time without allowing it to spoil?

5. Since pioneers were traveling on the plains, they might go days without seeing trees or wood. How can you build a fire without wood?

6. What could you do if you ran out of supplies?

7. What could you do if your oxen could not pull your wagon up a high mountain?

8. There were some very steep mountains along the trail. How could you prevent your wagon from rolling down the mountain too fast?

Bonus Box: How do you think we know so much about what it was like to travel west in a wagon? Write your answer on the back of this page.

Note To The Teacher: Use with *"Now* What Do We Do?" on page 21.

Name_____ Critical thinking

TRAITS ON THE TRAIL

The people who faced the dangers and difficulties of moving west probably shared some of the same personality traits. On the lines below, brainstorm a list of what those traits might be. Choose three from your list and write each one in the center of a different wagon wheel. In the spaces between the spokes of each wheel, write five ways that kids today can demonstrate that trait.

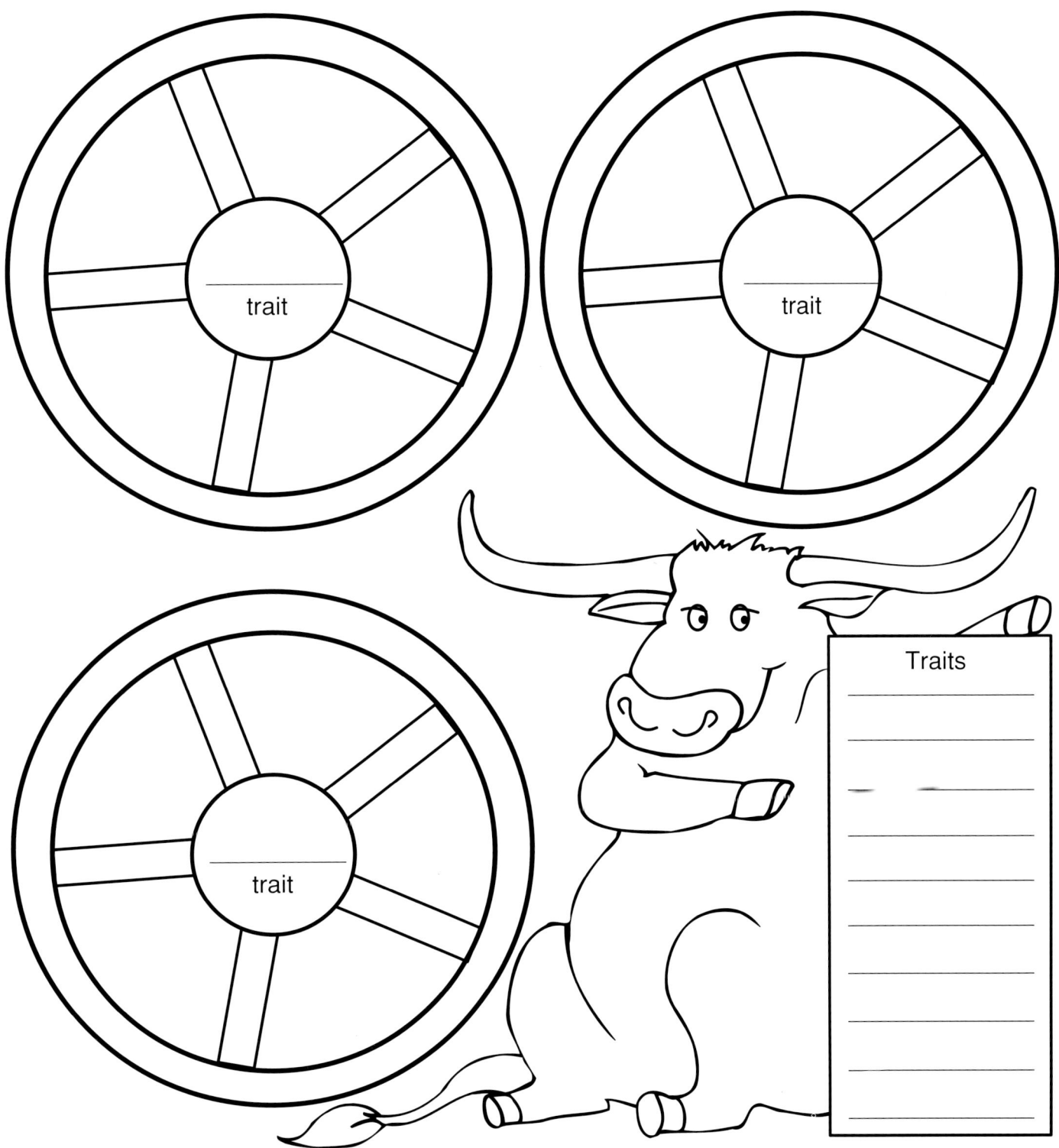

Bonus Box: On the back of this page, list three adjectives to describe how the pioneers might have felt when they finally reached the Oregon Territory.

A Nation Torn

Thematic Activities For Studying The Civil War

It was a time when brother fought against brother, cities were razed, farms were ravaged, and more Americans lost their lives than during any other war in history. From the destruction of the Civil War rose a new Union, the abolition of slavery, and the promise of equality. Use the following ideas to introduce students to this tragic chapter in our nation's history.

with ideas by Becky Andrews and Liz Hagner

To Secede, Or Not To Secede

Historians agree that the Civil War was the result of complex economic, political, and social issues. One of those issues involved the right of a state to make its own decisions. *States' rights* was a popular position in the Southern states, as was a state's right to *secede* (withdraw) from the Union. In December of 1860, South Carolina became the first state to secede.

To help students understand secession, present the following scenario: One of your school's teachers has just announced that her class is seceding from your school. This means that the teacher and her students will be a part of the school in location only. Have small groups discuss the following questions: What problems will the seceded class create for the school? What problems might the seceded class face? How might this secession affect you as a student? After several minutes of discussion, meet as a class to share students' conclusions. Point out that President Abraham Lincoln believed that secession was illegal. When South Carolina seceded, Lincoln announced that he would hold all federal possessions. One such possession was Fort Sumter, which lay in the harbor of Charleston, South Carolina. Confederates fired on Fort Sumter and forced its federal troops to surrender. Lincoln then called for additional federal troops to enforce the nation's laws. Southerners saw this act as equivalent to a declaration of war. Other Southern states quickly joined the Confederacy, and the Civil War was born.

Extra! Extra! Point-Of-View Newspapers

Bring the Civil War period to life with an unusual writing project. Post the following list of topics:

- slavery
- Robert E. Lee
- the Dred Scott decision
- Harriet Tubman
- Jefferson Davis
- Fort Sumter
- surrender at Appomattox
- states' rights
- abolitionist movement
- Fugitive Slave Laws
- Frederick Douglass
- *Monitor* and the *Merrimack*
- the economy in the South
- results of the Civil War
- 1860 presidential election
- Underground Railroad
- Missouri Compromise
- *Uncle Tom's Cabin*
- life on the home front
- the economy in the North
- costs of the Civil War

Have each student (or pair of students) choose a topic and write a newspaper article about it from the point of view of a Confederate sympathizer. (Provide research time as needed.) Have students compile their finished articles into a class "Confederate Times" newspaper, adding original illustrations. Next have students write newspaper articles on the same topics, but from a Northerner's point of view. Publish the finished articles in a class "Union Gazette" newspaper. Have small groups compare and contrast the different viewpoints presented in the newspapers.

Betty Bowlin, Henry Elementary, Ballwin, MO

The Music Of The Civil War

One of the most popular forms of entertainment in both the Union and Confederate armies was music. The war song of the South was "Dixie." Julia Ward Howe put new words to "John Brown's Body" to create "The Battle Hymn Of The Republic," the anthem of the Union army. Other popular tunes included "Yellow Rose Of Texas," "Eating Goober Peas," "Tenting Tonight," and "When Johnny Comes Marching Home." Ask your music teacher to provide students with copies of these songs. Have students read the lyrics to find information about the Civil War. Let interested students perform the songs for the rest of the class.

American composer Aaron Copland wrote a composition called "Lincoln Portrait," an orchestral work with narration based on the famous words of Lincoln. This work employs parts of popular Civil War tunes. Check a public library for a recording of "Lincoln's Portrait." Listen to portions of the piece; then have each student write his reaction in a journal. *(See the ready-to-duplicate journal cover on page 30.)*

A Soldier's Life

Students may be surprised to learn that each Civil War soldier had to carry at least 40 pounds of equipment and personal items, including a nine-pound musket, a bayonet, a bowie knife, a canteen, a cartridge box, and a knapsack. To give students a better picture of the hard life of a soldier, label index cards with the following items (one per card): underwear, soap, towels, a comb, a brush, a looking glass, a toothbrush, paper and envelopes, pens, ink, pencils, shoe blacking, photographs, smoking and chewing tobaccos, pipes, twine, string, cotton strips for wounds, needles and thread, buttons, a knife, a fork, a spoon, two blankets, and a rubber ground cloth. Place the cards in a knapsack or large bookbag. Pull out each card, reading it aloud as you do. Place the cards in a chalk tray. When you've emptied the knapsack, point out that it was no fun carrying such a load on a hot day—and when it was soaked with rain, the knapsack became even heavier!

Follow up this activity by reading excerpts about a soldier's life from *Behind The Blue And Gray: The Soldier's Life In The Civil War* by Delia Ray (published by Lodestar Books) *The Boys' War: Confederate And Union Soldiers Talk About The Civil War* by Jim Murphy (published by Houghton Mifflin) is a spellbinding account of the war from the youngest soldiers' point of view, with excerpts from authentic diaries, letters, and journals of that time.

Civil War Correspondents

His photographs preserved forever the grim reality of the Civil War. Mathew Brady, famed Civil War photographer, felt compelled to go to war "to preserve the moment of experience for the future." That he did, with hundreds of photographs taken with the help of several photographic teams.

Tell students to pretend that they are members of one of Brady's photographic teams. A newspaper has asked each of them to keep a journal during the photographic trip. The journal will be reprinted in newspapers to give readers information about the war. Duplicate the journal cover pattern on page 30 on brown construction paper for each student. Have the student fold the pattern in half; then have him staple white paper cut to size between his covers. Give each student the list of writing topics on page 31 (or conserve paper by posting one copy at a center). Have students write in their journals during free time or writing workshop, using reference books as needed. Encourage students to add items such as sketches, diagrams, and poems in their journals. Let students read excerpts from their journals during a special sharing session. Later use the journals to assess your students' grasp of important concepts.

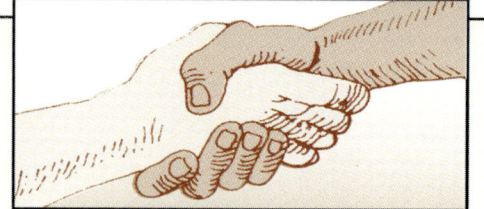

A Tale Of Two Soldiers

For an unforgettable reading experience, find a copy of Patricia Polacco's picture book, *Pink And Say* (Philomel Books). It tells the true story of two young Civil War soldiers: one a wounded boy left for dead in a battlefield, and the other a young black soldier who takes him to his mother's home to heal.

On the last page, Polacco tells readers, "This book serves as a written memory of Pinkus Aylee since there are no living descendants to do this for him." Discuss ways that famous people are remembered or memorialized today: statues, songs, poems, scholarships, buildings, highways, etc. Tell students to pretend that, like Polacco, they heard the story of Pinkus Aylee; but unlike Polacco, they have decided to remember Pinkus in a manner other than writing a book. Have each child describe his idea in a written proposal. Let students share their ideas; then post the ideas on a bulletin board.

Women And Minorities In The War

Women, African Americans, Native Americans, Hispanic Americans, European immigrants—all played important roles in the Civil War. For example, more than 440,000 European immigrants fought for the Union. Native Americans, treated harshly during the war, proved to be some of the Union's toughest soldiers. Introduce some of the brave women and minority heroes of the Civil War with the essay-writing reproducible on page 32. Publish finished essays in a class book entitled "A Brave Bunch."

For more information about women and minorities during the Civil War, look for *A Separate Battle: Women And The Civil War* by Ina Chang (Lodestar Books). Also look for *The Civil War To The Last Frontier: 1850–1880s* by William Loren Katz (part of the "A History Of Multicultural America" series published by Raintree Steck-Vaughn Publishers).

Civil War Flash Cards

Let your students make learning aids about the Civil War that you can use from year to year. Assign each of several small groups one of the categories listed below; then give each group a supply of large, unlined index cards. Have the students research each topic in its category. On one side of each card, have students write a topic and illustrate it. On the back of the card, have the students write a short description or definition. Place the cards at a center so students can drill each other during free time.

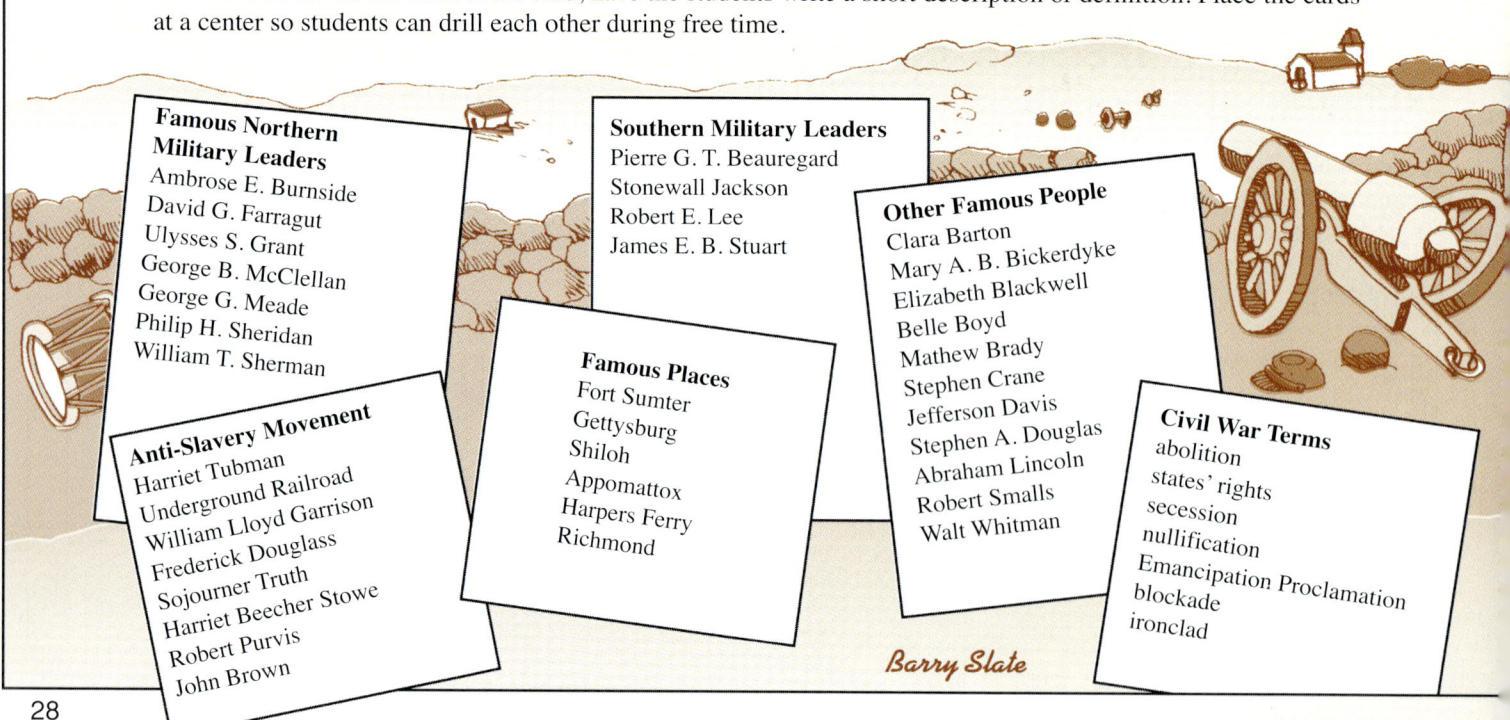

Famous Northern Military Leaders
- Ambrose E. Burnside
- David G. Farragut
- Ulysses S. Grant
- George B. McClellan
- George G. Meade
- Philip H. Sheridan
- William T. Sherman

Anti-Slavery Movement
- Harriet Tubman
- Underground Railroad
- William Lloyd Garrison
- Frederick Douglass
- Sojourner Truth
- Harriet Beecher Stowe
- Robert Purvis
- John Brown

Southern Military Leaders
- Pierre G. T. Beauregard
- Stonewall Jackson
- Robert E. Lee
- James E. B. Stuart

Famous Places
- Fort Sumter
- Gettysburg
- Shiloh
- Appomattox
- Harpers Ferry
- Richmond

Other Famous People
- Clara Barton
- Mary A. B. Bickerdyke
- Elizabeth Blackwell
- Belle Boyd
- Mathew Brady
- Stephen Crane
- Jefferson Davis
- Stephen A. Douglas
- Abraham Lincoln
- Robert Smalls
- Walt Whitman

Civil War Terms
- abolition
- states' rights
- secession
- nullification
- Emancipation Proclamation
- blockade
- ironclad

Barry Slate

A Nation Torn In Two

The Civil War was the result of years of disagreements between the states in the North and those in the South. When the war began, the North was clearly at an advantage. Use the chart and crayons or markers to fill in the bar graph.

INFORMATION CHART

Key:
Color N bars **blue**.
Color S bars **red**.

Population:
North—71%
South—29%

Wealth Produced:
North—75%
South—25%

Railroad Track:
North—72%
South—28%

Factories:
North—85%
South—15%

Bank Deposits:
North—81%
South—19%

Farms:
North—67%
South—33%

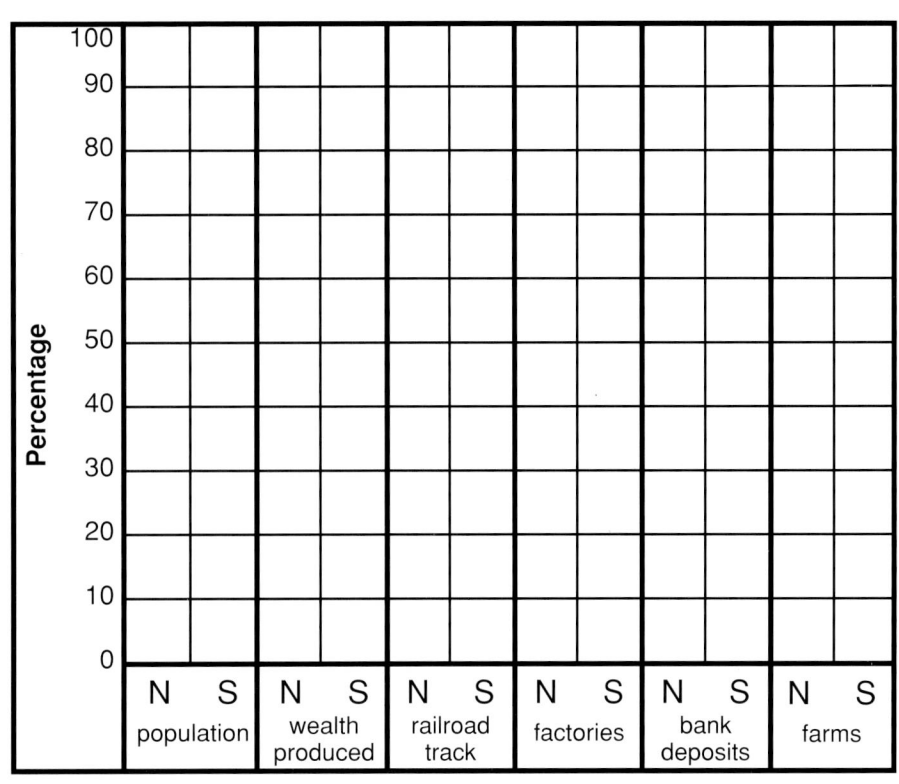

Write your answers to these questions on the back of this page.

1. Why do you think railroads were so important to both sides?
2. Compare the percentages of factories in the North and in the South. What problem would this create for southern cotton growers?
3. Which parts of the graph tell you that the South had trouble getting enough food during the war?
4. What difference do you think wealth and bank deposits made for the North in the war?
5. The one advantage that the South had during the war was that the South fought almost the entire war on its own soil. Why do you think this was an advantage?

Bonus Box: Look at a map of the United States. Take a close look at the eastern coastline. Which side of the war—the North or the South—do you think had the most shipyards and seaports? What difference do you think this made in the war?

Note To The Teacher: Use with "Civil War Correspondents" on page 27 and the reproducible on page 31. Duplicate on brown construction paper for each student. Have the student fold the pattern in the middle to make the front and back covers of a journal; then have him staple white paper cut to size inside the covers. Instruct the student to write his name at the bottom of the front cover.

Name _____

Civil War: research, writing

Civil War Correspondent

Mathew Brady was a photographer known for the photos he took of the Civil War. Pretend that you are one of Brady's assistants. You've been asked by a newspaper to keep a journal while on a photographic trip. The newspaper will print excerpts from your journal as a way of telling its readers about the war. First make a journal for your entries (your teacher will help you with this step). Choose one topic from Box A. Use research books or encyclopedias to help you write about this topic in your journal. Then choose three topics from Box B. Write about them in your journal.

Box A

- You've witnessed the battle of the *Monitor* and the *Merrimack*. Describe the ships and the battle that took place between them.
- You've just interviewed General Robert E. Lee at his headquarters. What did he say about the war and about leading the Confederate army? What was your impression of him?
- You've photographed a black soldier who has been in the Union army for a few months. What did he say about his time in the army? What hardships has he faced? Why did he join the army?
- You've just heard President Abraham Lincoln give the Gettysburg Address. What did you think of his speech? How did the rest of the audience react? Summarize what Lincoln said.
- You've arrived in Atlanta hours after the Union army has devastated the city. Describe what you see and experience there.

Box B

- Write your opinions about the war. Which side do you support? Why?
- Write about a day when you almost got caught in the middle of a battle while taking photographs. How did you react and feel?
- How do you think the North and South could have settled their differences without going to war?
- You've been away from home for months taking photographs. Are you homesick? Why or why not? What's the first thing you want to do when you get home? Why do you want to do this first?
- You've witnessed a lot of death and destruction on this trip. Now that it's over, how do you feel about the war? Explain your answer.

Note To The Teacher: Use with "Civil War Correspondents" on page 27 and the reproducible journal cover on page 30. Provide students with reference books about the Civil War (see the suggestions mentioned on pages 27–28).

Name_____   Civil War: critical thinking

A Brave Bunch

Women and minorities played a huge role in the Civil War. Below are the stories of six brave people who took part in this conflict. Read each story. With a crayon or marker, outline the box of the person you would nominate as "The Bravest Of The Bunch." On the back of this page, write a paragraph explaining why you chose this person.

Clara Barton
Collecting and delivering supplies to Northern troops was something that Clara Barton was very good at doing. A former schoolteacher, Barton once heard that injured Union soldiers who were her former students had arrived in Washington, D.C. These soldiers had no place to stay and no supplies. Immediately Barton found volunteers and supplies to care for the men. When other people who wanted to help the Union army heard about this, they began sending supplies to Barton. She loaded the supplies into wagons and took them straight to the camps and battlefields.

Robert Smalls
Robert Smalls grew up as a slave in South Carolina. He was trained to work as a sailor. Smalls was forced to work on a Confederate paddle steamer called the *Planter*. One night Smalls and the other slaves on the crew watched the white officers leave the ship for the evening. Then they brought their families aboard. Smalls secretly sailed the *Planter* out of the harbor until it met a Union ship. Smalls surrendered the Confederate ship to the Union captain. Later Smalls was made captain of the *Planter*, which became part of the Union navy.

Charlotte Forten
In 1861, the Union army invaded South Carolina's Sea Islands. The white plantation owners on the island fled. They left behind 10,000 slaves. When word got out that these slaves had been freed, other slaves flocked to the island. Charlotte Forten also went. She was a free black from the North who worked to end slavery. Forten went to the Sea Islands to teach the freed slaves. Many of these slaves didn't even know what a book was or how to hold one. Forten devoted her life to teaching and to working for civil rights.

Opothle Yahola
Life was hard for Native Americans during the Civil War. Many Native Americans were pressured to join the Confederacy. One Creek chief—Opothle Yahola—would not be pressured. He gathered African and Native Americans who either were *neutral* (did not take sides) or favored the North. Yahola asked President Lincoln to protect the group from the Confederates. When the Confederates heard of this, they attacked Yahola's group. Yahola escaped and led his people to safety across Union lines. Yahola's men who survived joined the Union army. They became some of its toughest soldiers.

Charles Zagony
Charles Zagony moved to America from the European country of Hungary. He became a major in the Union army. When the war started, Zagony organized trappers, hunters, and pioneers into three companies. He became famous for "Zagony's Death Ride." In this battle, Zagony and his 300 soldiers defeated a force of almost 2,000 Confederates!

Mary Ann Bickerdyke
Conditions in Civil War hospitals were terrible. Mary Ann Bickerdyke had a cause—to improve the conditions in the Union army's hospitals. "Mother Bickerdyke" did everything she could to make sure her patients were clean, well fed, and warm. She even helped remove the wounded from battlefields. One night after rescue parties had gone to bed, an officer saw a light on the abandoned battlefield. It was Mother Bickerdyke, alone out looking for more survivors!

Bonus Box: On another piece of paper, design a certificate that you would like to have awarded to one of these brave people.

World At War
A Thematic Teaching Unit On World War II

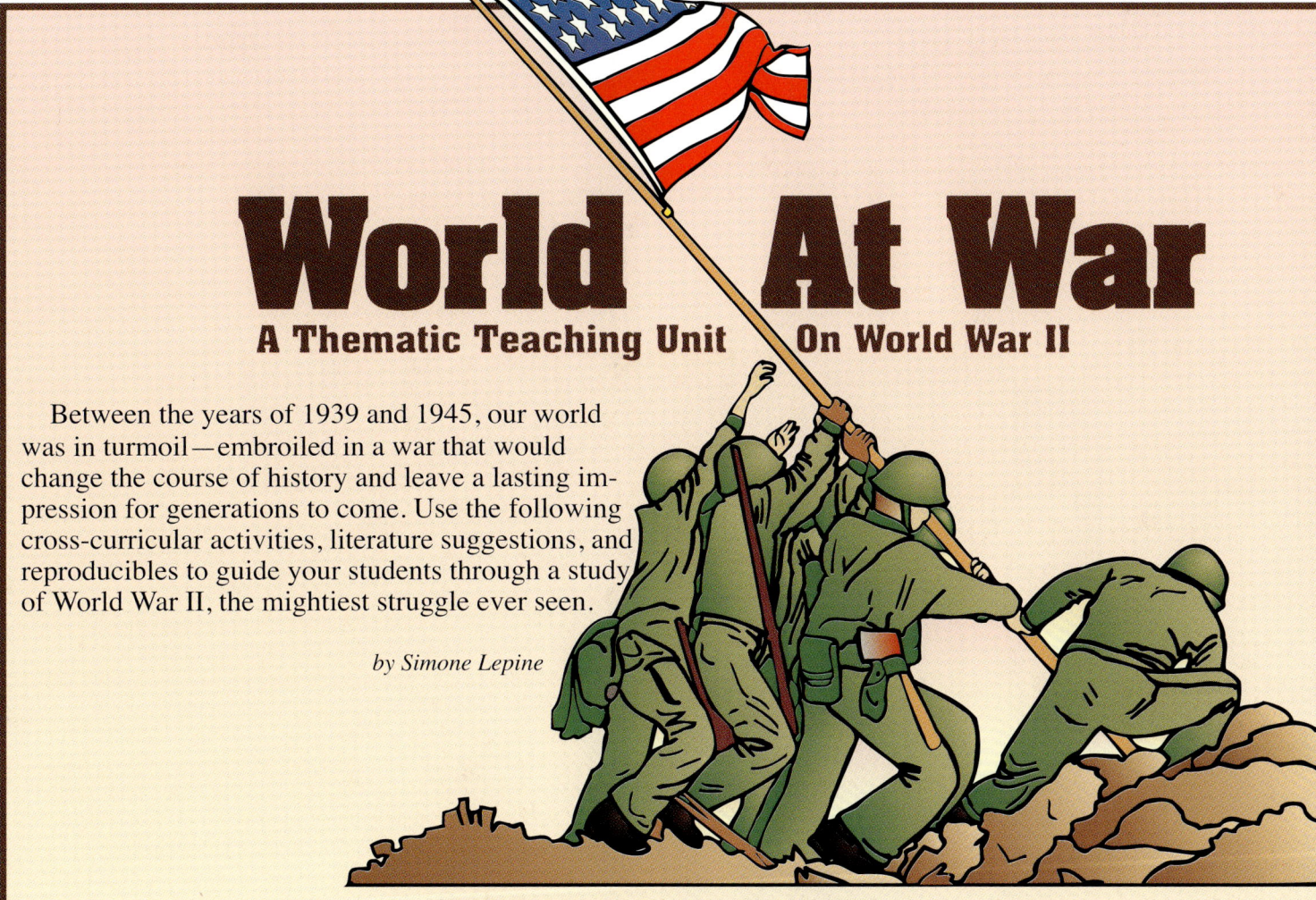

Between the years of 1939 and 1945, our world was in turmoil—embroiled in a war that would change the course of history and leave a lasting impression for generations to come. Use the following cross-curricular activities, literature suggestions, and reproducibles to guide your students through a study of World War II, the mightiest struggle ever seen.

by Simone Lepine

Background Information

The war in Europe began in September 1939 when Germany attacked Poland. The United States did not enter the war right away, but was supportive of the *Allies* (Great Britain, China, Russia, and two dozen other countries by January 1942) in their fight against the *Axis* powers (Germany and its eight allies, including Italy and later Japan). On December 7, 1941, the Japanese bombed Pearl Harbor, Hawaii. The next day the United States declared war on Japan. A few days later Germany and Italy, in support of Japan, declared war on the United States. Thus America was drawn into the conflicts in the Pacific and in Europe. The war officially ended with Japan's surrender on September 2, 1945.

Plenty Of Patriotism

The Pearl Harbor attack unified the people of the United States to take action against a common enemy. The war gave birth to a spirit of patriotism and national unity. The government encouraged this patriotic fervor through posters, comic books, radio shows, movies, and music.

Discuss with students what they think it means to be patriotic and how "team spirit" can help overcome adversity. Explain that during World War II the U.S. government created many advertising tools aimed at encouraging patriotism and sacrifice for the war effort. Help your class better understand the team spirit that was encouraged on the home front with a fun group project. Have students brainstorm a list of slogans that would send a positive message about your school to the entire student body. Divide students into groups according to the type of motivational items they would like to make: posters, comic strips, radio commercials, or original songs. Display students' finished products—including tape recordings of the songs and radio commercials—in the media center, cafeteria, or other common area. After the display has been up for one week, discuss whether students think it was effective in terms of raising school spirit.

Mapping Out The European Theater

To give students a full picture of how the Axis powers took over most of Europe, give each child a copy of the reproducible on page 38. After students have completed the map-reading activity, have them tell why they think Hitler was able to acquire so many countries before the other nations of the world stepped in. *(Europe was war wary and didn't want to start another war.)* Have students note the uncolored countries, such as Switzerland and Turkey. Discuss what it means to be a *neutral* country during wartime. Also have students think about how the Allies were able to defeat the Axis powers who had so much more land. *(The Axis powers may have possessed the land, but they did not possess the will of the people who lived in the occupied countries.)*

The Secret War

Behind the battle lines of World War II, courageous men and women carried on a secret war. Many *resistance groups*—comprised of citizens from countries that were occupied by the Axis powers—sprang up to fight the enemy "underground." These brave people often risked their lives to fight, sabotage, hide spies, and steal information to help the Allies.

Give students an opportunity to reflect on the courage and convictions of resisters with a role-playing activity. Have volunteers improvise the following conversations. After the activity, begin reading aloud Lois Lowry's award-winning novel, *Number The Stars*, which tells about one family's experience with Nazi occupation.

Role-Playing Situations:
- Your father has announced that your family will go into hiding rather than be forced to work in an ammunitions factory taken over by German forces. This will mean living like outlaws. Respond to your father's decision.
- Your older brother has seemed unusually secretive lately and has been acting suspiciously. You suspect that he might be working for the local resistance group. You know that if he's caught, he will be executed immediately. Confront your brother with your suspicions.
- Your uncle works at a local railway. While eavesdropping, you heard him tell your aunt that he switched labels on a railway car, which resulted in a German commander being sent a railway car full of fruit instead of necessary airplane parts. Share this information and your feelings about it with your big sister, who shares a room with you.
- You and your best friends are members of the Danish Resistance. You are sitting in the back of a truck that is traveling to a nearby bridge. You are going to blow up the bridge so that the German soldiers cannot use it. It will be a very dangerous mission. If caught, you will be executed. Talk with your buddy about why you are willing to go on such a risky mission.

Top Secret

During World War II, most military information had to be sent in coded form so that the enemy would not learn of its adversary's next move. A *cipher code*—in which the alphabet is rearranged—was one of the most common ways to send a message. To give your class a taste of espionage, have each pair of students complete the following cipher, rearranging the alphabet on the blank line in order to create a code.

Alphabet: A B C D E F G H I J K L M N O P Q R S T U V W X Y Z
↓ ↓
Code: _____

Once the code is developed, have students practice sending and deciphering messages. Explain to students that this type of cipher worked well until a German officer developed a method for breaking it.

The United States military discovered another form of sending coded messages using the language of the Navajo Indians. Because the Navajo language is so complex and unlike any other language, the code proved to be unbreakable. Learn more about this fascinating aspect of World War II by reading *Navajo Code Talkers* by Nathan Aaseng (published by Walker and Company).

Prisoners In Their Own Country

After the surprise attack on Pearl Harbor, there rose an ungrounded suspicion about the Japanese Americans who lived on the West Coast. Though they had done nothing wrong, the U.S. government reacted to the hysteria by uprooting and imprisoning 120,000 West Coast Japanese Americans, two-thirds of whom were American citizens. These people were "relocated" to ten bleak internment camps further inland, where they stayed for three years. In the late 1980s, the U.S. government officially acknowledged the injustice of the camps, apologized, and made symbolic restitution to the families whose rights had been ignored.

To introduce students to this "stain on American democracy," share a touching picture book entitled *Baseball Saved Us* by Ken Mochizuki (Lee & Low Books). This tale conveys the stress, frustration, and prejudice experienced by relocated Japanese Americans. After reading the book aloud to students, list the amendments to the Bill of Rights on the chalkboard; then discuss the questions below:
- Was this policy of internment fair? Why or why not?
- Was this policy constitutional? Why or why not?
- How would you feel if you had been a relocated Japanese American?
- Could a situation like this happen today? Why or why not?
- How would you define *prejudice?* Why do you think prejudice is still a problem today?

The Holocaust

As part of his scheme to conquer the world, Adolf Hitler planned to wipe out the entire Jewish population in Europe. By using propaganda to create distrust and stir up German nationalism, Hitler convinced many Germans that Jews were enemies to a stronger Germany. By the end of the war, Hitler had almost accomplished his mad dream. Six million Jews had been killed, along with approximately five million non-Jews. This tragic mass murder will certainly disturb students and raise many questions. Explore the Holocaust with the following activities:

- To help students fathom such a huge loss of life, have them find the seating capacity of a local stadium, concert facility, movie theater, or other large arena. Have students use calculators to find out how many "full houses" in the building would equal the number of people who lost their lives in the Holocaust. Despite the depressing overtones of this activity, it will help students conceptualize the depth of devastation caused by the Holocaust.

- One can't help but wonder how the world would have been different if the 11 million Holocaust victims had lived. Would their grandchildren be sitting in your classroom? Would there have been more books to read, art to appreciate, songs to sing, or medical breakthroughs to celebrate? Would there have lived a leader who would help bring peace or feed the starving? Though there will never be answers to these questions, it is important that students realize that each of those 11 million people held the potential to add something positive to the world. Have students create a bulletin board entitled "People Who Make A Difference." Direct your class to collect pictures, articles, or personally written accounts about people in the news or in their own lives who have made a positive mark in the world. Before displaying each item, have the student share why he feels the person is special and how life is better because he/she exists.

- For a story that demonstrates the power of the individual in making a positive difference in others' lives, share the picture book *The Lily Cupboard* by Shulamith Levey Oppenheim (HarperCollins Children's Books). This is a gentle tale about a young Jewish girl who was put into hiding by her parents during the Nazi occupation. The book explains how a non-Jewish family risked their lives to make sure the girl lived. For more advanced readers, try *Behind The Secret Window: A Memoir Of A Hidden Childhood During World War Two* by Nelly S. Toll (Dial Books) or *Sheltering Rebecca* by Mary Baylis-White (Dutton Children's Books). Or share an unforgettable photo essay about the children who lived and died during the Holocaust by reading *The Children We Remember* by Chana Byers Abells (Greenwillow Books).

Hiroshima

After the war with Germany ended on May 8, 1945, the United States continued to battle in the Pacific against Japan. It was projected that the Allies would eventually win, but that the loss of life would be massive. On August 6, 1945, a U.S. Army plane dropped the first atomic bomb on the Japanese city of Hiroshima. More than 92,000 people were killed or missing. Because Japanese leaders hesitated to surrender, a second bomb was dropped three days later on Nagasaki, killing 40,000 more Japanese citizens. Japan reluctantly accepted defeat and officially surrendered on September 2, 1945.

1995 marked the 50th anniversary of the dropping of the atomic bombs on Hiroshima and Nagasaki. Incorporate the following thought-provoking activities into your World War II unit:

- The decision to drop the atomic bomb was a difficult one for President Harry Truman. Involve students in the decision-making process with the reproducible on page 39. Review with students what is meant by *pros* and *cons*. Explain that weighing the pros and cons of a situation is a good way to make a decision. After students complete the reproducible, have them share their responses and how they came to their conclusions.

- The picture book *My Hiroshima* (Viking Children's Books) is a story written by Junko Morimoto, who was a child in the Japanese city at the time of the bombing. Although the tale is disturbing and graphic, it clearly describes the type of destruction rendered by the bomb. After sharing and discussing the book with students, have each child write his reaction to the story in his journal. Share with students that Hiroshima was rebuilt after the war and is once again a vital Japanese city.

- Another book that addresses the Hiroshima bombing is *Sadako And The Thousand Paper Cranes* by Eleanor Coerr.

Birth Of The United Nations

After World War II ended, the devastation it left in its path led many to agree that the nations of the world could not survive another world war. A step toward assuring peace was the formation of the United Nations in October 1945. One of the areas that the United Nations has focused on since its formation is the issue of human rights. Use the following activities to focus on human rights during World War II and now:

- The world was appalled at the abuse of human rights which characterized the Holocaust, and the United Nations dealt with the issue early on. On December 10, 1948, the UN adopted the Universal Declaration of Human Rights. This document outlined the basic rights that all human beings are entitled to regardless of race, sex, language, or religion. Discuss with students the meaning of *rights;* then have them brainstorm a list of basic rights they would have included in the UN's document. After the brainstorming, have students or small groups complete the reproducible activity on page 40.

- The famous autobiography, *Anne Frank: The Diary Of A Young Girl,* includes descriptions of the rights denied the Jews during World War II. Read aloud to your class the entries for June 20, 1942, and November 19, 1942. Using page 40, discuss how the things mentioned by Anne could be in violation of the Universal Declaration of Human Rights.

- Sadly there are still places in the world today where people live in subhuman conditions. The United Nations is actively involved in many of these situations. Direct your students to skim current newspapers or newsmagazines to find articles involving the United Nations. After discussing the articles, post them on a bulletin board.

Preamble To The United Nations Charter
We the peoples of the United Nations determined:
- to save succeeding generations from the scourge of war...
- to reaffirm faith in fundamental human rights...
- to establish conditions under which justice and respect... can be maintained...
- to promote social progress...

Let There Be Peace

At the conclusion of your unit on World War II, focus on the positive with a creative-thinking activity on peace. Duplicate the reproducible pattern on page 41 on various colors of pastel construction paper (one pattern per child). On his pattern, have each student write a short poem about peace, human rights, or the victims of World War II. Have students cut out their patterns and mount them, pyramid-fashion as shown, on a bulletin board or wall space. Explain to students that the pyramid is like a delicate support system in which each individual matters. To have peace we must help and support each other.

Literature Suggestions

In addition to the books mentioned in the preceding activities, look for these fine titles to use as resources for your World War II unit.

Holocaust/World War II Germany
Waiting For Anya by Michael Morpurgo; published by Viking Children's Books
Daniel's Story by Carol Matas; published by Scholastic Inc.
Anne Frank: Life In Hiding by Johanna Hurwitz; published by William Morrow & Co., Inc.
Rescue: The Story Of How Gentiles Saved Jews In The Holocaust by Milton Meltzer; published by HarperCollins Children's Books

The Home Front
Love You, Soldier by Amy Hest; published by Puffin Books
The Cookcamp by Gary Paulsen; published by Orchard Books

Hiroshima
Hiroshima And The Atomic Bomb by Wallace B. Black and Jean F. Blashfield; published by Crestwood House
Hiroshima No Pika by Toshi Maruki; published by Lothrop, Lee & Shepard Books

Japanese American Internment Camps
The Moon Bridge by Marcia Savin; published by Scholastic Inc.
The Journey by Sheila Hanamaka; published by Orchard Books
The Bracelet by Yoshiko Uchida; published by Philomel Books

Name _____   Reading a map

The European Theater

In 1936, German dictator Adolf Hitler invaded the area along the Rhine River between Germany and France. This invasion was only the beginning of what Hitler had planned. Germany and Italy—the Axis powers—would eventually invade many other European countries. This part of the war was known as the *European Theater.* World War II was also fought in Africa and Asia.

Directions: Using an up-to-date or older map of Europe, fill in the blanks with the names of the countries occupied by German forces during World War II. Color each country after you spell it.

1. _____
2. _____
3. _____
4. _____
5. _____
6. _____
7. _____
8. _____
9. _____
10. _____

11. _____
12. _____
13. _____
14. _____
15. _____
16. _____
17. _____
18. _____
19. _____

Bonus Box: Using an up-to-date map, list at least five ways that Europe has changed since World War II. Write your list on the back of this page.

©1999 The Education Center, Inc. • *The Best Of The Mailbox*® *Social Studies* • *Intermediate* • TEC1474 • Key p. 158

Note To Teacher: Use with "Mapping Out The European Theater" on page 34.

Name _____   Critical thinking

Tough Decisions

President Harry Truman had to make a difficult decision before using the atomic bomb against Japan in World War II. He had to weigh the pros and cons of each argument. Then he had to decide which option would be best for the United States. Not everyone agreed with President Truman's decision. Read the information in the chart below; then explain what decision you would have made if you had been president.

	Option 1: Use the atomic bomb.	Option 2: Don't use the atomic bomb.
PROS	It would probably end the war with Japan and save the lives of hundreds of thousands of American soldiers.	Thousands of innocent Japanese civilians would not be killed.
CONS	It would mean the death of thousands of innocent Japanese civilians. It would do extensive damage to the city of Hiroshima.	The American military would have to invade Japan. About 500,000 American soldiers would probably die in this attack. Even more Japanese civilians and soldiers would also die.

If you had been president of the United States, what would you have decided? _____
_____
_____

Why? _____
_____
_____

When you make a decision, it is important to consider the pros and cons of your different options. Below are some choices you make as a student every day. Choose A or B; then fill out the chart to help you decide what to do. On the back of this page, write what you decided to do and why you think it is the best decision.

Pick only A or B:

A) Option 1 = Do my homework.
    Option 2 = Don't do my homework.

B) Option 1 = Read a favorite book.
    Option 2 = Watch a favorite TV show.

	Option 1:	Option 2:
PROS		
CONS		

©1999 The Education Center, Inc. • *The Best Of The Mailbox® Social Studies • Intermediate* • TEC1474

Note To Teacher: Use with the "Hiroshima" activity on page 36.

Name _____   Critical thinking

Honoring Human Rights

The United Nations Flag
The branches symbolize peace.

Because of the Nazis' horrible treatment of the Jewish people during World War II, the United Nations declared that there are some things that all humans must have in order to live. These needs are called *human rights*. Today the United Nations observes countries to see that their governments are providing these rights to their citizens.

Directions: In the boxes at the bottom of the page are some of the human rights that all people of the world are entitled to, according to the UN. Above the boxes are listed some of the crimes committed against the Jewish people during World War II. Read each sentence and decide which of the human rights of the Jewish people were being violated. Write the number of the sentence in the box (or boxes) that you believe best describe(s) the right(s) being violated.

1. Jews were kicked out of Germany's civil service and army.
2. The Nuremberg Laws of 1935 took away the citizenship of Jewish citizens in Germany.
3. Hitler used starvation as one way to kill Jewish people.
4. Jews were forced out of their homes and imprisoned in concentration camps.
5. Jews were forced to work in German factories as slave laborers.
6. The Nazis prohibited Jews from gathering together to pray.
7. Jews were not allowed to open schools.
8. Jewish shops and businesses were boycotted.
9. Jews had to wear a yellow star or other special symbol on their clothes.
10. The Nazis killed thousands of Jews in specially designed gas chambers.
11. Jews were forced to live in fenced-in, crowded areas called *ghettos*. Jews who were caught outside the ghettos were killed.
12. Jews were not allowed to engage in trade or work as artisans.

Freedom from slavery	Right to an education	Freedom from torture or degrading punishment
Freedom of movement	Right to take part in government	Freedom of religion
Right to work	Right to an adequate standard of living	Right to life, liberty, and the security of a person
Right to privacy	Right to hold meetings	Right to rest

©1999 The Education Center, Inc. • *The Best Of The Mailbox® Social Studies • Intermediate •* TEC1474

Note To Teacher: Use with "Birth Of The United Nations" on page 36. Accept any answers students can reasonably support. You may wish to review the meanings of the terms *civil service, boycott, ghetto, concentration camp,* and *artisan* before completing this page.

Name_____ Writing poetry

Building A Pyramid Of Peace

World War II taught the world how important it is to maintain peace. It also taught that we can never let hatred and prejudice destroy so many lives again. The United Nations's main goals are to promote and maintain peace and to ensure that all human beings are treated fairly. To achieve these goals, all nations of the world must support each other and work together.

Directions: Inside the pattern below, write a short poem or slogan that sends a message of peace. Your message can be about human rights, fighting racism and prejudice, or those who died in World War II. After you've written your message, cut out the pattern. Use it to build a pyramid of peace with your classmates. (Your teacher will give you instructions about this step.)

©1999 The Education Center, Inc. • The Best Of The Mailbox® Social Studies • Intermediate • TEC1474

Note To Teacher: Use with "Let There Be Peace" on page 37. For each student, duplicate a copy of this page on pastel construction paper.

41

The Road To

Activities For Exploring The Presidential Election Process

The road to the White House has been called both "the road to glory" and "the torture trail." Either way, whoever aims for the highest office in our land must be willing to work hard for that honor. Use the following fun activities to help your class explore the presidential election process that directs candidates along this winding road.

by Chris Christensen

✓ Do You Have What It Takes?

What does it take to be a leader? Explore this important question as it applies to the office of the president. Prepare a set of ten cards for each group of three or four students. Label five of the cards with the qualities of leadership listed below; leave the other five cards blank. Give each group its set of cards with instructions to discuss the five qualities and why they're important for a president to possess. Then have each group brainstorm five more leadership qualities that a president should have and list them (one per card) on the five blank cards. Have each group rank all ten qualities from most to least important. Invite each group to share its insights and rankings. Next duplicate the pattern on page 46 for each student. Instruct each student to write a definition of *leadership* on the pattern. Arrange these patterns on a bulletin board titled "To Be A Leader."

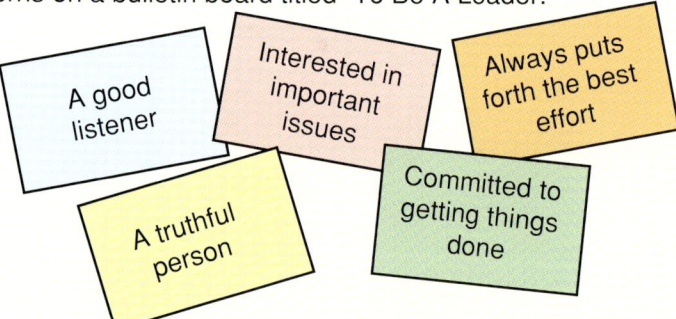

✓ Public Opinion Pollsters

To get a handle on which direction public opinion is leaning, pollsters survey groups of individuals to find out how they'd vote if the election were held today. Imitate this process in your class or school by taking three polls during the last weeks before the election.

Begin by enlarging a photograph of each candidate. Mount each photo onto poster board, and write in the candidate's name and party. On a third poster draw a large question mark (for "Undecided"). One day in early September, set up three milk- or lunch-count stations—one under each candidate's poster and one under the Undecided poster—in your school's cafeteria.* Instruct each student to "vote" for the candidate of his choice by buying milk or lunch from the station under his candidate's or the Undecided poster. Have each money collector keep track of the number of votes cast for her candidate. Tally the "votes" after the collection. Repeat this poll in early October and at the end of October. Have students compare the results of the three polls. Did the votes remain consistent or change with each poll? If they changed, what factors do students think may have contributed to the change?

If you don't wish to combine this activity with milk or lunch count, simply set up the posters and stations on one side of the cafeteria so students can vote before or after eating their lunches.

The White House

✓ The Many Hats Of The President

Ask students: "Are you someone's brother, sister, son, daughter, friend, student, or teammate? What are some of your responsibilities for each role?" Point out that almost everyone has a variety of responsibilities that go with the roles he plays. The president also has several roles: head of state, commander in chief, chief diplomat, national leader, party leader, chief executive, and legislative leader. Duplicate page 45 for each student; then discuss the definition for each of the presidential roles on that page. After students have completed the page, discuss their answers, making sure that students have a clear understanding of each role.

Next divide the class into seven groups. Assign each group one of the hats from page 45. Instruct each group to draw an illustration of the hat in the center of a sheet of poster board. Mount the posters on the wall. Then provide the groups with newspapers. Instruct the groups to comb the papers to find articles that contain information about the president. Have each group skim each article it finds to determine which role the president is playing. Then have the group glue each article to the appropriate poster.

✓ The College Of Choice

The electoral college plays a key role in the presidential election. Demonstrate the difference between the popular vote and the electoral vote with this fun experiment. Gather five shoeboxes. Label one box with the name of your school's home state. Label another box "California." (If your home state is California, select another state to be your home state.) Label the three remaining boxes with three states that border—or are close to—your home state. On each box write that state's electoral votes; then place slips of paper equal to that number in the box.

Beginning with one state, simulate a popular vote by using a coin toss. First decide which candidate will be represented by "heads" and which by "tails." Instruct each student to flip a coin and report the resulting vote. Tally the votes; then determine which candidate received at least 51 percent of the total popular vote for that state. Award all of the electoral votes from that state to the winning candidate. Repeat this process with the other four states. Add up the electoral votes gained by each candidate. Compare that number to the number of popular votes. Ask students: "Is it possible for a candidate to win the popular vote and lose the electoral vote? Why would a candidate spend a great deal of time and money campaigning in California and other states with large populations?"

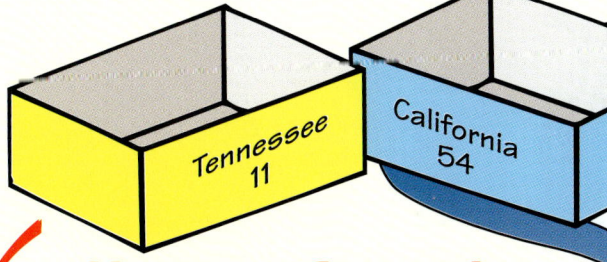

✓ Literature Connection

Looking for resources to help you teach about elections? These books are sure to get your vote!

The Election Book: People Pick A President by Tamara Hanneman (Scholastic Inc.)
Facts And Fun About The Presidents by George Sullivan (Scholastic Inc.)
Our Elections by Richard Steins (The Millbrook Press)
Our Presidency by Karen Spies (The Millbrook Press)
Presidential Campaign by Thomas R. Raber (Lerner Publications Company)

☑ Are You Qualified?

What is required of a person if she wants to become the president of the United States? Duplicate "Can I Become The President?" on page 46 for each student. After students have completed the page, tell them that only three of the qualifications listed on the page are actually required by the Constitution of the United States. Have students guess which qualifications are absolute. Then read them the following excerpt from the Constitution:

"No Person except a natural born Citizen, or a Citizen of the United States, at the time of the Adoption of this Constitution, shall be eligible to the Office of President; neither shall any Person be eligible to that Office who shall not have attained to the Age of thirty five Years, and been fourteen Years a Resident within the United States."

Follow up by having each student write her opinion about these qualifications in her journal. Are these qualifications sufficient for such an important office? If so, why? If not, what other qualifications should be included and why?

☑ My Hat's In The Ring

Once a candidate throws his hat into the ring, he must jump over a series of political hurdles to become his party's presidential candidate. Help students follow a candidate's path by taking a closer look at the individual stages involved in a presidential election. Duplicate the bottom of this page for each student to use as a guide. Divide the class into five groups. Assign each group one of the five stages listed on the reproducible. Have each group research the individuals and groups that take part and the events that take place during this stage of the process. Then have each group prepare a one- to two-minute video presentation showing the life of a typical candidate during this stage of the election process. Record the presentations in order so that you can show them together to make a documentary of the political process. Share your film with other classes.

Four score and seven years ago...

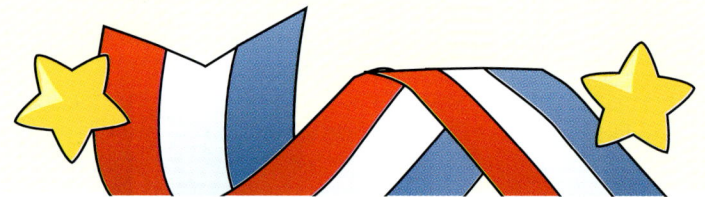

In Search Of A President

1 January–June
Caucuses, Primaries, And State Conventions

2 July–August
National Conventions

3 September–October
Final Campaign Between Main Opponents

4 November
Election Of President And Vice President

5 December
Electoral College Vote

©1999 The Education Center, Inc. • The Best Of The Mailbox® Social Studies • Intermediate • TEC1474

Name _____

Elections: critical thinking

The Many Hats Of The President

The job of the president is not a simple one. Each day he performs many different roles. He may discuss foreign policy in the morning and hand out awards to outstanding students in the evening. Read the descriptions of the president's seven main roles. Then complete the activity below.

Chief Diplomat
The president has the power to make treaties and appoint ambassadors with Senate approval. He determines how the United States will recognize and treat other countries. He helps warring nations find peaceful solutions to their conflicts.

Commander In Chief
As leader of our armed forces, he makes decisions about our country's defense and national security. He oversees all our military actions. He is responsible for deciding whether or not to use nuclear weapons in battle.

Party Leader
As head of his political party, the president helps decide its positions on various issues. He also supports the campaigns of his other party members. Sometimes a president appoints faithful party members to government positions.

Directions: Listed below are tasks that a president must perform. Compare each task with the roles described on this page. Write the name of the matching role next to each task.

1. _____ He works with business leaders.

2. _____ He attends the funeral of a foreign leader.

3. _____ He recommends a new law to Congress.

4. _____ He decides which military bases will remain open or close down.

5. _____ The president and his wife greet world leaders who visit the White House.

6. _____ He campaigns for other party members.

7. _____ He asks Congress for money to increase the number of troops or weapons.

8. _____ He helps labor leaders work out their problems so American workers won't go on strike.

9. _____ He invites foreign dignitaries to special White House events.

10. _____ He appoints advisors to help him run his programs.

11. _____ He vetoes certain congressional acts.

12. _____ He helps other world leaders work out peace agreements.

National Leader
In his decision making, the president must consider what is best for our country. He promotes American businesses and products. He shares America's ideals and beliefs with the rest of the world.

Chief Executive
The president makes sure that all laws and court rulings are obeyed. He appoints officials in the executive branch. He also prepares budgets and reorganizes governmental agencies.

Head Of State
He is our nation's representative to the world. He maintains relationships with leaders from other countries. He gives out awards to outstanding citizens, attends historical celebrations, and participates in symbolic ceremonies.

Legislative Leader
The president does not have the power to pass laws. However, he can recommend bills that he'd like to see made into laws. He can also say "No" to, or *veto*, certain bills sent to him by Congress.

©1999 The Education Center, Inc. • *The Best Of The Mailbox® Social Studies • Intermediate •* TEC1474 • Key p. 158

Note To The Teacher: Use this page with "The Many Hats Of The President" on page 43.

Elections: critical thinking

Name _____

Can I Become The President?

What qualifies someone to be president of the United States? Must a person be a male? Or have worked as a lawyer? The following activity will get you thinking about what's required to hold the highest office in the land.

Directions: Complete the following sentence with each phrase below. Check each phrase that you think describes a requirement for becoming the president of the United States.

A person who wants to become president should:

1. have a driver's license.
2. be a millionaire.
3. first be a lawyer.
4. be married.
5. be a natural-born citizen.
6. never have been arrested.
7. have served in the military.
8. have a college degree.
9. be termed "in good health" by a doctor.
10. be 35 years old or older.
11. be a registered voter.
12. first be a senator, congressperson, or governor.
13. have a social security number.
14. know how to read.
15. own property.
16. have been a resident of the United States for 14 years.
17. be 60 years old or older.
18. know how many words are in the Declaration of Independence.

©1999 The Education Center, Inc. • *The Best Of The Mailbox® Social Studies • Intermediate •* TEC1474

Note To The Teacher: Use this page with "Are You Qualified?" on page 44.

Pattern
Use with "Do You Have What It Takes?" on page 42.

Celebrate Your State!
Creative And Motivating Projects To Learn About Any State

Our nation is a hodgepodge of cultures and traditions. Yet each state has a unique identity and heritage of which its people are immensely proud. Whether you're studying your home state, a region, or all 50 states, you're sure to find an enticing idea in this collection of state ideas from our subscribers!

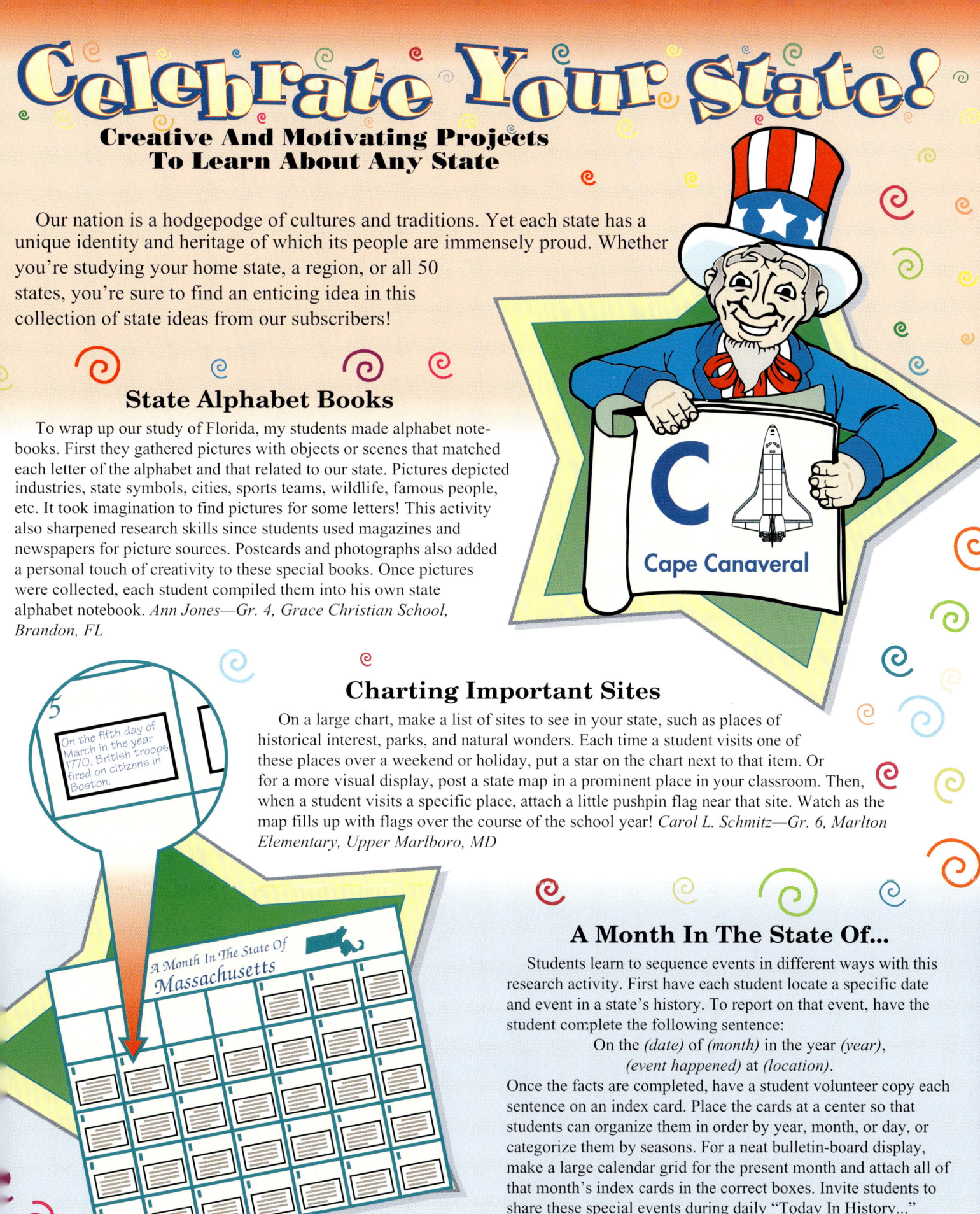

State Alphabet Books

To wrap up our study of Florida, my students made alphabet notebooks. First they gathered pictures with objects or scenes that matched each letter of the alphabet and that related to our state. Pictures depicted industries, state symbols, cities, sports teams, wildlife, famous people, etc. It took imagination to find pictures for some letters! This activity also sharpened research skills since students used magazines and newspapers for picture sources. Postcards and photographs also added a personal touch of creativity to these special books. Once pictures were collected, each student compiled them into his own state alphabet notebook. *Ann Jones—Gr. 4, Grace Christian School, Brandon, FL*

Charting Important Sites

On a large chart, make a list of sites to see in your state, such as places of historical interest, parks, and natural wonders. Each time a student visits one of these places over a weekend or holiday, put a star on the chart next to that item. Or for a more visual display, post a state map in a prominent place in your classroom. Then, when a student visits a specific place, attach a little pushpin flag near that site. Watch as the map fills up with flags over the course of the school year! *Carol L. Schmitz—Gr. 6, Marlton Elementary, Upper Marlboro, MD*

A Month In The State Of...

Students learn to sequence events in different ways with this research activity. First have each student locate a specific date and event in a state's history. To report on that event, have the student complete the following sentence:

On the *(date)* of *(month)* in the year *(year)*, *(event happened)* at *(location)*.

Once the facts are completed, have a student volunteer copy each sentence on an index card. Place the cards at a center so that students can organize them in order by year, month, or day, or categorize them by seasons. For a neat bulletin-board display, make a large calendar grid for the present month and attach all of that month's index cards in the correct boxes. Invite students to share these special events during daily "Today In History..." mini-reports. *Kevin S. Spencer—Gr. 5, Raleigh Court Elementary, Roanoke, VA*

Computing Your State

Try this kid-pleasin' math activity when studying your state. Assign each letter of the alphabet a whole number or fractional value. Write each letter/number pair in a square on one-inch graph paper. Then duplicate the graph for your students and instruct them to cut apart the squares. Have students use the letters to spell out the names of cities, historical sights, famous people, or other words associated with your state. Next use the numbers with those letters in a variety of math exercises. For example, have students spell out the capital city, then add the total value of its letters. Challenge students to find another city in your state that is "worth" half or two times that total. Have students create equations involving subtraction, division, and multiplication using the letter values. Or make up word equations for students to solve, such as those shown. Then have students solve the equations based on the values of the letters in each word.
Pam Doerr—K–6 Substitute Teacher, Lancaster County Schools, Lancaster, PA

Harrisburg – Lancaster = ?
William Penn – Philadelphia = ?

Two Helpful Resources

For an excellent networking opportunity—plus an abundance of resources—join your state's historical society. Fellow historical society members are good resources for teachers' names and addresses. After you receive a list of names, have each student select a teacher from whom to request a pen pal. Decorate a bulletin board with your state map and pinpoint the home of each pen pal, along with a summary of each letter received.

Another good source of information is the county clerk's office of each individual county. Request the names and addresses of county clerks from your state capital. Then have each student choose one clerk's office to write to requesting information. You'll be surprised at the responses you'll receive! *Elaine Jordan—Gr. 4, Abraham Lincoln School, Indianapolis, IN*

Compare A State With A Country

For our school's International Week celebration, my cooperating teacher and I developed a social studies unit that integrated the study of our state with the study of a foreign country. First we took a survey of students' backgrounds, then chose a country based on the results. Our students loved comparing and contrasting our state with the selected country, Italy.
Jonathan S. Cohen—Gr. 4 Student Teacher, Maple Shade, NJ

Ahh, Kansas!

For a study of Kansas, I enlarged a map of our state's counties and displayed it in a hallway. Each student located the city in which she was born and placed a dot on the map at that location. Then each student made a sunflower (our state flower) with yellow yarn and brown construction paper, and placed a photo of herself in its center. Long pieces of yarn were used to connect the sunflowers to the cities of birth. For those students not born in our state, we added each of their birth states to the display—on the sides of the map.
Ruth Menzer—Gr. 4, Haskins Elementary, Pratt, KS

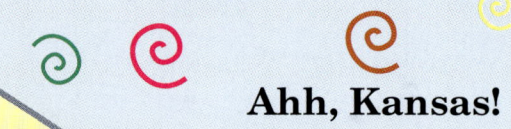

Unusual Cities

For a fun letter-writing activity, I have each student choose a city in our state that has an unusual name from a zip code directory. The student writes to that city's chamber of commerce, introducing herself and explaining our project. She also asks how the city got its name and requests a map and additional information. As replies come in, students share the information about their cities and locate them on our state map. *Nancy Cutforth, Orland Center School, Orland Park, IL*

Piecing The States Together

After completing a state report, each of my students writes her final copy within an outline map of that state. Some students complete more than one report to ensure that all the states are covered. When all reports are finished, students cut out their map outlines and assemble their individual puzzle pieces to make a giant map of the United States. *Elise Nash—Gr. 5, Delaware Academy, Delhi, NY*

A Map Good Enough To Eat!

Celebrate your state's birthday in a special way. Have each teacher in your grade provide a sheet cake cut in the shape of your state and frosted with white icing. Let students use cereal, raisins, nuts, and gumdrops to mark the locations of cities and special sites. Identify rivers with licorice, and use a sprinkle of rice cereal to represent hills. Have students make a map key to accompany their creation. If desired, label small flag cutouts attached to toothpicks with the names of special sites; then give one to each child to insert in the cake. How exciting to go home and say you took a bite of the capital city! *Neva J. Doerr—Gr. 4, Creighton Community Schools, Creighton, NE, and Lindsey Roman—Gr. 4, Shannock Valley Elementary, Rural Valley, PA*

Welcome To This State!

For a creative-writing project, have each student create a newsletter about travel in a particular state. Suggest that the student include advertisements for the state, letters to the editor persuading tourists to visit, a food section outlining the state's specialties, a garden section explaining the state's agriculture, and a weather graph for each season in the state. Post all of the newsletters on a bulletin board so that students can enjoy each other's final products. *Kelly A. Wong, Berlyn School, Ontario, CA*

Our Patchwork State

Fourth graders in our state study the counties of New Jersey. For a fun art/map project, I supply each student with a poster board–size shape of our state, plus precut oaktag patterns for each of our 21 counties. Students collect all types of wrapping paper, which they cut into 5" x 7" rectangles. Each student traces each county pattern onto the colored side of the wrapping paper. The wrapping-paper shape is then cut out and glued in its appropriate place on the state map. Students glue the counties around the perimeter of the state first, then fill in the interior. My kids love to take their patchwork maps home to decorate their rooms! *Brenda Hanuschik—Gr. 4, Antheil Elementary, Ewing, NJ*

State Floor Map

When studying Pennsylvania, I began with its geography so that students would have insight into the locations of landmarks as they were studied. First we created a classroom-size floor map of our state. I determined its dimensions in inches, then scaled it to feet. We used white athletic tape to outline the state on the floor. (It works best since it comes up easily.) We discussed political and natural boundaries, then made dashed lines on the tape to represent political boundaries and bold blue lines to represent natural boundaries. Next I assigned an important city to each small group to research and locate on a road map. Each city was then plotted on our map with a large or small black dot, depending on its population. Next students designated rivers with tape and mountains with paper cups. A map key was made on a piece of white poster board so that visitors could understand the symbols. Making this huge map took four days and was a successful motivator for everyone. *Lindsey Roman—Gr. 4, Shannock Valley Elementary, Rural Valley, PA*

Top 10 Lists

This fun activity helps students distinguish trivial facts from important ones. Ask each student to write ten facts about a state—facts that are obscure as well as those that are obvious. After completing the list, have the student rank his facts from 1 (most common info) to 10 (most unusual). Next have him rewrite his list in order with fact #10 first. For a game, divide students into two teams. Have a player read the first clue (#10) from his list. If the opposing team guesses the correct state based on that clue, it wins 10 points. If not, the player reads clue #9. If the opposing team guesses on that clue, it earns 9 points. Clues are read down to #1 until the team identifies the state.

As an alternative activity, have each student make a minibook with his facts. Page 1 should have the most unusual fact, continuing to page 10 with the most common fact. Have the student identify his state on the book's last page. Place these books at a reading center for everyone to enjoy during free time. *Kevin S. Spencer—Gr. 5, Raleigh Court Elementary, Roanoke, VA*

A Big Book About Vermont

Instead of assigning an essay as the end product of research, I have my class create a big book. For example, when we studied Vermont, I had each student research one county. I provided each child with a large sheet of poster paper and an outline of what the finished poster should feature. I encouraged students to include words and pictures to make the posters complete and attractive. When the posters were finished, students presented them to their classmates. Then they assembled the posters into a "Big Book About Vermont." After each student signed the cover, the book was ready to share with other classes. *Julia Alarie—Gr. 6, Essex Middle School, Essex, VT*

My State Jumper

After studying our state's famous places and landmarks, I had each student choose one to illustrate. Students drew their illustrations on paper using fabric crayons. I then made a simple jumper and ironed the drawings onto it. I wore this unique dress to our Open House and to other special events during the school year. Be sure to use fabric that is not 100% cotton, or the crayon drawings will wash out. *Deborah Hartman, Bethel Park, PA*

Native Americans Of The Pacific Northwest

Towering totem poles decorated with mystical beasts and wide-eyed faces. Huge canoes that could speed through the ocean chasing immense whales. Elaborate celebrations held to establish rank and status. Such was the culture of the Native American tribes that lived in the Pacific Northwest. Investigate these fascinating people and their unique heritage with the following activities and reproducibles.

by Simone Lepine and Becky Andrews

Background For The Teacher

The Pacific Northwest Indians* lived in a narrow band of coastal land that stretched from the southern tip of Alaska to northern California. The warm, moist climate made the region one of dense mists, lush evergreen forests, abundant vegetation, and numerous game animals. Rich fishing grounds and a variety of sea animals provided most of the people's food supplies. Huge trees furnished the people with material for almost all their needs, including tools, clothing, transportation, and shelter.

Due to the abundance of natural resources, the Native Americans who lived in the Pacific Northwest did not need to farm or spend all year hunting for food. Instead, they spent much of the winter enjoying ceremonial and social activities, including the practice of various arts and crafts such as carving, weaving, and basketry.

*The terms *Native American* and *Indian* are both used in this article. Explain to students that *Indian* was coined by Christopher Columbus who—upon reaching the New World—mistakenly thought that he had reached the Indies and so named its inhabitants *Indians*. The word *Indian* was not in the vocabulary of Native Americans since almost every tribe had its own name. Today many Indians refer to themselves as Native Americans.

The Gift-Giving Ceremony

The Pacific Northwest Indians were the most status-conscious tribes in North America. At the center of this strict social structure was an important ceremony called the *potlatch*. During a potlatch, the host chief would give his guests "gifts" to demonstrate his great wealth and status. The gifts were carefully selected so that their value would match the status of the recipient. Often the host would give away all of his possessions. Sound unwise? Not really, for in this system the guests were obligated to invite the chief to their potlatches and give him even more valuable gifts in return. The potlatch ceremony thus became a banking system of giving out loans that collected interest.

Demonstrate this fascinating ceremony by holding a mini-potlatch session. Have each student cut ten slips of paper and label each with a valued possession. Next have the student number the strips in order from most to least valuable. Share information about the potlatch with the class; then divide students into groups of four to ten. Have each group sit in a circle. Choose one student to be the first chief. Have that student distribute his gifts to the other children in his group. Designate that the person sitting to the chief's left will be the most important guest and then, moving clockwise around the circle, the status of the guests decreases. After a chief has given away his gifts, have the person sitting to his right host the next potlatch.

At the end of the activity, each student will have hosted a potlatch, given away his possessions, and received other gifts in return. Let students share some of the items they ended up with and their thoughts about the ceremony. Guide students to draw the conclusion that the potlatch tradition was similar to a banking system that used goods instead of money.

Fish, Fur, And More

Start your Native American unit with a research activity centering on the animals important to the Pacific Northwest Indians' lifestyle. Have student pairs choose an animal to research from the list that follows. Instruct students to research their animals following the instructions on the reproducible on page 53. Ask a local pizzeria to donate a small pizza box for each student pair. Have each pair cover its box with paper; then have the students illustrate the outside of the box with pictures of their animal. On one side of the box, have the students write the name of their animal. Inside the box, have students glue their completed index cards (see page 53), along with any additional pictures. After students have shared their information, stack the boxes in a reading center. Refer to the projects throughout the unit as students learn about the use of animals in the Indians' lives, study the centrality of animals in their religious beliefs and artwork, and read legends featuring animal characters.

Animals: raven, eagle, black bear, grizzly bear, caribou, moose, beaver, raccoon, mountain goat, elk, mink, bobcat, porcupine, squirrel, marmot, weasel, wolf, seal, sea lion, sea otter, gray whale, sperm whale, salmon, halibut, herring, sardine, eulachon (candlefish), clam, mussel, oyster

Tales Of The Totems

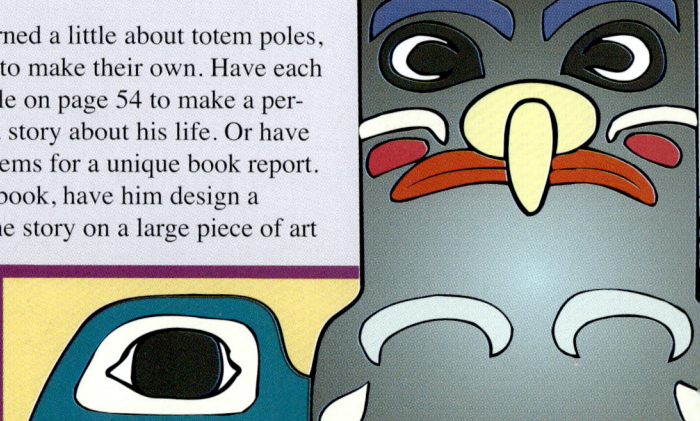

The Native Americans who lived in the Pacific Northwest are perhaps best known for their fantastic totem poles. Contrary to popular misconceptions, the totems were not religious icons, but were instead carved designs of animals, supernatural beings, or humans that represented each clan. A totem pole was a way that a chief could tell his family legends and ancestral histories, while also illustrating his status in the community. To give students a better understanding of the totem pole and tools used to carve it, share Anne Siberell's picture book *Whale In The Sky* (E. P. Dutton, 1985). The book demonstrates in a simple format how a story can be seen in a totem pole.

Once students have learned a little about totem poles, give them the opportunity to make their own. Have each student use the reproducible on page 54 to make a personalized totem that tells a story about his life. Or have students create original totems for a unique book report. After a student has read a book, have him design a totem pole summarizing the story on a large piece of art paper. Remind students that a totem is read from top to bottom and that the carvings show only key illustrations to the tale being told. Have students color and cut out their finished totems before stapling them to a bulletin board. Set aside a storytelling time during which each student tells the tale of his totem.

Fun And Games

Due to the abundant natural resources, Native Americans of the Pacific Northwest had more leisure time than did most North American Indians. They used this extra time for ceremonies, storytelling, and playing games. Spend a Friday afternoon playing the following games:

Laughing Competition: Played by both adults and children, the object of this game was to make an opponent laugh. Divide students into two teams. Have the teams stand in lines facing each other. At your signal, have team A make silly faces and noises; if anyone on Team B smiles or laughs, Team A earns a point. If, after one minute, no one on Team B smiles or laughs, Team B earns a point. Another variation is to have one player from each team stand in front of the opposing team. The opposing team tries to make the player laugh or smile before a minute is up.

Stick Game: This game used 10–100 sticks. One or more of the sticks was decorated at one end with a small mark or carving. A player would divide the sticks in half, holding one half in each hand. His opponent would guess which hand held a particular marked stick. Have students play this game using tongue depressors, one or more of which is marked on one end. Another variation played by the Native Americans had a player try to guess whether an opponent was holding an even or odd number of sticks in one hand.

Names_____ Research skills, taking notes

Fish, Fur, And More!

The animals of the Pacific Northwest were important to the Native Americans because they were a source of food, clothing, and fur to trade. The Native Americans also believed that the animals were their ancestors. They honored the animals in the legends they told, the totems they carved, and the names they called their clans. To understand the Native Americans' culture, you also need to learn about the animals with whom they shared the land.

Use a variety of sources to answer the following questions about your animal. Write your notes in the boxes below. Once you have completed each box, rewrite your notes on an index card in paragraph form. Glue the paragraphs inside an empty pizza box. Decorate the outside of the box with pictures of your animal.

What is the name of your animal? Is your animal a vertebrate or an invertebrate?	What is your animal's habitat?
What does your animal eat?	What special features does your animal have that help it to survive?
What does your animal look like? (size, shape, color, etc.)	Sketch and color your animal.

©1999 The Education Center, Inc. • *The Best Of* The Mailbox® *Social Studies* • Intermediate • TEC1474

Note To Teacher: Use with "Fish, Fur, And More" on page 52. Provide each pair of students with an empty pizza box, six index cards, glue, construction paper, and various art supplies with which to create illustrations.

My Totem Tale

Art project

Like the Native Americans of the Pacific Northwest, you can make a totem pole that tells a story about your life. Think of three important goals you have accomplished. Write a brief description about each accomplishment in a totem below. Color around your writing on the totems. Cut out the pole along the thick black lines ONLY. Roll the sides of the paper; then glue the shaded areas together to make a tube. Share your totem tale with the rest of the class!

©1999 The Education Center, Inc. • The Best Of The Mailbox® Social Studies • Intermediate • TEC1474

Name _____

Note To Teacher: Duplicate this page on construction paper. Provide each student with crayons or markers, scissors, and glue.
Use with "Tales Of The Totems" on page 52.

The Other Americans
Getting To Know Our Latin American Neighbors

What covers almost 8,000,000 square miles and is home to over 400,000,000 people? If you answered "Latin America," you're right! Introduce your students to this colorful and diverse region with the following south-of-the-border activities.

by Mary Beth Rollick and Christine A. Thuman

Background: Latin America

In 1507, a German mapmaker named Martin Waldseemüller suggested that the New World be named *America* in honor of the Italian-born explorer Amerigo Vespucci. Waldseemüller and others believed Vespucci's claim that he had been the first European to discover the *Mundus Novus* (New World). Although his claim was eventually disputed by historians, the name America stuck. Citizens of the United States often refer to themselves as Americans; however, that term really applies to everyone who lives south of the U.S.-Canadian border. The majority of people who live in Mexico, Central America, the islands of the West Indies, and South America speak either Spanish, Portuguese, or French—languages that have developed from Latin. Consequently, this region is typically called *Latin America*.

¿Habla Usted Español?

Nearly two-thirds of the people who live in Latin America speak Spanish. This common language creates a bond between the various cultures. Extend your students' understanding of the people of this region by incorporating Spanish into your unit. First provide Spanish resource books such as *Spanish For Beginners* by Angela Wilkes, a phrase dictionary, or a Spanish language study guide. Next challenge your students to learn a new Spanish phrase each day for several weeks. As each student selects a useful phrase from the resource books, instruct him to record the phrase, its meaning, and its use on an index card. Have the student use his card to introduce one new phrase per day to the class. Gather the cards and use them for review or as a learning center activity. Instruct students to practice all the phrases. At the end of a designated time period, see how many students can accurately use the phrases in conversation. Reward successful students with "¡Yo Hablo Español!" badges using the patterns on page 59.

Latin American Treasure Hunt

Numerous adventurers came to the New World in search of treasure. Have your students conduct research to find a treasure load of facts about Latin America. Duplicate a supply of the coin pattern on page 59 on yellow construction paper. Instruct each student to write one fact in sentence form on a coin pattern; then have him cut out the pattern. Display this historical, geographical, and cultural bullion on a bulletin board under the title "Treasures Of Latin America."

Latin American "Info-mercial"

Latin American countries rely heavily upon tourism as a means of income. How do entrepreneurs in each country encourage people to visit their homeland? They advertise, of course. Have each of your students try her sales skills by conducting an advertising campaign for the Latin American country of her choice. After conducting research and listing the pertinent facts about her country, have the student work alone or with a small group to devise a three- to five-minute commercial about her country. This "info-mercial" should be informative and entertaining, and should arouse the interest of the listener. Use the fact-gathering sheet on page 60 to help your students get started. Videotape the final products, and let students check out the tape to share at home.

Contemporary Issues

How is the region of Latin America changing? By exploring the nine topics below, your students will gain a clearer understanding of how the cultures of our southern neighbors are changing and developing as we enter the 21st century.

Divide your class into nine groups. Assign each group one of the topics to research. Have each group gather resources and prepare its report. Spend several days listening to the presentations. As each report is presented, ask the students to relate its information to that of previous reports. For instance, after listening to the report on common markets, ask students to identify how an individual country's climate or government might affect its participation in a common market.

Topics To Research:

- Who were the Mayas, Incas, and Aztecs? When and where did they live? What were they like? Where are they now? What influences have their cultures had on modern Latin American society?
- Develop an outline and timeline of the first European explorers to "discover" the region of Latin America. What influences did the Europeans bring with them? What effect did the Europeans have on the existing cultures?
- Study a climate map of Latin America. Identify at least five different climate regions. Also compare and contrast the rainfall, temperature, population, and animal and plant life of each region. Record each region's natural resources as well as its man-made products. Discuss the effect that climate has on production in that region.
- Describe the government of each Latin American country. How are these governments alike and different? Why do countries located on the same continent have different governments? Who are some of the most popular Latin American leaders in history? What made them popular? What role has the military played in governing these countries?
- What is a *common market*? Which Latin American countries belong to a common market and which do not? What are the advantages and disadvantages of membership? How does a common market operate? What agreements and laws are necessary to regulate it? What happens if a country breaks a rule?
- What is the Pan American Highway? Where is it? When, how, and why was it constructed? Through which countries and near which cities does it pass? What positive and/or negative effects has it had on the communities and environment of Latin America?
- What is the Organization of American States (OAS)? When and for what reason was it founded? Which Latin American countries belong to it? What are the advantages and disadvantages of membership?
- What is the Panama Canal? Who built it and why? How has it affected the economy of the Americas? Who owns this canal now and who will own it in the year 2000? Based on your research, do you think this new ownership will bring about any significant changes?

The United States recently signed a free trade agreement with Mexico. What is *free trade*? What are its advantages and disadvantages for the United States? For Mexico? What other country(ies) enjoy free trade with the United States?

Latin American Mosaics

The art of creating mosaics is currently experiencing a revival in Latin America. This is due in part to renewed interest in the work of famous artists such as Diego Rivera, who designed the mosaic on the Olympic Stadium in Mexico City, and Juan O'Gorman, whose historical mosaic appears on the library of the University Of Mexico.

Have students explore this art form by constructing their own mosaics. First have each student draw a large, simple, easily recognizable design on a 9" x 12" sheet of construction paper. After choosing the colors for their designs, instruct the students to cut 1/2-inch pieces from construction paper, wrapping paper, foil, or magazine pictures. Have them sort the pieces in small paper plates or bowls according to color. Using patience and a little glue, instruct the students to carefully glue the colorful pieces onto their drawings, filling in the spaces to complete their designs. Display the completed designs under a banner entitled "Magnífico Mosaics."

Latin American Fiesta

Between national holidays and religious festivals, Latin Americans celebrate many fiestas. Have your students practice planning strategies as they design the events for their own festival. During this finale, have students present projects, display models and artwork, entertain each other with skits and songs, and eat delicious Latin American food.

Divide your class into three to six groups. Have each group use the Group Fiesta Planning Sheet on page 62 to plan its portion of the festival. Listed below are some activities for your students to consider:

- Dress up as a fictional or nonfictional Latin American character and give a report about your life.
- Construct a three-dimensional model of landforms, ancient or modern architecture, or the Panama Canal.
- Create artwork that reflects the style of either ancient or modern artisans.
- Present a traditional song or dance.
- Present a persuasive essay on a current Latin American issue.
- Dramatize a Latin American folktale or a historical event.
- Create the flags of Latin American nations using construction paper.
- Plan a Latin American menu and cook the food.
- Select traditional prerecorded music to play during lunch.
- Design table decorations for the festival luncheon: placemats woven from construction paper, napkins with sponge prints of Latin American designs, and napkin rings cut from paper-towel rolls and colored with paints or markers.
- Design a program outlining the festival events.
- Design invitations requesting that parents and/or another class join in the festivities.

Use with "¿Habla Usted Español?" on page 56.   **Patterns**

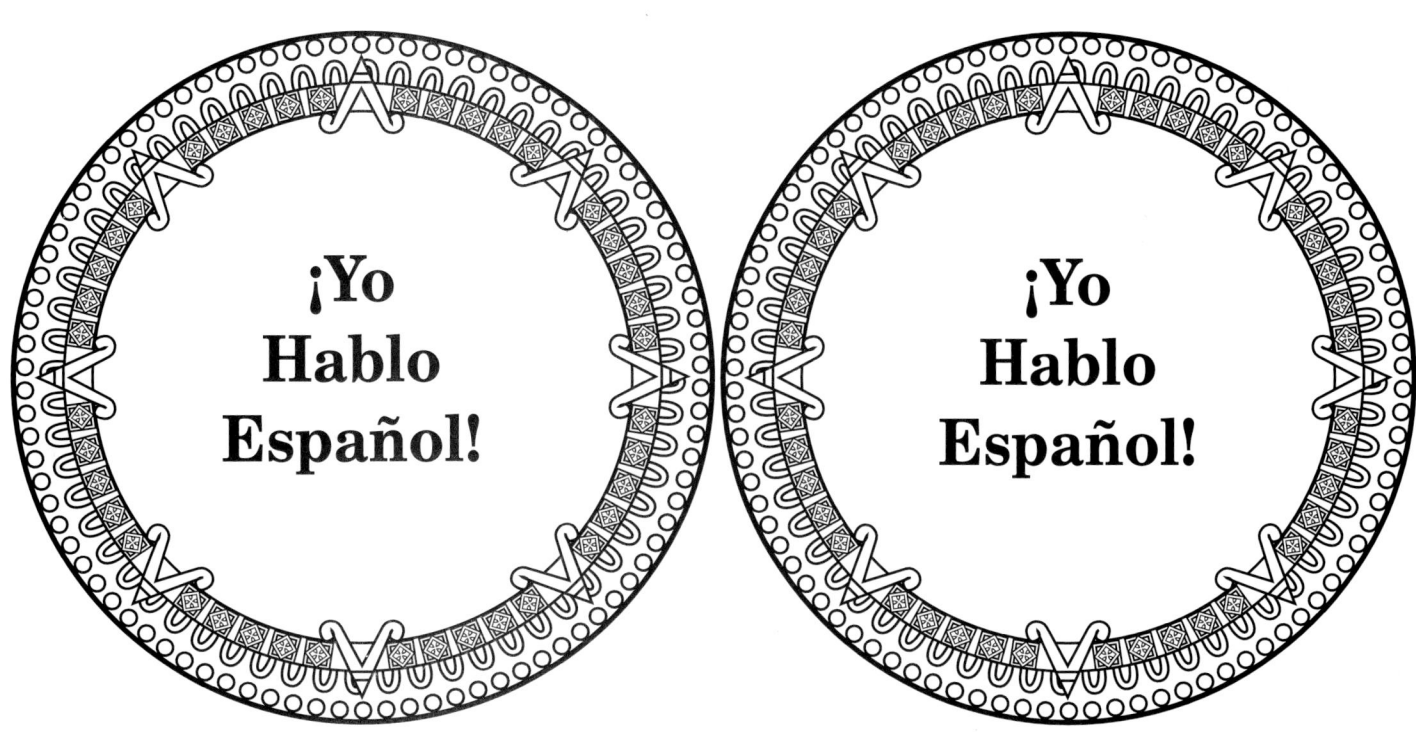

Use with "Latin American Treasure Hunt" on page 56.

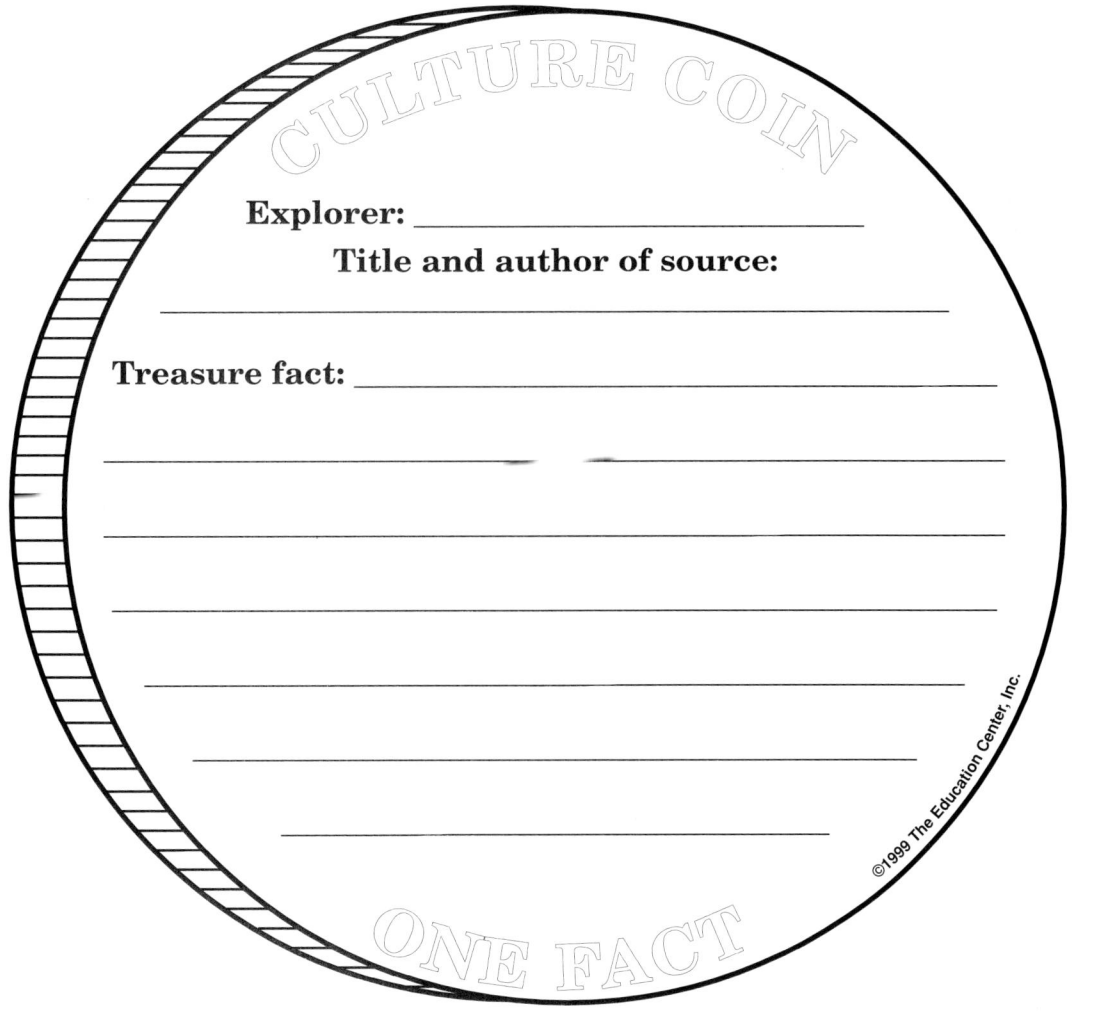

Name_____   Research: creating an advertisement

The Most Fascinating Place In The World

You have been selected to write a commercial for the following country. How can you make your commercial message informative and appealing? Use the following form to help you gather facts, brainstorm catchy phrases, and create inviting descriptions. Invite tourists to come and see the most fascinating place in the world!

Name of country: _____

Describe the location using descriptive phrases ("Nestled on the east coast, tucked between, etc.,..."): _____
_____
_____
_____
_____
_____

What special activities are available for people interested in exercising, history, shopping, etc.?
_____
_____
_____
_____
_____
_____

What are the people like (physical characteristics, ancestries, attitudes, occupations, etc.)?
_____
_____
_____
_____
_____
_____

Write a *slogan*—a brief, attention-getting phrase—to promote tourism in your country.
_____
_____
_____
_____
_____

Describe particular customs, special celebrations, or holidays.
_____
_____
_____
_____
_____

Draw a simple logo or design to represent your country.

List five words that describe the climate.
_____
_____

What should tourists pack to wear while visiting?
_____
_____
_____

List the props you will need to present your commercial.
_____
_____
_____
_____

©1999 The Education Center, Inc. • *The Best Of The Mailbox® Social Studies • Intermediate* • TEC1474

Note To Teacher: Use with "Latin American 'Info-mercial'" on page 57.

Name _____   Writing: comparing and contrasting

A Capital Comparison

Two important cities, two different cultures. But just how different are the cities of Brasília (the capital of Brazil) and Washington, DC? Research to find out about these two capital cities. Include the information listed below in a paragraph comparing and contrasting Brasília with Washington, DC. Write your final copy neatly below. Use the back of this page if you need more space. Include a title on the line provided.

- location within nation
- date that city was built on that site
- previous location of nation's capital and reason for relocating capital
- city planner(s) who designed layout of city
- architect(s) who designed government buildings
- facts about the layout design of the city
- name of president's home
- population
- nearby rivers

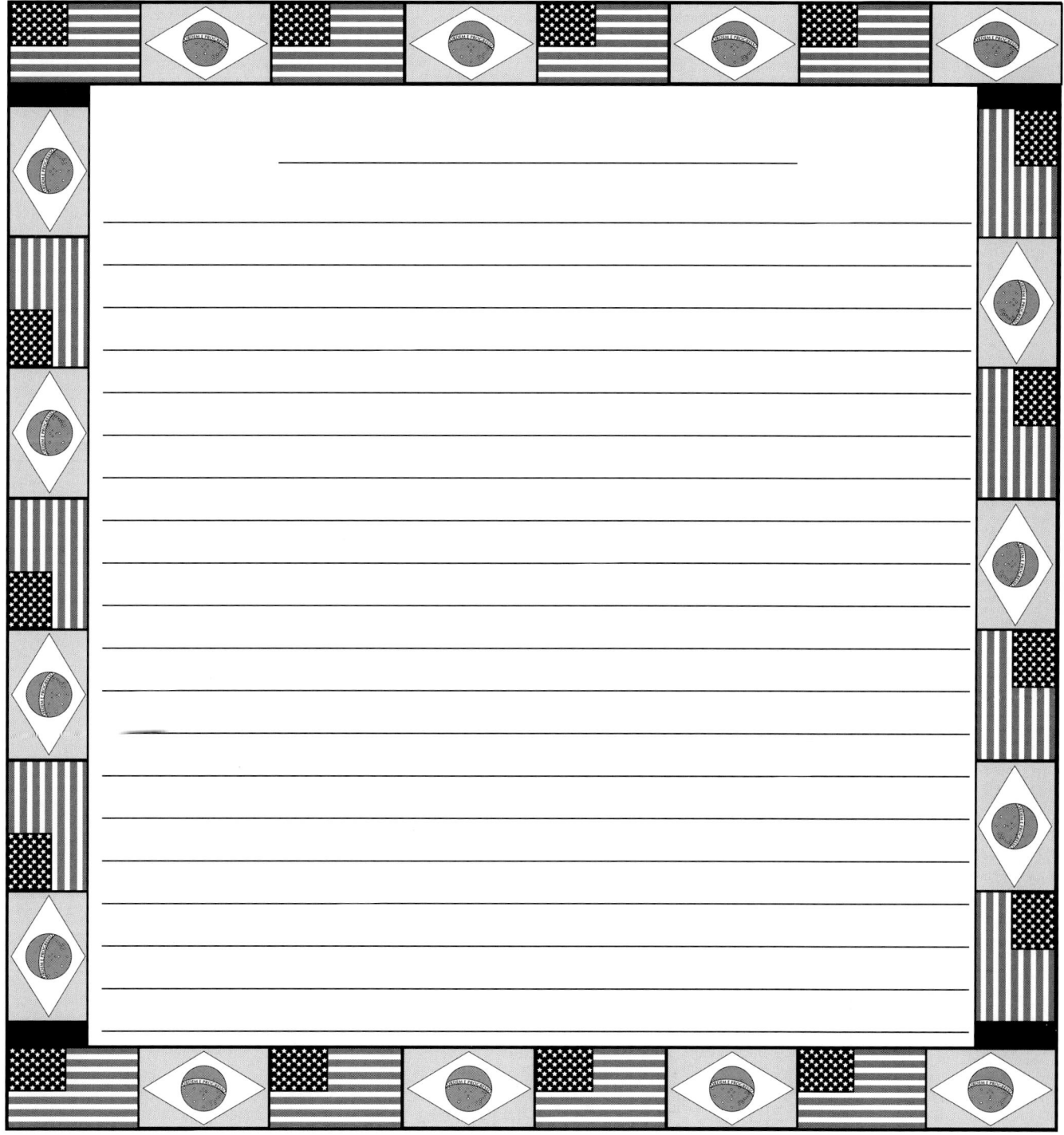

Bonus Box: Choose one of the cities above. Draw a map showing the city's layout as seen from an airplane.

Group Fiesta Planning Sheet

Group Members: _____

Date Of Fiesta: _____

Food: *Which foods will your group prepare and bring?*

    A. Main Course: (Circle one.)   Vegetable   Meat   Fruit

    Name of recipe: _____
    Write the recipe on an index card and attach it to this form.

    B. Side Dish: (Circle one.)   Bread   Dessert   Drink
    Other: _____

Dramatic Presentation: *Circle the letter of your group's choice. Write its title in the space provided.*

    A. Skit about a historical event: _____

    B. Traditional song: _____

    C. Traditional dance: _____

    D. Other: _____

Report: *Circle the letter of your group's choice. Be sure to include visuals: map, model, table, diagram, etc.*

    A. Contemporary issue facing several Latin American countries: _____
    _____

    B. Biography of a famous Latin American: _____

    C. Highlight a specific Latin American group of people, focusing on one aspect of its culture.
    Name of group: _____

Note To Teacher: Use this page with "Latin American Fiesta" on page 58.

Voyages, Explorations, And Conquests

Student-Centered Activities That Explore The First Voyages To The New World

People knew very little of their world for thousands of years. Europeans knew nothing of the continents of North and South America. Native Americans knew nothing of Europe, Africa, and Asia. This changed when the Spanish began exploring western routes across the Atlantic Ocean to Asia. Use the following creative contracts to help your students get a better understanding of the world in the late 1400s and 1500s.

by Thad H. McLaurin

Tips For Using This Unit

This unit is designed so that you can make it as short or as long as you need in order to fit your schedule and curriculum needs. The student contracts—"Spanish Conquests," "France In The New World," and "English Explorers"—can be used in a variety of ways:

- Complete each contract or parts of it as a whole-class activity.
- Divide the class into pairs and have each pair complete all or just selected items on each contract. Pairs can be regrouped after each contract.
- Assign a due date and have students complete all or just selected items on each contract independently.
- Divide the class into six groups. Give two groups a Spanish contract, two groups a French contract, and two groups an English contract. Instruct students to complete all or just selected items on the contracts; then have each group present its findings.

Exploration Literature

Include the following books in your Exploration unit:
- *Pedro's Journal* by Pam Conrad (Scholastic Inc., 1992)
- *Morning Girl* by Michael Dorris (Hyperion Books For Children, 1994)
- *The Double Life Of Pocahontas* by Jean Fritz (Puffin Books, 1987)
- *The Story Of Sacajawea: Guide To Lewis And Clark* by Della Rowland (Dell Publishing, 1989)
- *Voyages To The New World, The Spanish Conquests In The New World,* and *The Search For A Northern Route* by Peter Chrisp (Thomson Learning, 1993)
- *Where Do You Think You're Going, Christopher Columbus?* by Jean Fritz (Putnam Publishing Group, 1981)
- *Exploration And Conquest: The Americas After Columbus, 1500–1620* by Betsy and Giulio Maestro (Lothrop, Lee & Shepard Books; 1994)
- *Who Really Discovered America?* by Stephen Krensky (Scholastic Inc., 1987)
- *Against All Opposition: Black Explorers In America* by Jim Haskins (Walker & Company, 1992)
- *The Accidental Explorers: Surprises And Side Trips In The History Of Discovery* by Rebecca Stefoff (Oxford University Press, 1993)

Name_____   Contract: Spanish explorers

Spanish Conquests

RESEARCH

1. Research four of the following explorers. Find where they went, why they went, and what they found. Record your findings on "Fast Facts" cards. Using a blank world map, trace the routes taken and label them with the explorers' names and dates of their voyages.

Explorers For Spain
- Christopher Columbus
- Hernando Cortés
- Francisco Pizarro
- Ferdinand Magellan
- Juan Ponce de Léon
- Vasco Nuñez de Balboa
- Hernando de Soto
- Francisco Coronado
- Estevanico

2. Find out what foods Columbus discovered in the New World that were unknown to Europeans. Also find out what European foods were brought to the New World.

3. Research to find out what large Native American empire of Mexico was conquered by Hernando Cortés. What large Native American empire of Peru was conquered by Francisco Pizarro? What did these two groups have that the Spanish wanted? How did the Spanish get it? What happened to the two empires?

WRITE

1. *Pedro's Journal* by Pam Conrad (Scholastic Inc., 1992) is about a fictitious ship's boy, Pedro, who is aboard Christopher Columbus's ship, the *Santa María*. Pretend you are Pedro's shipmate, keeping your own journal. On a separate sheet of paper, write a journal entry for the day Columbus discovered what he thought was Asia. Describe what you see, how you feel, and the feelings of the crew at the sighting of land!

2. What if Ponce de Léon had found the Fountain of Youth? What would have happened? Rewrite history and tell what you believe would have occurred.

3. Columbus's return from his first voyage caused quite a sensation in Spain. Write a news article with a headline announcing his return. Include in the article items that Columbus brought back from the New World.

CREATE

1. Create a New World buffet. Bring in examples of food the Spanish found in the New World. Provide plates and napkins. Cut the food into bite-sized pieces for your classmates to sample.

2. Create a three-dimensional model of Tenochtitlán, the Aztec capital, or of Columbus's ship, the *Santa María*.

3. Use the information on your Fast Facts cards to create a trifold display of Spanish explorers. Use three large pieces of cardboard. Hinge the sections together with tape or string. Paint the backgrounds a bright color. Make sure the display has a title and tells *who, what, when, where,* and *why*.

©1999 The Education Center, Inc. • *The Best Of* The Mailbox® *Social Studies • Intermediate •* TEC1474

Note To The Teacher: For the first "Research" activity, each student or group will need two copies of page 67 (four "Fast Facts" cards in all). Each student or group will also need one blank world map to trace the voyages of the Spanish explorers. Ask parent volunteers to help provide food for the first "Create" activity.

Name _____ Contract: French explorers

France In The New World

RESEARCH

1. Research four of the following explorers. Find where they went, why they went, and what they found. Record your findings on "Fast Facts" cards. Using a blank world map, trace the routes taken and label them with the explorers' names and dates of their voyages.

Explorers For France
- Giovanni da Verrazano
- Jacques Cartier
- Samuel de Champlain
- Father Jacques Marquette and Louis Joliet
- Jean Baptiste Pointe du Sable
- Robert de La Salle

Giovanni da Verrazano

Jacques Cartier

2. Unlike other European countries, France developed a good relationship with the Native Americans. Find out why this happened. Which European countries had poor relationships with the Native Americans?

3. Samuel de Champlain founded the first permanent French settlement in the New World—Quebec. Today Quebec is one of the leading cities of Canada. How has this modern city kept its French heritage?

WRITE

1. During the 1600s Frenchmen came to explore the wilderness of the New World, not to conquer it. Many were known as *coureurs de bois* (runners of the woods) or *voyageurs* (travelers). They befriended the Native Americans and adopted their hunting and survival techniques. Pretend you are a voyageur learning how to survive in the wilderness. Write a letter to your family in France of your adventures.

2. Jean Baptiste Pointe du Sable (a well-known black explorer) set up a trading post on the Chicago River in 1779. Why was this a good area for him to settle? Pretend you are du Sable writing in your journal. Explain why you've decided to set up a trading post along the Chicago River.

3. What would have happened if the Native Americans had sailed to Europe first? How would the Europeans have felt about being *discovered*? Would the Native Americans have tried to conquer the Europeans, or would they have befriended them?

CREATE

1. The French fur trade was booming by the 1600s. Hats made of beaver and otter pelts were in great demand in Paris. Research other animal skins that were in demand and the garments made from them. Create a poster advertising goods made from North American furs. Describe each garment and the type of animal fur used.

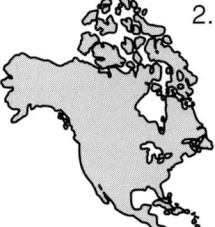

2. Create a map of North America in the late 1600s showing land claimed by the French. Label major landforms explored and claimed by French explorers. Also show who had claimed land to the west and east of the French.

3. If you were a French explorer, what supplies would you need? Create two lists of supplies. First list supplies needed for an expedition in the 1600s. Then list supplies needed for an expedition in the 1990s. Compare the two lists. Which items are still needed in the 1990s that were used in the 1600s?

©1999 The Education Center, Inc. • *The Best Of The Mailbox® Social Studies • Intermediate • TEC1474*

Note To The Teacher: For the first "Research" activity, each student or group will need two copies of page 67 (four "Fast Facts" cards in all). Each student or group will also need one blank world map to trace the voyages of the French explorers. Make copies of the pattern on page 68 for students to use with the first "Write" activity.

Name_____ Contract: English explorers

English Explorers

RESEARCH

1. Research four of the following explorers. Find where they went, why they went, and what they found. Record your findings on "Fast Facts" cards. Using a blank world map, trace the routes taken and label them with the explorers' names and dates of their voyages.

   Explorers For England
   - Henry Hudson
   - John Cabot
   - Sir Francis Drake
   - Sebastian Cabot
   - Martin Frobisher
   - John White
   - John Smith

John Smith

Martin Frobisher

Sebastian Cabot

2. Native Americans suffered from diseases brought to the New World by the English and other European settlers. Research the following diseases: smallpox, bubonic plague, typhus, cholera, measles, and diphtheria. Why were Native Americans so helpless against these diseases?

3. Research England's use of piracy to gain wealth from the Spanish. Who were some of England's most notorious pirates of the 1570s and 1580s? What was taken from the Spanish ships that helped England become so wealthy?

WRITE

1. In the 1570s Martin Frobisher sailed for England looking for a northern route to China. He encountered the Inuit people of the Arctic. The English thought the Inuit were simple savages, yet the Inuit were able to live and thrive in the Arctic. Write a paragraph explaining what you think about the English views of the Inuit people.

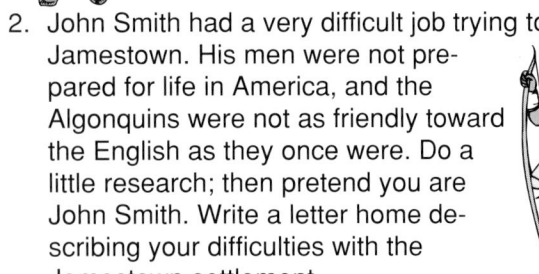

2. John Smith had a very difficult job trying to settle Jamestown. His men were not prepared for life in America, and the Algonquins were not as friendly toward the English as they once were. Do a little research; then pretend you are John Smith. Write a letter home describing your difficulties with the Jamestown settlement.

3. The English Company of Virginia raised money and attracted people to come and settle in Jamestown. The advertisements made America sound too good to pass up! Write an advertisement recruiting settlers for Jamestown.

CREATE

1. Create a timeline of English expeditions. Include the name of the explorer, plus the destination and purpose of his voyage. Add illustrations of the explorers or their expeditions.

2. The English looked for gold but soon realized there was very little to be found. Jamestown needed a way to make money for survival. The solution was tobacco. Tobacco was new to the English. Create an advertisement poster that may have been used by an English merchant to entice customers into trying this new product. The health hazards of smoking were unknown to the British. Research the hazards of smoking; then add a warning to the bottom of your poster.

3. Create a travel brochure for a new English colony. First think about where your colony should be located. What is its name? How is it going to make money? What will interest new settlers in your colony? Fold an 8 1/2" x 11" piece of paper into thirds. Include illustrations and information on both sides of the sheet.

©1999 The Education Center, Inc. • *The Best Of The Mailbox® Social Studies • Intermediate* • TEC1474

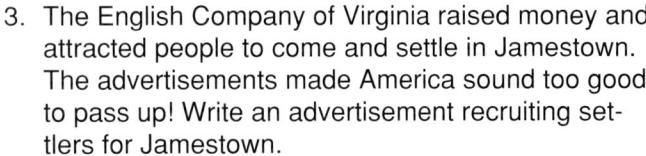

Note To The Teacher: For the first "Research" activity, each student or group will need two copies of page 67 (four "Fast Facts" cards in all). Each student or group will also need one blank world map to trace the voyages of the English explorers. Make copies of the pattern on page 68 for students to use with the second "Write" activity.

Fast Facts

_____
(Explorer's name)

(Draw a picture of the explorer or a scene from his voyage, and paste it here.)

Purpose of the voyage: _____
_____
_____
_____
_____
_____
_____
_____
_____
_____
_____
_____
_____

Destination: _____
_____
_____
_____

Discoveries: _____
_____
_____
_____
_____
_____
_____
_____
_____
_____

Was the voyage a success? Explain. _____
_____
_____
_____

©1999 The Education Center, Inc.

Fast Facts

_____
(Explorer's name)

(Draw a picture of the explorer or a scene from his voyage, and paste it here.)

Purpose of the voyage: _____
_____
_____
_____
_____
_____
_____
_____
_____
_____
_____
_____
_____

Destination: _____
_____
_____
_____

Discoveries: _____
_____
_____
_____
_____
_____
_____
_____
_____
_____

Was the voyage a success? Explain. _____
_____
_____
_____

©1999 The Education Center, Inc.

Note To The Teacher: To complete the first "Research" activity on each contract, give each student or group two copies of this page (four "Fast Facts" cards in all).

Pattern

Use with the first "Write" activity on page 65 and the second "Write" activity on page 66.

_____ (date)

_____,
(greeting)

_____,
(closing)

_____
(signature)

©1999 The Education Center, Inc. • *The Best Of* The Mailbox® *Social Studies • Intermediate •* TEC1474

Folding Directions:

Fold in.

Fold down. / Fold up.

Seal the envelope with a sticker. Do not use glue.
(Back)

return address / stamp / mailing address
(Front)

Note To The Teacher: Provide students with stickers for sealing the letters.

The Road To Ancient Rome

Engineering brilliance, exquisite art and architecture, and military might—words that describe one of the most advanced civilizations and greatest powers the world has ever known. Lead your students on a journey to the fascinating world that was ancient Rome with the following innovative activities and reproducibles.

written by Cynthia Wurmnest and Elizabeth H. Lindsay

Background Information

Believed to have begun as a small village in 753 B.C., Rome soon grew into a magnificent and vast civilization. At its height in about 100 A.D., it spanned the entire area of the Mediterranean coast, parts of Central Europe, North Africa, and the Middle East. This great empire—filled with the rich and diverse cultures of its nearly 80 million citizens—was linked together by an impressive network of roads (some of which still exist today). Thus the saying "All roads lead to Rome" was truly fitting.

"Rome-in' " Through The Library

Get your study of ancient Rome moving with a challenging scavenger hunt that will polish even the rustiest of library skills! Give a quick review of how to use an index, a table of contents, and an alphabetically arranged resource like an encyclopedia or biographical index. Then divide the class into teams of four. Give each team a copy of "On The Road To Rome" on page 72. Then direct each team to scavenge reference materials like those discussed to find the answers to the listed questions. Emphasize the need to identify a key word or words in helping locate information. Check the answers of the first team to finish; then continue the competition for the remaining teams. Reward the first team to answer all of the questions accurately with a special treat or prize.

The Roman Wall Of Fame

Legendary people—are they always good, or are they sometimes not-so-good? Direct students to identify legendary people throughout history who exhibit either positive or negative characteristics, such as Davy Crockett and Jesse James. Then discuss the characteristics of each one.

Next write the names of some famous Romans like those listed below on the board. Pair students; then supply each pair with a 4" x 6" index card, a six-foot sheet of bulletin-board paper, and markers or colored pencils. Direct the pair to choose a person from the list to research for information such as who he was, when and where he lived, and why he was famous. Have the pair record its information on its index card. Next have the pair create a life-size portrait of the person in action. Instruct one student to lie on the bulletin-board paper while the other student traces an outline of his body. Finally have the pair add detail and color to its figure. (See the example shown on the left.) After each pair has shared its information, display the figures and summaries on a large wall in the classroom or hallway titled "The Roman Wall Of Fame."

- Romulus and Remus
- Trajan
- Spartacus
- Julius Caesar
- Augustus
- Tiberius
- Nero
- Hadrian
- Mark Antony
- Constantine The Great
- Virgil
- Cicero
- Horace

Spartacus was a famous Thracian gladiator. He fought other gladiators and wild animals in an arena to entertain the Romans. When he fought, he wore a helmet and used a shield and sword. He later led many gladiators in a rebellion against the Roman forces. He died in battle in 71 B.C.

Amazing Aqueduct Engineering

The city of Rome had millions of gallons of water pumped daily to its households, bathhouses, fountains, and public toilets. This water was brought from high in the mountains by massive man-made channels called *aqueducts*. Some of the aqueducts that brought water to Rome still stand today and continue to service the city's fountains.

Demonstrate the principle of the aqueduct system with the following experiment. Provide each group of students with two small buckets and a six-foot piece of clear, plastic aquarium tubing. Fill one bucket with water; then add a small amount of food coloring to the water so that students may more easily see it flow through the tubing. Direct each group to place the water-filled bucket on a desk and the empty one on the floor beside the desk. Next direct one member in each group to place one end of the tubing into the water. Instruct the student to siphon the water from the bucket by gently sucking on the tubing until the water appears at the edge of the bucket. Then tell the student to quickly place the tubing into the empty bucket. Finally discuss how—like an aqueduct bringing water down from the mountains—the pressure brought on by the higher elevation of the water-filled bucket causes the continuous flow of water to the bucket placed at the lower level.

Cafe Roma!

Fast food in ancient Rome? You bet your *popinas!* Although wealthier Romans ate their dinners in the *triclinium* (a room with a dinner table surrounded by three couches), most ate at local "take-away bars" called *popinas* or bought food from street vendors. Their diet consisted of foods grown in their area and those imported from conquered lands. The result was a diverse menu of fruits, vegetables, meats, and grains, such as those listed at the right.

Invite your students to sample the flavor of the Roman diet by arranging your own take-away bar. About a week in advance, enlist the aid of parents in purchasing the foods and supplies for your bar. On the day of the activity, have students set up the bar and create posters advertising the foods being offered. Then feast in a fashion fit for an emperor!

Foods:
Eggs, nuts, cheese, breads, honey, wine (grape juice for students), figs, dates, apples, grapes, cabbages, carrots, cherries, peaches, pears, plums, leeks, olives, lettuces, beef, pork, chicken, fish; other special favorites included small birds, fattened snails, peacock brains, flamingo tongues, and a sauce made of fish guts called *liquamen!*

Trading Places

Roman citizens belonged to one of three main classes. These classes included the high-ranking *patricians,* wealthy landowners from the original families of Rome; the middle-ranking *equites,* rich merchants and traders; and the lower-ranking *plebeians,* the ordinary working class. Other people were allowed to live in the city, but did not have full-citizen's rights. This group included *slaves* who might be prisoners, captives of war, or people purchased from a slave dealer.

Divide students into groups of four. Direct each member of a group to research one of the classes for information on topics such as home, family life, work, leisure activities, and rights and privileges. Two good sources are Mike Corbishley's *Growing Up In Ancient Rome* (Troll Communications L.L.C., 1993) and *What Do We Know About The Romans?* (Peter Bedrick Books, Inc.; 1992). Then direct each member to prepare a two-minute talk for his group in which he becomes that member of society. If desired, give students time to construct props in order to enliven their speeches; then videotape them in action! After all speeches are shared, discuss students' findings as a class.

Mosaic Art

Roman walls and floors were covered with detailed pictures made from small, brightly colored glass, stone, or ceramic tile. These *mosaics* were a popular art form in ancient Rome and often detailed Roman life—a baker placing bread in the oven or a Roman god or goddess, for example. Challenge your students to become creators of their own mosaics. Provide each student with a variety of colorful half-inch-wide strips of construction paper, a sheet of 9" x 12" light-colored construction paper, scissors, glue, and a pencil. Direct each student to first draw a simple outline of a figure—such as a flower vase, an animal, or a hot-air balloon—onto the sheet of construction paper. Next instruct the student to cut the construction-paper strips into 1/4-inch squares. Have the student use glue to fill in the figure with the squares. Display the mosaics on a wall or bulletin board.

E Pluribus Unum (One Out Of Many)

Out of one language come many of the words in the English language—one-third to be exact! That language is none other than *Latin*—the language of ancient Romans. As the Romans conquered new lands and their empire grew, they brought their language with them.

Have each student bring in a brown paper grocery bag. Direct the student to cut out the bottom of her bag, cut along one side, and then lay the bag flat. If desired, have the student tear the outside edges of the bag to make it look like the papyrus paper on which the Romans often wrote. Next explain to students how to find the *etymology,* or origin, of a word in the dictionary. Share several examples of words that originate from Latin. Then direct each student to write the letters from *A* to *Z* on her bag. Instruct the student to search a dictionary to find a word that is of Roman origin for each letter. Have the student write the word, its Latin counterpart, and a definition in her own words next to each letter as shown. Display each student's collection of words. Before you know it, your students will be speakin' and writin' in Roman!

When In Rome—Do As The Romans Do!

Would you believe that graffiti written on public buildings is not just a problem of today's world? The ancient Romans were notorious for the messages they engraved on stone walls throughout their cities! Invite your students to take part in this Roman tradition—but in a more productive manner! Obtain a six-foot sheet of bulletin-board paper and draw a wall on it like the example shown. Post the paper on a large wall or bulletin board. Next direct each student to research a specific Roman contribution or achievement. Instruct each student to draw an illustration or symbol representing the contribution on the wall, then write a descriptive sentence or two beside his picture. After the wall is finished, have each student share his graffiti art.

A—abbreviate, abbreviatus, to shorten
B—beast, bestia, a four-footed animal
C—cellar, cellarium, basement
D—document, documentum, official paper
E—exceed, exedere, overdo
F—
G—
H—
I—
J—
K—
L—
M—
N—
O—
P—
Q—
R—

Latin phrases such as status quo (things as they are), and et cetera (and the rest) are still used today.

Civilians accused of a crime were tried by a jury. The jury listened to evidence about the crime, and then a judge passed a sentence according to the law.

OCTAVIAN WAS HERE, 13 A.D.!

Plants and animals are often classified using Latin names. **Ranunculus** is the scientific name for a buttercup.

Veni, vidi, vici! (I came, I saw, I conquered!)

Names_____ Research

On The Road To Rome

Looking to find some fascinating facts about ancient Rome? Then get ready to roam the library! First, underline the key word or words in each question that will help you start your hunt. Then, using the words, search through reference materials to find the answer to each question. Write your answers on another sheet of paper.

1. Did the Etruscans live in Italy before or after the rise of the Roman Empire?
2. In what year did Romulus and Remus supposedly found Rome?
3. On what continent was the city-state of Carthage located?
4. What sea did the Roman Empire surround?
5. For what was the forum in the city of Rome used?
6. Did the Roman Empire include England?
7. What was the date of Julius Caesar's assassination?
8. What was the main military road that led out of Rome?
9. How were the Roman public bathhouses heated?
10. What volcano buried Pompeii in mud and ash?
11. For what were aqueducts used?
12. Who were the gladiators and what did they do?
13. What was a centurion?
14. What animal was used to pull a chariot?
15. What is Trajan's Column?

Note To The Teacher: Use with " 'Rome-in' ' Through The Library" on page 69.

Name_____ Critical thinking

Unearthing Your Bedroom

Would you believe that a whole city in ancient Rome was buried in 79 A.D. by a layer of volcanic mud and ash? When scientists finally dug up the city about 1,700 years later, they found things exactly as they were before the volcano erupted! Guard dogs were at doorways, bread was in ovens, and people were trying to escape with jewelry or money. This enabled scientists to piece together a picture of the day-to-day life of a typical Roman family.

Imagine that your house is completely covered by a strange and mysterious substance that will preserve it for years to come. Then, 1,700 years later, scientists uncover artifacts in your bedroom. What would they discover about you?

Directions: In the box below, draw and color pictures of ten items depicting you and your life that you would want scientists to uncover. Then, on the back of this sheet, write a sentence for each item explaining why you chose it.

1.	2.	3.	4.	5.
6.	7.	8.	9.	10.

Name_____ Using Roman numerals

Roman 'Rithmetic

The ancient Romans did not use a place value system for numeration—they used symbols to name numbers. The seven symbols used for naming the numbers from 1 to 1,000,000 were read from left to right. The numbers were identified by adding and subtracting the symbol values.

Example: Add the values when the symbol representing a larger number appears before a symbol representing a smaller number. LX → 50 + 10 = 60; so LX = 60

Example: Subtract the values when the symbol representing a smaller number appears before a symbol representing a larger number. IX → 10 – 1 = 9; so IX = 9

Directions: Write a Roman numeral for each number described below. Write your answer on the blank before each number.

ROMAN NUMERALS:

I	II	III	IV	V
1	2	3	4	5

VI	VII	VIII	IX	X
6	7	8	9	10

XX	XXX	XL	L
20	30	40	50

LX	LXX	LXXX	XC	C
60	70	80	90	100

CC	CCC	CD	D
200	300	400	500

DC	DCC	DCCC	CM
600	700	800	900

M	M̄
1,000	1,000,000

_____ I. Your age

_____ II. Number of students in your class

_____ III. Number of days in the present month

_____ IV. Number of eggs in one dozen

_____ V. Number of days in a year

_____ VI. Number of states in the United States

_____ VII. Michael Jordan's jersey number (23)

_____ VIII. Number of players on a baseball team (9)

_____ IX. 656

_____ X. 1,347

_____ XI. Year in which you were born

_____ XII. Number of pages in your math book

_____ XIII. Number of feet in one mile (5,280)

_____ XIV. The current year

_____ XV. 2,000,000

Bonus Box: On the back of this sheet, write three of your Roman numerals answers from above. Add the numbers together; then write your sum in Roman numeral form.

A European Travelogue
Bringing The Grandeur And Diversity Of Europe To Your Classroom

From the majestic, snow-capped peaks of the Alps to a country that lies mostly below sea level, no other continent can rival the physical diversity of Europe. And with dozens of ethnic groups who speak over 50 different languages, no other region of the world is more culturally diverse.

Take your students on a whirlwind tour of our second most populous continent with the following creative group activities and reproducibles.

by Irving P. Crump

Where In The World?

The geographical boundaries of Europe are harder to define than those of the other continents. Europe is a large peninsula that projects from the huge Eurasian land mass. In the west and north, it is bound by the Atlantic Ocean and the Norwegian and Barents seas. To the south, the Mediterranean Sea seems to be the boundary; although the area around the Mediterranean is cut off from the rest of Europe by mountains, and its climate and topography are like those of North Africa and the Middle East. To the east, Europe is separated from Asia only by the Ural and Caucasus mountains, both of which run through portions of the former Soviet Union. Throughout this unit—and for simplicity—Europe will be defined by these boundaries.

Taking The Mystery Out Of Maps

Collect a variety of maps that depict Europe: a globe, a current world map, an outdated world map, and several others. Include maps in encyclopedias that show how the boundaries of some European countries have changed during this century. Ask students to bring to school maps that they may have at home. Next divide the class into small groups and provide each group with one map. Ask each group to study its map and answer this question: "What can you learn about Europe from your map?" Have a group recorder list all of the information that the group brainstorms.

Afterwards, lead a discussion about the different kinds of information that maps include, and how maps—like some books—can become outdated. Include these questions:

- Which map best represents Europe?
- From which map(s) can we learn Europe's longitudinal and latitudinal extent?
- From which map(s) can we learn the hemispheres in which Europe is located?
- Which maps include the names of Europe's countries? Major cities? Rivers?
- Which maps show landforms?
- Which maps show major population areas and population density?
- Which map of Europe is the most current?

Regions Within A Region

Europe has the second smallest land area of the seven continents. But in terms of landforms, it is the most diverse. As an ongoing project during your study of Europe, make a bulletin-board size enlargement of the outline map on page 78. Write the letters A-H at equal intervals across the top of the map; then add the numbers 1-8 vertically at equal intervals along the left side. Discuss with students how the other six continents are often described geographically (for example, "South America is described as the large land mass south of Panama"); then ask students to describe Europe.

Next divide your class into seven research teams. Assign each team one of the distinct regions identified within the continent and by a color (see the box below). Provide each team with a copy of pages 78 and 79. Have each group follow the directions for completing its map. After you check Part 3 of each group's work, have the group complete Part 4 by transferring the information onto the large classroom map.

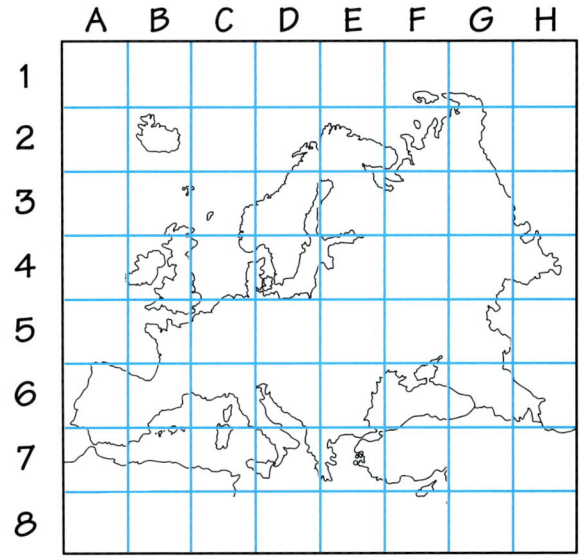

- **Mediterranean south**: Greece, Italy (which includes Vatican City and San Marino), Malta, Spain, Portugal, and the western part of Turkey *(pink)*
- **The western fringe**: Belgium, Luxembourg, France, Andorra, Monaco, and the Netherlands *(purple)*
- **The islands of Britain and Ireland** *(red)*
- **Germanic core**: Germany, Austria, Switzerland, and Liechtenstein *(orange)*
- **The eastern zone** (or Eastern Europe): Albania, Bulgaria, Hungary, Poland, Romania, Czechoslovakia, and the countries of the former nation of Yugoslavia *(yellow)*
- **The northern frontier**: Denmark, Finland, Iceland, Norway, and Sweden *(green)*
- **The European Soviet Union** (areas west of the Ural and Caucasus mountains and north of the Caspian Sea): made up of the most densely populated and economically developed republics of the former USSR *(tan)*

Team Tours

Provide each research team (see the preceding activity) with a copy of the geography themes outline on page 98. Have each team use the outline as a guide in researching its region of Europe. Although students will discover physical and cultural similarities among the countries in a region, each country also has a uniqueness of its own. In addition, provide each team with several copies of the current events reporting form on page 77. Have each group be on the lookout for newspaper and newsmagazine articles about their regions.

Suggest the activities on page 76 for each cooperative group to complete. If desired, duplicate the activities for each group.

Where Am I?

Use the numbers and letters on the large classroom map of Europe to create five clues about locations of countries, cities, rivers, and landforms in your region. For example: "I am a capital city located at B-5. What is my name?" Write each clue on a small index card.

Make an answer key for your clues by folding an index card in half. List the five sets of coordinates on the outside of the card; then list the answers on the inside. With the card folded, punch a hole in the top left corner and hang it on a pushpin that is attached near the map. Punch a hole in the top left corner of each clue card and hang the cards on top of the answer key card.

Visit the bulletin-board map and try to figure out your classmates' clues.

Flying Proudly

Draw the flag of each country in your region on a large index card. On a small index card, write the country's name and a description of its flag: its shape, designs, colors, symbols, etc. Display your flags, along with those of other research groups, above the bulletin-board map of Europe; display the descriptions of the flags below the bulletin board.

Visit the bulletin board and try to match other groups' flags with their written descriptions.

Country In A Box

Obtain a small box for each country in your region. With each box positioned as shown, cover the inside, bottom, and two sides with magazine and newspaper pictures and original drawings about the country. Choose pictures that show the games, hobbies, celebrations, and sports of the people, as well as ones that depict the country's natural resources and products. Display items that represent the country inside the box, such as dolls, products, models, and souvenirs. Stack the boxes as shown to create a striking display of your region!

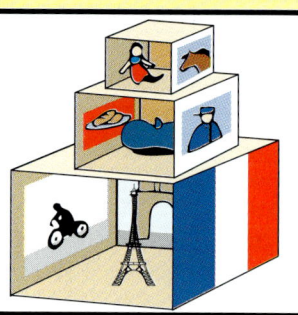

Mmmmmm, Good!

Name some special foods that are associated with your region. Choose 3-4 foods and write recipe cards for each one. Are the ingredients needed for each recipe grown in the region?

As a group, select your favorite recipe, collect the needed ingredients, and prepare it for your classmates. With your teacher's assistance, choose a special day in which all groups can bring in their dishes for an international tasting party.

The Top Ten

Brainstorm with your group the top ten reasons to visit your region. Consider climate, vacation spots, historical significance, tourist sites, interesting geographical features, and other appealing aspects of your region. With your group, decide the order of the ten reasons. Write your list on a large sheet of art paper, adding drawings and symbols to illustrate each reason.

Thanks For The Words

Have any of the words that we use come from a language spoken in your region? Research the *etymology* (word history) of each word listed below. Then try to find others that came from your particular area. (Your teacher has an answer key.)

kindergarten	broccoli	beret	delicatessen	circus	balcony	chili
skate	balloon	camouflage	fahrenheit	dialect	cocoa	sleigh
stampede	hamburger	genesis	chef	rodeo	psyche	studio
champagne	cruise	loafer	phobia	trombone	machete	garage
schooner	waltz	nausea	violin	mustang	cadet	waffle

(Note To Teacher: The key for this activity is on page 159.)

Name _____ Current events

It's happening in... EUROPE

Europe may be the second smallest continent in land size, but it has the second largest population. And despite its troubles during the 1900s, Europe continues to be a leading industrial and agricultural center of the world.

Complete this news article to report on an important news event in your region of Europe. After you answer the items, color the letters in the banner with your team color.

★★★★★★★★★★★★★★★★★★★★

Name the country (and city) in which this news story took place.

★★★★★★★★★★★★★★★★★★★★

Describe the country's location.

★★★★★★★★★★★★★★★★★★★★

Name the individuals or groups of individuals that the story is about.

Briefly describe the event.

★★★★★★★★★★★★★★★★★★★★

How will this event affect neighboring countries?

Will this event affect the United States or Canada? Explain.

★★★★★★★★★★★★★★★★★★★★

Describe how you feel about this event.

Note To Teacher: See "Team Tours" on page 75 for information on how to use this reproducible.

Name(s) ______________________________

Europe

Note To Teacher: Use with the activity on page 75 and the reproducible on page 79.

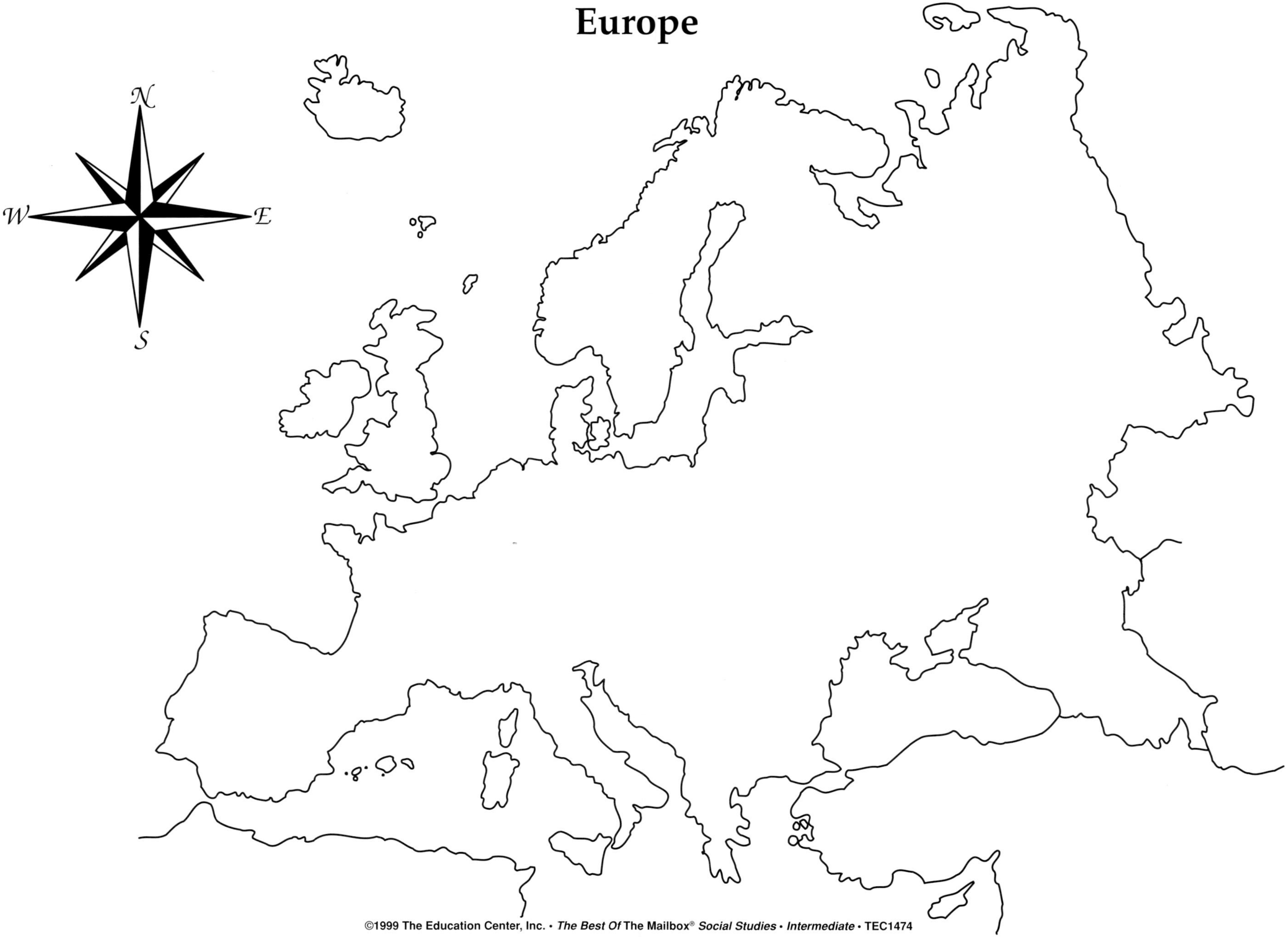

Name(s) _____ Map skills: Europe
Countries _____

Backpacking Through Europe
Follow the directions below to complete the map on page 79.

Part 1: Exploring Bodies Of Water
Label the following on your outline map of Europe. Then color all waters light blue.

Mediterranean Sea	Black Sea	North Sea	Adriatic Sea
Caspian Sea	Baltic Sea	English Channel	Aegean Sea
Atlantic Ocean	Bay of Biscay	Strait of Gibraltar	Barents Sea

Which bodies of water touch the countries in your region? _____
_____

Part 2: Exploring Mountains
Add ⋀ on your map to show the following mountain ranges. Label each mountain range. Use reference books to help you.

The **Pyrenees** lie between Spain and France.
The **Alps** cover part of southeastern France and northern Italy, most of Switzerland, and part of southern Germany, Austria, and the northern part of the former nation of Yugoslavia.
The **Apennines,** south of the Alps, cover much of Italy.
The **Caucasus Mountains** stretch between the Black and Caspian seas.
The **Ural Mountains** form the eastern border between Europe and Asia.

Part 3: Exploring Your Region
- Draw your group's countries on the map, using a pencil. If the countries have names or boundaries that have changed over the past few years, be sure to make those changes. Use a recent almanac or other up-to-date resource for the most current information.
- Write each country's name on the map.
- Add a small star for the capital of each country. Write the capital city's name near the star.

Part 4: Putting It All Together!
After your teacher checks your map, color the countries with your team color. Then draw the same information on the large bulletin-board map of Europe. Label each country and place a star in the location of the capital. Write the capital near the star. Then color the region on the large map with your team color.

©1999 The Education Center, Inc. • *The Best Of The Mailbox® Social Studies • Intermediate* • TEC1474 • Key p. 159

Note To Teacher: Use with the activities on pages 75 and 76 and the map on page 78.

Exploring The Medieval World

Creative Activities For Studying The Middle Ages

Knights in shining armor, towering castles surrounded by murky moats, and mystical legends of King Arthur and the famous Round Table—all these images and much more make the Middle Ages a period of history that intermediate students find captivating. Sort out the fact from the fiction during your study of the medieval world with the following creative activities, literature suggestions, and reproducibles.

with contributions by Terry Healy

Background Information: The Middle Ages

The Middle Ages is generally defined as the time period in western Europe between the A.D. 400s and the 1500s. The early part of this period was marked by the decline and fall of the Roman Empire, the invasions of the Germanic peoples from northern Europe, and the rise of Christianity. The strong central government of the Roman Empire was replaced by tribal rule. By the 800s, most of western Europe was divided into large areas of land called *manors,* ruled by wealthy landowners known as *lords*. Under this system of *feudalism,* the lords were served by other titled people known as *vassals,* who became independent rulers of their own *fiefs* (grants of land). The majority of the people were peasants who worked and lived on the land.

But Why?: An Introductory Activity

Before beginning a study of the Middle Ages, ask your librarian to help you gather plenty of reference books. Write intriguing statements such as the ones that follow on large cut-out flags attached to rolled-up newspapers or dowel rods as shown. Scatter the flags on your classroom walls. On the first day of your unit, give each student multiple copies of the open reproducible on page 86. Have each child bind the pages between two construction-paper covers to make a medieval-studies journal to use throughout the unit. Next have students guess the "why" behind each statement on the flags; then challenge them to use the reference books to answer each "why?" in their journals before the end of the unit (see page 159 for answers to the questions).

- Land was more important in medieval times than money. Why?
- By the 1200s, most castles were built of stone instead of wood. Why?
- A medieval town was a risky place to live. Why?
- A poor man in medieval times would likely never become a knight. Why?
- Hardly any medieval men or women could read. Why?
- The period between the 1000s and the late 1200s was a time of great achievement. Why?
- At least one-third of the entire population in western Europe died in the 1300s. Why?
- After 1500, castle-building stopped. Why?

Research Projects For Learning About The Middle Ages

With all the wonderful resources available on the medieval world, researching the Middle Ages can be a fascinating journey into the past. Choose one of the following group research projects for students to complete during your unit; or have students complete both projects for a real research workout.

Project #1—Go For The Guilds

During the latter part of the Middle Ages, craftsmen and merchants joined together to form unionlike organizations called *guilds*. Guilds were established for every craft from silversmithing to shoe making. Divide your class into cooperative groups; then have each group choose one topic from the list below. Explain that each group will form its own guild and work together to complete a research project on its topic. Give each guild a sheet of poster board and three same-sized pieces of cardboard cut from large boxes. Direct each guild to use packing tape to tape its three cardboard pieces together, making a standing display as shown. Also have each guild design a group emblem (used by medieval craftsmen to identify their guilds) on its piece of poster board. The emblem should represent the group's topic. Encourage each group to paint its display or glue colored paper to it; then have the group mount the emblem and a sentence strip labeled with its topic on the display.

After display boards have been made, challenge each group to display its information creatively on the standing display. When all displays have been completed, have guilds share them with the class. Invite other classes on your hall or grade level to examine the displays as well.

Topics:

Charlemagne	Castles	Black Death
Feudalism	Medieval Homes	Medieval Education
Knights & Knighthood	Medieval Farming	Medieval Food
Medieval Women	The Church	Medieval Art & Music
Life In A Medieval Town	Guilds	Medieval Clothing
Medieval Families	Peasant Life	Jousting & Tournaments
Life As A Noble	Fairs And Holidays	Trade & Industry
The Crusades	The Islamic World	Illuminations

Project #2—Giant Medieval Paper Dolls

To introduce the many different people who lived during the Middle Ages, divide the class into groups of two or three students each. Give each group a large piece of butcher paper, a copy of the reproducible planning sheet on page 83, and the other supplies listed in the "Note To The Teacher" at the bottom of the reproducible. After assigning each group one of the roles listed on page 83, instruct students to follow the steps to create a giant paper doll and a first-person letter detailing that medieval person's life. Have groups cut out their finished dolls; then display the dolls and letters on your classroom or hallway walls. Also have each group add any necessary labels to its doll, including the doll's name and role in medieval society.

We are sorely afraid for our lives. The Black Death has been reported in Lincolnshire. That town is only 20 miles from here! I...

Story-Starter Scrolls

Weave a writing workshop into your medieval studies with this easy-to-implement idea. Duplicate eight copies of the open reproducible on page 86. Dab each copy with a damp tea bag; then let the papers dry to give them an aged look. Use a black, fine-tipped permanent marker to label each paper with one of the following writing prompts:

- Tonight is my first night as a page. I have never been away from my family before. I pray that I might do well with my new duties. Oh, to become a knight! I....
- The jousting tournament begins tomorrow. The hall is bustling with anticipation of the upcoming events. As one of the knights who will be participating in the event, I....
- We are sorely afraid for our lives. The Black Death has been reported in Lincolnshire. That town is only 20 miles from here! I....
- What joyous news! My father has obtained an apprenticeship for me with a master craftsman. My future is now secure. I....
- It's hard to watch my brothers head to school at the monastery today—as it is every day. Here I am, stuck at home to help with all the housework and to look after my little sister. Everyone says that girls don't need to go to school, but I....
- I'll never forget my first visit to the town. Since my father works the land for Lord Highsmith, we've never needed to go to town. But one day, my father decided to take me. I couldn't believe what I saw. I....
- Living at my uncle's castle has been a real adventure! It's so huge, and there are so many people who work and live here or nearby. I....
- "What is it like being the lady of the castle?" I was surprised by my niece's question. Being the lady of the castle means....

Next have student volunteers use colored pencils or fine-tipped permanent markers to color the border of each sheet. Roll each finished page into a scroll; then tie it with a bright ribbon and place it in a basket with the other scrolls. At the start of a writing workshop, announce that a local historian recently found the scrolls—which appear to be unfinished journals—in a relative's house in Europe. Inform students that their job will be to finish the journal entries. Unfurl each scroll and read it aloud; then have a student volunteer pin each one to a bulletin board titled "Writings From The Medieval World." Have each student choose one prompt to copy and then finish on a copy of page 86. (Again, you may wish to stain the pages with tea bags before distributing them to students.) Post the finished stories on the bulletin board.

By Blazon!

Because armies in medieval times did not have standard uniforms, each knight wore his own design, called a *coat of arms*. These colorful, emblazoned designs were put on a knight's shield, banner, and outer coat to let others know who he was. Heralds—who served as messengers, reporters, and historians of the times—were skilled in the special language of *Blazon*, a language that described the coats of arms.

Give your students a hands-on taste of heraldry with the creative reproducible on page 85. Post the completed coats of arms on a bulletin board or on your classroom walls.

Names _____ Group research project

Making A Giant Medieval Paper Doll

Work with your group to complete a giant paper doll of one of the medieval people listed below. Circle the person your group will research; then follow the steps given below to complete your paper doll.

Medieval Roles:

A monk who lives in a monastery
A medieval peasant woman
A lord of a manor
A craftsman who lives in a town
A young boy training to be a knight
A medieval noblewoman
A knight
A bailiff who works on a manor
A stonemason helping to build a castle
A soldier fighting in the Crusades

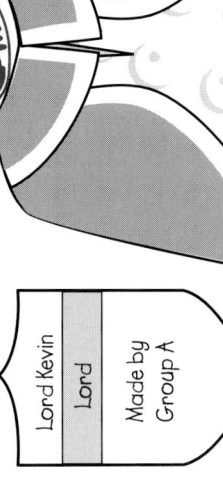

Lord Kevin
Lord
Made by Group A

Steps:

1. Have one group member lie on a large piece of paper; then trace his or her body to make the outline of a giant paper doll.
2. Research the following information about your medieval person:
   • In what kind of home did this person live?
   • What did this person wear?
   • What did this person eat?
   • How did this person spend his or her day?
   • What hardships did this person face?
   • In what way was this person important to medieval society?
3. After your group has answered each of these questions, draw eyes, hair, and other facial features on your paper doll. Decide on a name for your person.
4. Work together to "dress" your paper doll with clothing that matches the information you learned while researching. Draw on the clothing with crayons or markers. Or glue on clothing that you've cut from paper or fabric scraps.
5. Cut out your paper doll.
6. On another piece of paper, work as a group to write a letter from your person to the class. In the letter, give information that answers the questions above. Write the letter as if your person wanted to let your class learn about his or her life in medieval times.
7. After you've proofread your letter, rewrite it on one or more copies of the stationery your teacher will give you.
8. Share your letter and paper doll with the class.

©1999 The Education Center, Inc. • *The Best Of The Mailbox® Social Studies • Intermediate* • TEC1474

Note To The Teacher: Use this page with "Giant Medieval Paper Dolls" on page 81. Give each group a large piece of butcher paper, scissors, glue, markers and crayons, and one or more copies of the open reproducible on page 86. To make the letters in step 6 look more authentic, first have each group dab a damp tea bag on one or more copies of page 86. After the page has dried, have the group rewrite its letter on the aged-looking paper.

Name _____ Vocabulary

Become A Vocabulary Knight!

In the Middle Ages, a boy who wanted to become a knight had to go through quite a bit of training. First he became a *page*. As a page, he learned how to behave and how to ride. When he was about 14, a page was apprenticed to a knight and became a *squire*. As a squire he looked after his knight's horses, armor, and weapons. He also learned how to fight. If a squire was successful, he became a *knight* when he was about 21 years old.

In the banners and shields below are important vocabulary words that will help you learn about the Middle Ages. Work your way from being a page all the way to knighthood by following the steps below!

To become a page:
- Use a crayon to circle 15 of the words. Create a crossword or other puzzle using the words and their meanings.

To become a squire:
- Use a different-colored crayon to circle 10 more words. Make a set of flash cards to help you learn their meanings.
- Draw a medieval scene that includes at least 15 of your circled words in some way. Label your scene with the vocabulary words that are illustrated.

To become a knight:
- Use a different-colored crayon to circle 10 more words, making a total of 35 words.
- Make a mini dictionary that includes each circled word, its definition, a sample sentence using it, and an illustration. Be sure to organize your dictionary so that words are listed alphabetically. Add an attractive cover.

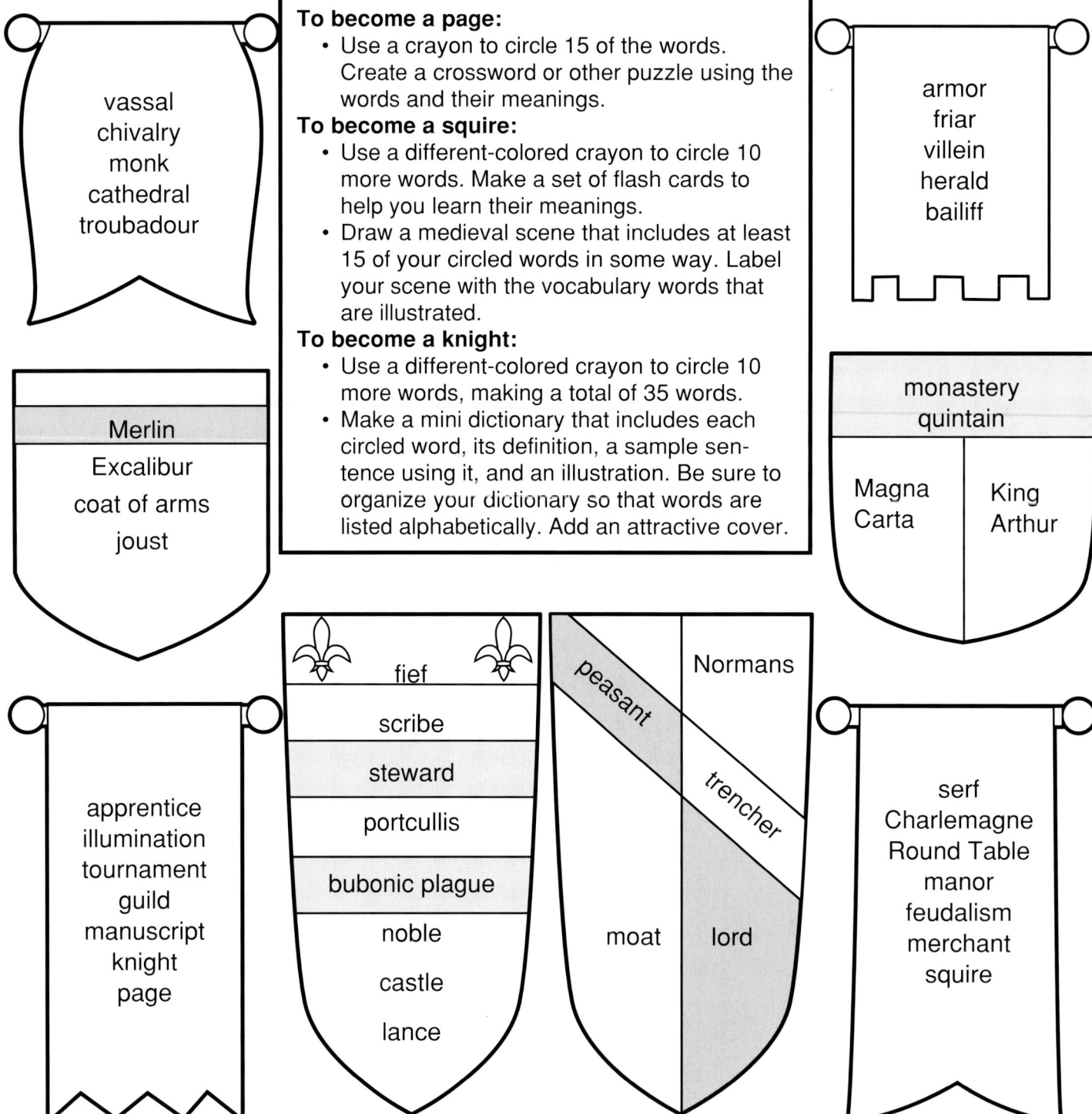

Banner 1:
vassal
chivalry
monk
cathedral
troubadour

Banner 2:
armor
friar
villein
herald
bailiff

Shield 1:
Merlin
Excalibur
coat of arms
joust

Shield 2:
monastery
quintain
Magna Carta | King Arthur

Banner 3:
apprentice
illumination
tournament
guild
manuscript
knight
page

Shield 3:
fief
scribe
steward
portcullis
bubonic plague
noble
castle
lance

Shield 4:
Normans
peasant
trencher
moat
lord

Banner 4:
serf
Charlemagne
Round Table
manor
feudalism
merchant
squire

84 ©1999 The Education Center, Inc. • *The Best Of The Mailbox® Social Studies • Intermediate* • TEC1474

Name _____ Creative thinking

Friend Or Foe—How Did Knights Know?

During the Middle Ages, there were frequent wars. These were fought by knights and other soldiers. Knights were usually covered from head to toe in armor. So how did a knight know whether another knight was a friend or an enemy? He would know by looking at the knight's coat of arms. A *coat of arms* was a special design on a knight's shield, flag, and outer coat. Each knight wore his own special coat of arms. Knights learned to recognize each other's designs so they wouldn't hurt a friend during battle. Some knights used symbols on their coats of arms, such as these:

Knights often included animals—both real and make-believe—on their coats of arms. Some believed that an animal design revealed something about the personality of the knight who wore it. For example, a knight whose coat of arms was decorated with a dog would be considered loyal and willing to follow his master even to death. Other coats of arms included objects that had something to do with a person's job or talents. For example, a king once gave his favorite cook a special coat of arms that included three cooking pots!

Directions: On a large square of paper, use a ruler to measure three points as shown. Cut on the dotted lines (which should be slightly curved) to make a shield. Use some of the ideas listed above to design a coat of arms that could be used to describe you. In the box below, describe what the symbols tell about you.
IMPORTANT: Be sure to write your last name in large letters somewhere on the shield.

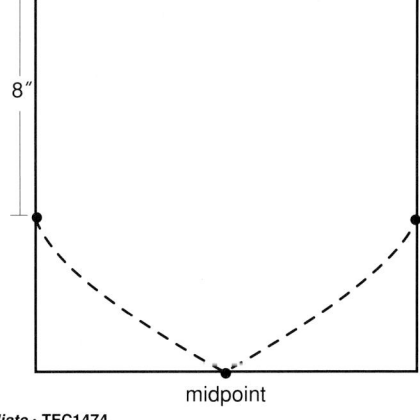

©1999 The Education Center, Inc. • *The Best Of* The Mailbox® *Social Studies* • *Intermediate* • TEC1474

Note To The Teacher: Use with "By Blazon!" on page 82. Provide each student with a 12-inch square of white drawing paper, scissors, a ruler, and crayons or markers. After a student has finished his design, have him glue it on a larger piece of colored paper, gluing the description box below or above it. Mount the shields on a bulletin board or on your classroom walls.

ANCIENT EGYPT: THE GIFT OF THE NILE

Giant tombs rising toward the heavens. Richly decorated coffins housing mysterious mummies. Ancient Egypt continues to intrigue historians and curiosity seekers who long to travel back to the time of pharaohs and pyramids. Explore this fascinating civilization with the following creative activities and reproducibles.

written by Beth Gress and Becky Andrews

THE NILE: LIFEBLOOD OF EGYPT

How could a thriving civilization survive in a land of sand and heat? That question can be answered in one word: Nile. Without the Nile River, ancient Egypt never would have existed. The Nile flooded its banks every year and deposited fertile soil along its banks. Ancient Egyptians were able to farm the otherwise arid land and grow huge amounts of food. The river also provided a vital means of transportation and water for irrigation.

To help students understand the location and importance of the Nile River, enlarge the map on page 91 and post it on a bulletin board. Along the top and bottom of the board, staple strips of brown butcher paper. Have student volunteers outline the Nile in blue chalk and label the map with the items listed on page 91. Have students guess why ancient Egypt was often called "The Gift Of The Nile." As students learn more about life along the Nile, let them draw scenes of Egyptian life on the border strips (similar to the friezes painted on the walls of ancient Egyptian tombs). If desired, have students copy the unique art style used by the Egyptians. Heads were drawn in profile, with a half-mouth and a full eye and eyebrow. The upper torso was shown facing front, while the waist, legs, and feet were in profile. Basic colors—black, white, red, yellow, blue, and green—were used, and outlines were usually drawn in black.

A PYRAMID OF FACTS

Create a giant visual of newly learned facts with a student-made display. Duplicate 100 copies of an equilateral triangle on tan construction paper. Place the triangles, a pair of scissors, a black marker, and resource books about ancient Egypt (see the list on page 89) at a center. During free time, a student can cut out a triangle and label it with a fascinating fact about ancient Egypt. Have students mount their triangles as shown (starting with a base of ten triangles) to build a giant pyramid on a wall or bulletin board. Remind students to check for the placement of their triangles before labeling them so that they'll label them correctly. For fun, have students predict how long it will take to complete their pyramid. No one really knows how long it took the Egyptians to finish theirs!

A PYRAMID CHALLENGE

Building a pyramid in ancient Egypt without the use of modern tools and machinery was truly a "monumental" feat! Give each pair of students a sheet of paper; then challenge them to create a one-piece pattern that—when cut, folded, and taped—will make a three-dimensional, four-sided pyramid. Remind students to add tabs to any edges that will be taped together. When everyone is finished, compare the different pyramid solutions; then ask students questions such as the following:
- ◉ How many blocks of stone do you think were needed to complete a pyramid?
- ◉ How do you think workers moved and lifted the huge blocks of stone?
- ◉ How do you think the blocks of stone were moved from the river's docks to the building site?
- ◉ How do you think the tunnels and burial chambers of a pyramid were constructed?

After students have offered their conjectures, share David Macaulay's wonderful book, *Pyramid* (Houghton Mifflin Company, 1975). Macaulay's easy-to-understand text and detailed drawings graphically explain the construction process of an imaginary pyramid. Discuss the tools and simple machines that the ingenious Egyptians used to make their unbelievable task a reality.

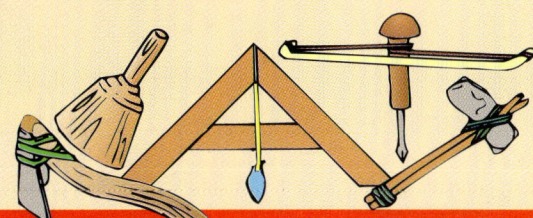

EGYPTIAN MYTHOLOGY FLIP BOOKS

Ancient Egyptians worshiped many different gods and goddesses. Familiarize students with the legends behind some of these mythological deities with *Gods And Pharaohs From Egyptian Mythology* by Geraldine Harris (Bedrick, 1982). After reading some of the legends aloud, divide the class into groups of three or four students each. Give each group three same-sized sheets of light-colored construction paper. Instruct students to stagger the pages so that the side edges are even, and the top and bottom edges of each page extend one inch. Fold the stack of papers so that all six ends of the pages are offset one inch as shown. Staple the folded edge to make the top of a flip book. With the book closed, write the name of a god or goddess on each page's flap. Decorate a title page for the book on the top flap. On each page, have the student draw a picture of the god or goddess and write a brief paragraph explaining his or her function in Egyptian society. Place the finished books at your reading center.

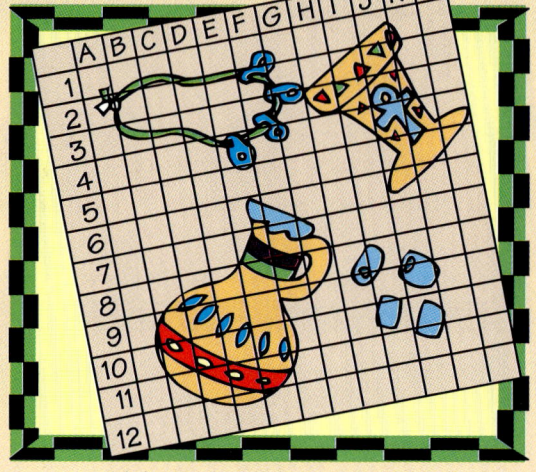

HANDS-ON DIGGING

Give students a little hands-on experience as archaeologists with this fun activity. Line a large cardboard box with garbage bags; then fill the box with sand. Hide some "artifacts" in the box, such as a small clay pot, some costume jewelry, beads, or a small vase. Explain to students that they will be excavating some artifacts and recording their locations on a chart similar to ones used by real archaeologists. Provide each group with a large piece of chart paper—approximately the same size as the box—on which is drawn a labeled and numbered grid of one-inch squares (see the illustration). Also provide students with several garden trowels, paintbrushes, and old toothbrushes. Allow students, working in small groups, to conduct a dig to uncover the artifacts. Remind students of precautions to take to preserve the artifacts, such as carefully brushing the sand off an artifact with a paintbrush and not tugging too hard to pull something out of the sand. As students remove items from the box, have them sketch each object as accurately as possible in its exact location on the chart, using a ruler to measure distances from the sides of the box. After each group has completed its dig, replant the artifacts in different locations for the next group.

MYSTERIOUS MUMMIES

No topic will grab your students' attention more than mummification. Because Egyptians believed that the invisible twin of the person, or *ka*, returned to the physical body after death, a corpse was meticulously preserved so that the ka would recognize it. Use Aliki's marvelous book *Mummies Made In Egypt* (Thomas Y. Crowell, 1979) or other resource books to introduce students to this ancient practice; then duplicate several copies of the mummy pattern on page 90 for each child. Have each student cut out his patterns and trace one copy onto a piece of tan or yellow construction paper. After cutting out the construction-paper tracing, have the student decorate it to resemble a real Egyptian coffin (see the example on page 90). Have students staple the lined copies behind their decorated covers to make shape booklets. Have each student choose one of the following topics to write about in his booklet:

- 👁 Write a tall tale describing what happened to the nose of the Sphinx.
- 👁 Rewrite a favorite fairy tale as an Egyptian legend, including Egyptian gods and goddesses, pharaohs, and an Egyptian setting.
- 👁 Pretend to be a worker helping to construct a pyramid. Write a journal entry telling about a day on the job.
- 👁 Pretend to be Howard Carter, the discoverer of King Tut's tomb. Write a diary entry telling about the day that you discovered the tomb.
- 👁 King Tut was only 18 or 19 years old when he mysteriously died. Write your theory of how and why he may have died so young. What kind of ruler do you think he might have been?

RESEARCH PYRAMIDS

Watch research skills reach new heights when your students build their own research pyramids. Assign a topic about ancient Egypt (see the list below) to each group. Have students in each group collect six same-sized boxes and rubber cement them together to make a pyramid. After researching its topic, have the group paint, wallpaper, or color the exposed sides of the pyramid's boxes; then have the group decorate the pyramid with maps, illustrations, diagrams, reports, and other items related to its topic. Inside each box, have the students place larger, three-dimensional items or create a diorama about their topic. Now that's a research project that reaches for the sky!

Possible topics to research:
Medicine and Law
Arts and Crafts
Tombs and Pyramids
Writing and Math
The Pharaohs
  and Palace Life
Food and Drink
Government
Home Life
Childhood
Fashion
Gods and Goddesses
Farming

THE LITERATURE LINK: LOOK FOR THESE!

- *Growing Up In Ancient Egypt* by Rosalie David; published by Troll, 1993
- *On The Banks Of The Pharaoh's Nile* by Corinne Courtalon; published by Young Discovery, 1988
- *Ancient Egypt* by Geraldine Harris; published by Facts on File, 1990
- *Ancient Egypt* by Judith Crosher; published by Viking, 1992
- *The Ancient Egyptians* by Vivian Koenig; published by Millbrook, 1992
- *The Riddle Of The Rosetta Stone* by James Giblin; published by Crowell, 1990
- *Fun With Hieroglyphs* by Catherine Roehrig; published by Viking, 1990
- *Hieroglyphs From A To Z* by Peter Der Manuelian; published by Rizzoli, 1993

HIEROGLYPHICS HAPPENING

The ancient Egyptians were noted for their unique picture writing, called *hieroglyphics*. Made up of about 750 signs, this style of writing frequently omitted vowels. For fun, have each child write a sentence without vowels; then have students trade papers with partners and try to decode the sentences. Next give each student a copy of the "Hieroglyphic Alphabet" on page 92. Explain that royal names were often encircled by an oval called a *cartouche* (see the illustration above). Have each student use the alphabet to design his own cartouche; then have students swap their cartouches and discuss the translation of each name. (There can be a variety of ways to write a single name.)

Note To Teacher: Use this pattern with "Mysterious Mummies" on page 88.

Pattern

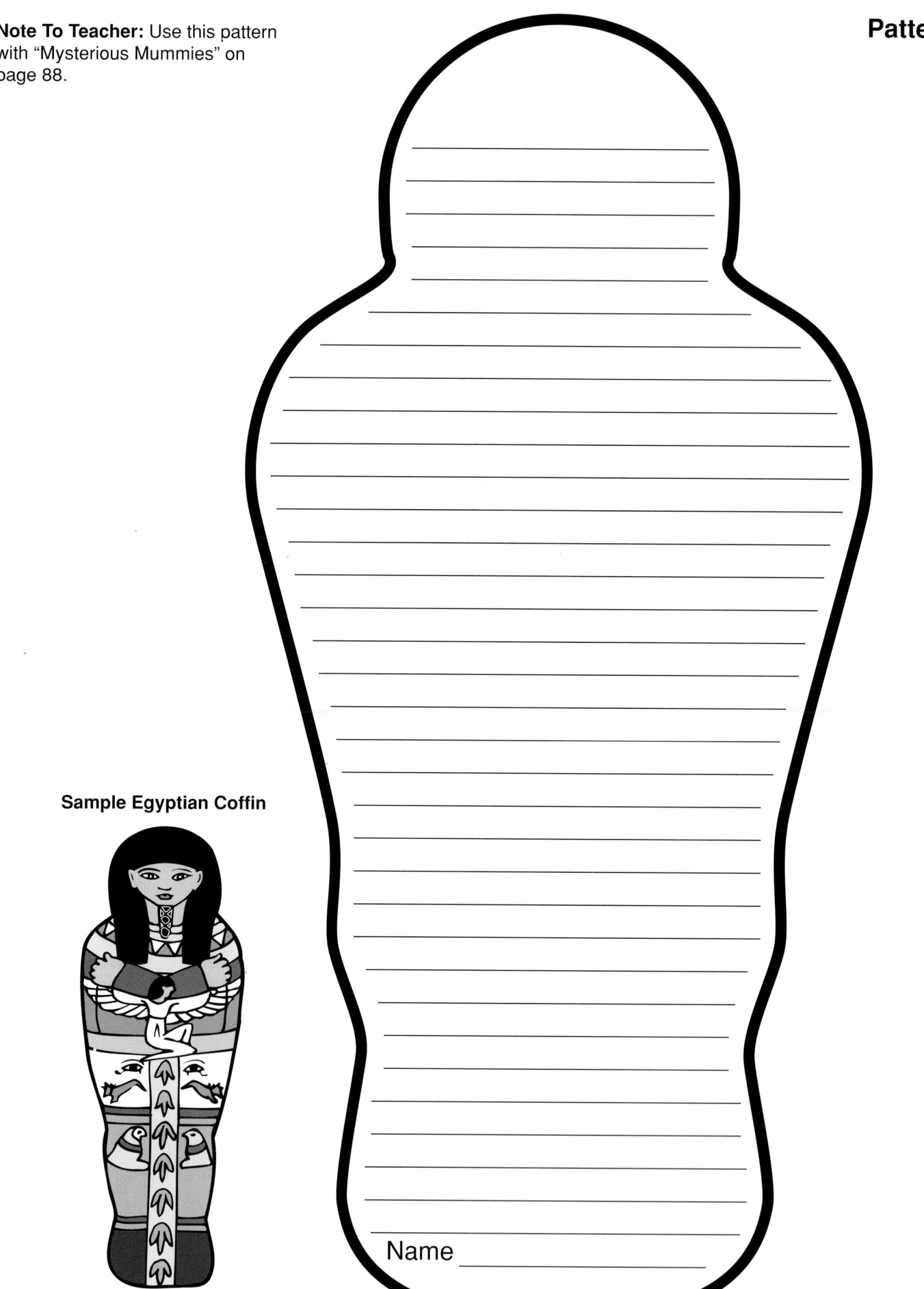

Sample Egyptian Coffin

Name _____

Name _____ Map skills

ALONG THE BANKS OF THE NILE

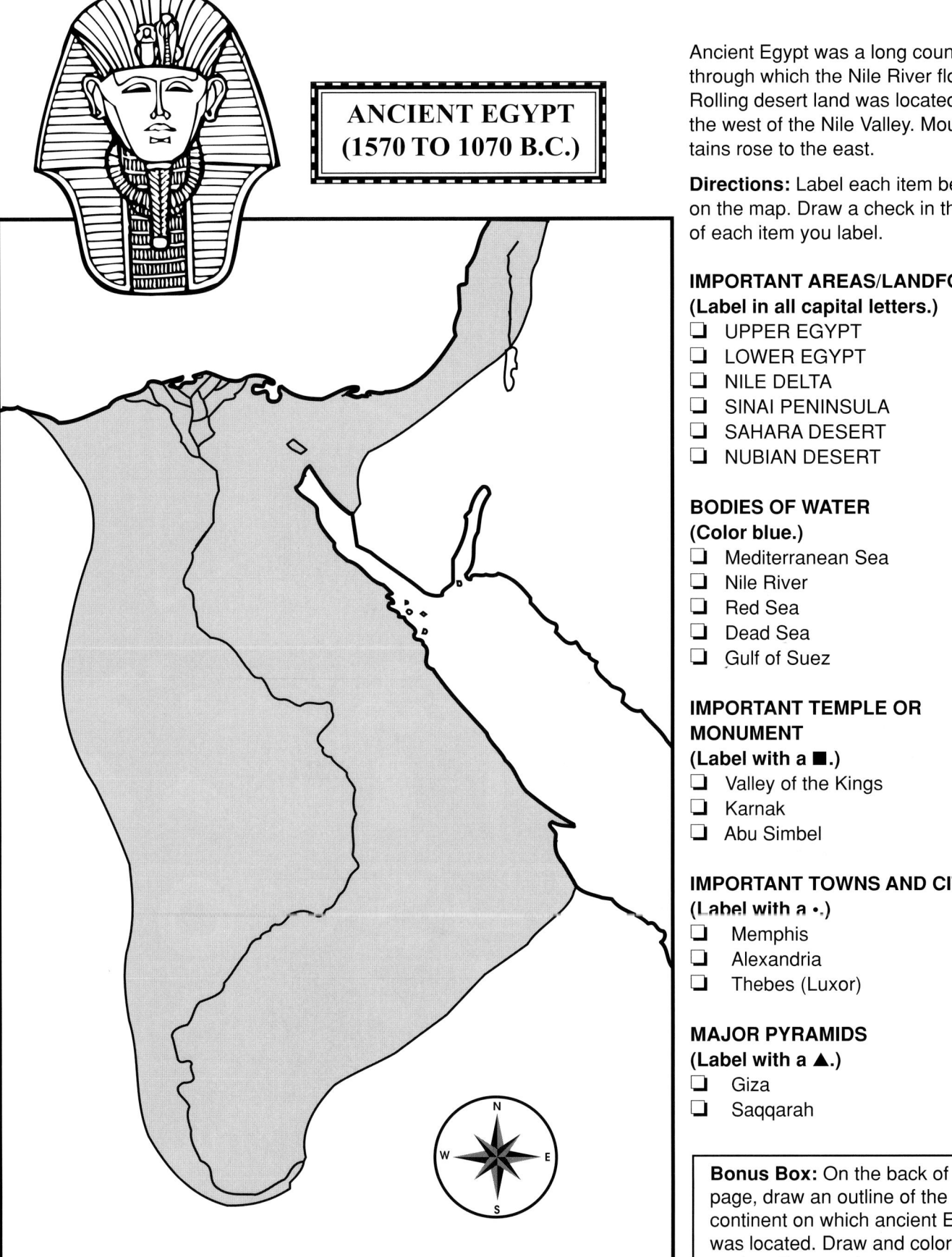

ANCIENT EGYPT (1570 TO 1070 B.C.)

Ancient Egypt was a long country through which the Nile River flowed. Rolling desert land was located to the west of the Nile Valley. Mountains rose to the east.

Directions: Label each item below on the map. Draw a check in the box of each item you label.

IMPORTANT AREAS/LANDFORMS
(Label in all capital letters.)
❏ UPPER EGYPT
❏ LOWER EGYPT
❏ NILE DELTA
❏ SINAI PENINSULA
❏ SAHARA DESERT
❏ NUBIAN DESERT

BODIES OF WATER
(Color blue.)
❏ Mediterranean Sea
❏ Nile River
❏ Red Sea
❏ Dead Sea
❏ Gulf of Suez

IMPORTANT TEMPLE OR MONUMENT
(Label with a ■.)
❏ Valley of the Kings
❏ Karnak
❏ Abu Simbel

IMPORTANT TOWNS AND CITIES
(Label with a •.)
❏ Memphis
❏ Alexandria
❏ Thebes (Luxor)

MAJOR PYRAMIDS
(Label with a ▲.)
❏ Giza
❏ Saqqarah

Bonus Box: On the back of this page, draw an outline of the continent on which ancient Egypt was located. Draw and color ancient Egypt red on your outline.

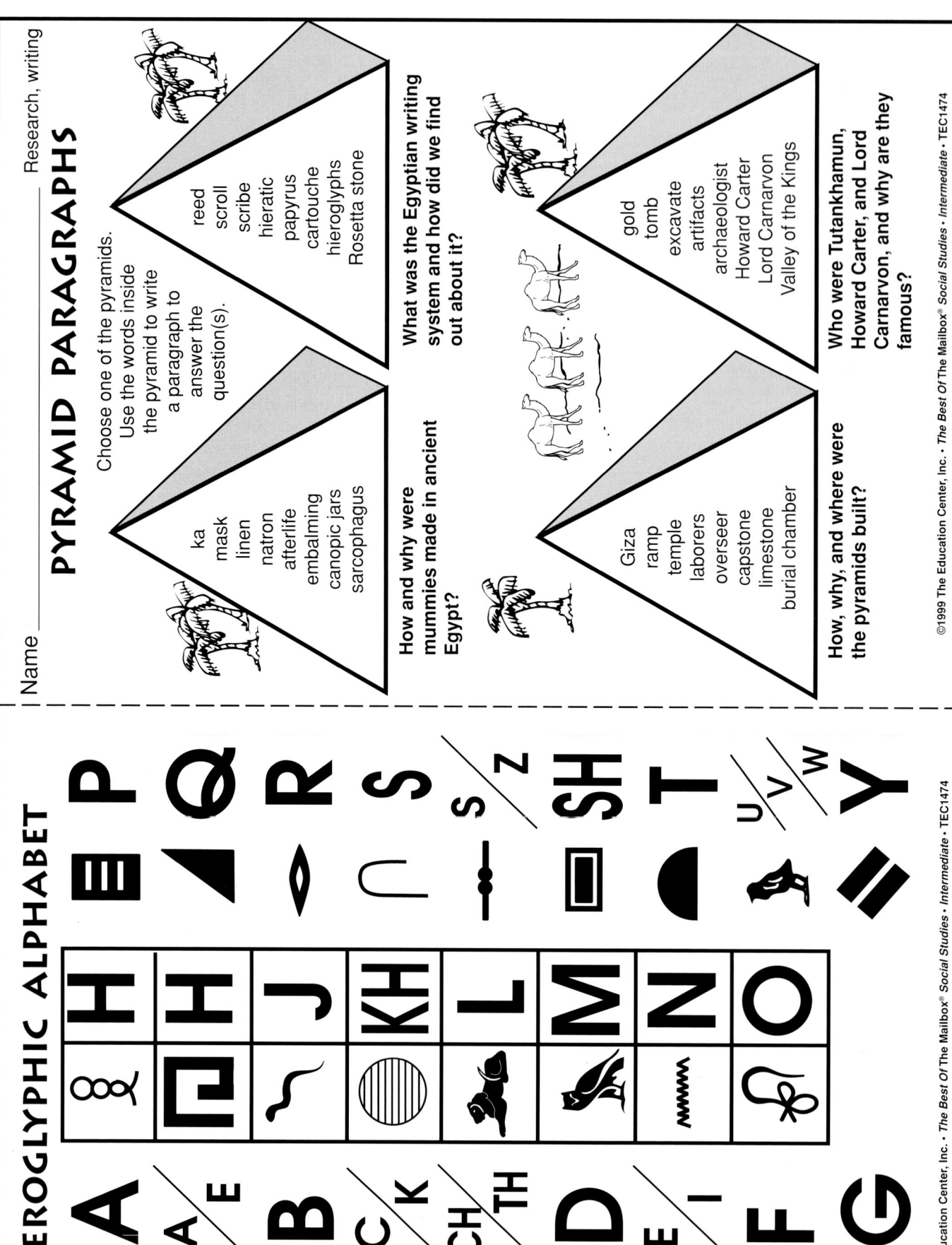

High-Altitude Research

Leading Students To Write Research Papers On Foreign Countries

"Why research?" Pose this simple question to your students and their first response may be "Because the teacher told us to." Students in the intermediate grades don't always see how academics relate to real life. Discuss the fact that people research to find answers and that finding answers is not difficult once one has mastered some basic research techniques. Then follow these guidelines and watch your students soar into successful report writing!

by Christine A. Thuman

Choose Topic → Locate Resources → Take Notes → Organize Notes → Draft → Share With Peers → Edit → Final Copy → Title Page And Bibliography → Publish And Print

In Search Of...

Help your students realize the importance of learning about foreign countries with the following activity. Save several newspapers and newsmagazines over a two-week period. Divide your class into small groups of three to four students each. Have each group look through several of the papers and magazines for articles that deal with U.S./foreign relations. Instruct the groups to list any countries named in those articles. Next have each group select one of its articles to read and summarize. Post a world map at the front of the classroom. As each group shares its list of countries, mark each country on the map. Then let each group share its article summary. As a class, discuss how each of the issues presented will affect people in the United States.

Reservations Only

Students who select their own topics will be more enthusiastic about research. Focus the selection by providing a list of countries from which to choose. (See page 75 for a list of European countries.) Then give each student a copy of "My Topic" on page 96. First have the student list any information that she already knows about her topic. This background information will be the stepping-off point for further research. Next have each student list any questions that she may have about her topic. Have her circle the question that would best summarize the purpose of her research. Spend a few minutes with each student after she completes this sheet to help her identify a clear purpose for research. Focusing and narrowing topic choices at the beginning of research will save you and your students a lot of headaches later!

Resource Runway

Prior to conducting any formal research, spend time introducing your students to such resources as atlases, almanacs, periodicals, the card catalog, and encyclopedias, as well as knowledgeable individuals. Contact local colleges for information on international students. Invite these people into the class as guest speakers, or have your students conduct interviews with them.

A current almanac is an excellent resource because it contains up-to-date information such as the addresses of consulates or embassies. Incorporate letter-writing lessons into your research by having students send away for information several weeks before you officially begin researching. The "Almanac Scavenger Hunt" on page 97 will help your students practice finding information in an almanac. Have your students write their scavenger-hunt answers as phrases; then have them practice the skill of rewriting facts by putting away the almanacs and rewriting each of their phrases in a complete sentence.

Pam Crane

Navigating Through Note Taking

The backbone of research is note taking. Help your students learn how to organize notes by using one of the following methods:

- Have each student use one sheet of paper for each subtopic in her report. As she takes notes, have her decide under which subtopic the fact fits and then write that fact on the appropriate sheet of paper. Later when she drafts a paragraph on that subtopic, she'll have all her notes in one place.

- Note cards can also be used to organize notes. First have each student list each resource used on a color-coded note card (a different color of card for each separate resource). These will be the student's *bibliography cards* (see the examples shown). Each time the student takes notes from a particular source, he writes them on a card that's the same color as the matching bibliography card. This helps the student track down a fact for clarification or elaboration. On the actual note card, have the student record the page(s) on which the fact was found. Facts should be written in short phrases so that later—when the student rewrites the facts into paragraphs—he will be less likely to plagiarize the original source.

Pomeray, J. K., Places And Peoples Of The World: Ireland, 1988, pp. 9–10.

page 13
United Kingdom:
• Scotland
• England
• Wales
• Northern Ireland

"Ireland, Republic of," Encyclopedia Americana, 1992, pp. 425–437.

Flying Through The Five Themes

One way that students can organize their notes is according to the five themes of geography: Location, Place, Relationships Within Places, Movement, and Regions. The following activity will familiarize your students with this tool. Provide each student (or pair of students) with a 12" x 18" sheet of colored construction paper. Have the student make five columns on his paper, labeling the top of each with one of the five themes. Duplicate "The Five Themes Of Geography" (page 98) and "Facts About The Emerald Isle" (page 99) for each student. Instruct each student to cut the fact cards on page 99 apart and then place each fact under one of the five themes listed in the columns. Let students use page 98 as a guide in placing the facts. Have small groups of students meet to compare notes before gluing the facts under the columns.

Location	Place	Relationships Within Places	Movement	Regions

Peer Copilots

Thinking, writing, speaking, and listening are interrelated, so give students time to talk to each other about their writings. This will help them process their research as well as get suggestions from classmates on ways to revise and clarify their writings. Form sharing groups of three to four students each. In turn, have each student state the purpose for his research, then read his draft to the group. Instruct the others in the group to listen carefully, noting (1) any facts that are particularly well written or interesting and (2) any facts that do not seem to fit the paper's purpose. Instruct the student to jot down his classmates' suggestions and consider them when he rewrites his draft.

Takeoff And Landing

A traditional research report includes *introductory* and *concluding* paragraphs. A good introductory paragraph grabs the reader's attention. How can that be accomplished? Have each student find one very interesting fact about his country; then have him begin the paragraph by asking a question or making a statement using that fact. For example, in a paper on Ireland the introductory paragraph might begin: *What do palm trees and shamrocks have in common? They both can be found in Ireland.* Introductory paragraphs also need to briefly state the purpose of the research, informing the reader about the points that will be covered.

The concluding paragraph summarizes the ideas presented in the body of the paper. Encourage students to try different ways of stating the same points so that the introductory and concluding paragraphs are not carbon copies of each other. If the purpose stated in the introduction was a question, the conclusion contains the answer to that question. The concluding paragraph may include an opinion based on the facts researched, but it must not contain any new information.

Final Destination

Once a student has edited and revised her paper, have her make a title page by neatly writing the paper's title and her name on a clean sheet of paper. Since the student has used several resources for her research, she will also include a bibliography page. If she listed her sources on note cards, the student simply arranges the cards in alphabetical order and then lists the sources in a column under the title "Bibliography." Let students use construction paper and other art materials to make creative covers for their reports. Or give each child a large manila envelope or folder to decorate; then have her slip her finished research paper inside.

To keep your students' efforts from going unnoticed by the rest of the school, share their reports with other audiences. The following options will let your students know how much you appreciate their hard work:
- Display the reports individually in the media center or in the front office.
- Bind all of the reports together into a book for public display.
- Have each student present his report orally to the class. Videotape the presentations; then let each student take a turn checking out the tape to share with his family at home.

For additional activities on studying foreign countries, see "A European Travelogue" on pages 74–79.

Name _____ Research planning

MY TOPIC

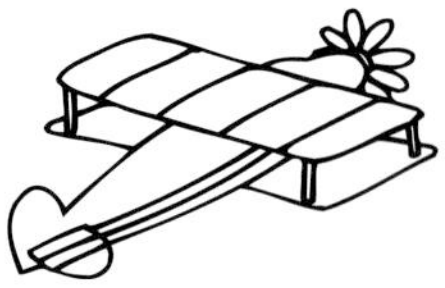

Topic: _____ Date: _____

List information that you already know about your topic.

_____
_____
_____
_____

What questions would you like to answer through your research?

1. _____
2. _____
3. _____
4. _____
5. _____

Circle the question above that you would like to use as the **purpose** of your research.

What sources will you use to conduct your research?

Title: _____ Author: _____ Page(s): _____
Title: _____ Author: _____ Page(s): _____
Title: _____ Author: _____ Page(s): _____
Title: _____ Author: _____ Page(s): _____
Title: _____ Author: _____ Page(s): _____

Other: _____
_____

©1999 The Education Center, Inc. • *The Best Of The Mailbox*® Social Studies • Intermediate • TEC1474

Note To Teacher: Use with "Reservations Only" on page 93. Use this page before students begin any research project to help them narrow and identify their topics.

Name _____   Using an almanac

Almanac Scavenger Hunt

One of the most useful resources for research is a world almanac. Finding information in an almanac is as simple as identifying the key word for your question, then looking up that key word or phrase in the almanac index.

Below are 12 almanac questions. The key words in the first six questions are in **bold**. Use the key words to help you find the correct listing in the almanac's index. See how many of these facts you can answer by using a current almanac. Then try your hand at answering the last six questions. Remember: First identify the key word(s) in your question; then look in the index for the key word(s).

1. What is the symbol for the **chemical element** aluminum?
2. The world's **tallest building** is located in Chicago, Illinois. What is its name and how tall is it in feet and in stories?
3. When and by whom was dynamite **invented**?
4. How much **water is used** by an average person each day?
5. From which countries does the United States get its supply of the **mineral** manganese?
6. What is the size (in square miles) of **Finland**?
7. Who won football's Heisman Trophy in 1963?
8. Name the hurricane that hit Louisiana and Mississippi on August 17–18, 1969. Tell how many deaths it caused.
9. When did the ancient Greek poet Sappho live?
10. Name the 15th president of the United States.
11. According to the Social Readjustment Rating Scale, which is more stressful: the death of a close family member or a major personal injury or illness?
12. What is the street address of the Department of Labor?

1. _____
2. _____
3. _____
4. _____
5. _____
6. _____
7. _____
8. _____
9. _____
10. _____
11. _____
12. _____

©1999 The Education Center, Inc. • The Best Of The Mailbox® Social Studies • Intermediate • TEC1474 • Key p. 159

Note To Teacher: Provide students with a copy of a current almanac to complete this worksheet. Use with "Resource Runway" on page 94. (These questions were developed using *The World Almanac® And Book Of Facts 1993* published by Pharos Books, 1992.)

The Five Themes Of Geography

Location: *the exact location of a place on the earth's surface*
- What are the latitude and longitude coordinates of this country?
- Where is this country located in relation to other countries, continents, or landforms?
- Where are this country's major cities, landforms, and resources?

Place: *the physical and human characteristics of a place that set it apart from other places*
- What is this country's official name, size, and population?
- What customs, religions, languages, and ethnic groups are found in this country?
- Describe this country's schools, homes, music, art, foods, national holidays, and types of recreation.
- Describe this country's landforms, natural resources, plants, and animals.
- Describe this country's climate and weather patterns.

Relationships Within Places: *how humans interact with the environment of a place—with both good and bad results*
- How have the people in this place adapted to the climate?
- How has the climate affected the settlement of people within this country?
- How do the people of this country use their natural resources?
- How do the people and industries treat their environment?
- What forms of energy do people of this country use?
- How do the different cultures in this country get along?
- How do the people of this country make their living?
- What economic issues face this country?
- Describe some of the important people and events in the history of this country.

Movement: *the movement of people, products, information, and ideas within a country and between countries*
- Where do the majority of people live in this country?
- How are goods, services, and people transported within this country?
- How are people, goods, services, and ideas moved to and from this country?
- What methods do people use to communicate ideas and information?
- How have traditions and customs passed from one generation to another?

Regions: *how regions form and change*
- What kind of government does this country have and how was it formed?
- What political regions are located within this country?
- What are some of the unique characteristics of these regions?
- What are some of the major tourist attractions found in this country?

©1999 The Education Center, Inc. • *The Best Of* The Mailbox® *Social Studies* • *Intermediate* • TEC1474

Note To Teacher: Use with "Flying Through The Five Themes" on page 94 and "Facts About The Emerald Isle" on page 99. Also use with "Team Tours" on page 75.

Facts About The Emerald Isle

1. Ireland's longest river, the Shannon, begins in the north central area and flows for 240 miles before emptying into the Atlantic Ocean.

2. Ireland trades most of its goods and services with the United Kingdom, western European countries, and the United States.

3. Both the Irish and English languages are spoken in Ireland.

4. By the middle of 1991, Ireland's population was 3,600,000.

5. The lowland regions of Ireland contain peat bogs which were formed when dead plant material built up over millions of years.

6. For many years conflict has existed between the people of the Republic of Ireland and their close neighbors, the people of Northern Ireland.

7. This island country, located in the Atlantic Ocean, is separated from Great Britain by the Irish Sea.

8. The Republic of Ireland has 26 counties. Irish people identify each other by their counties rather than by the few cities in the country.

9. Peat, one of Ireland's natural resources, is used as a fuel to generate electricity and for heating and cooking.

10. The major exports are livestock, dairy products, machinery, chemicals, and data processing equipment.

11. Ireland's government is called a *parliamentary democracy.*

12. Ireland's land is bowl-shaped with a central plain surrounded almost entirely by a ring of mountains.

13. Of the people in Ireland who work, 21% find jobs in forestry, fishing, and agriculture; 32% in industry; and 47% in service-oriented occupations.

14. Ireland is divided into four provinces: Leinster, Munster, Connaught, and Ulster.

15. Due to Ireland's mild, wet climate, farmers in the South and West enjoy a long growing season.

16. The island of Ireland is located between 51°N and 56°N latitudes, and 5°W and 11°W longitudes.

17. Ireland imports grains, metal products, chemicals, petroleum products, machinery, oil, textiles, motor vehicles, paper, and steel.

18. Most houses are made with brick and concrete. These materials continue to replace the more traditional thatched-roof cottages.

19. Goods, services, and people move through Ireland by using the roads, railroad, seaports, and airports.

20. Dublin, Ireland's capital and largest city, lies on the central east coast of this island.

©1999 The Education Center, Inc. • *The Best Of* The Mailbox® *Social Studies • Intermediate* • TEC1474 • Key p. 159

Note To Teacher: Use with "Flying Through The Five Themes" on page 94. Provide each student with a copy of "The Five Themes Of Geography" on page 98 also.

AFRICA:

Shedding Light On "The Dark Continent"

More than wild animals and tropical rain forests, our second largest continent is characterized by diversity and awesome beauty. Enlighten your students about this magnificent continent with the following activities and reproducibles.

with ideas by Beth Gress

Tearing Down Stereotypes

It is most important that any multicultural topic be approached with a desire to be accurate and culturally sensitive. Here are a few things to consider before talking with students about Africa and African countries:

- Africa is a continent of more than 50 independent countries.
- Rain forests and deserts make up relatively small parts of Africa.
- Thousands of Africans are well educated in the Western sense of the term.
- At least one-third of the African population resides in urban areas or cities.
- The African people belong to several racial groups, have varied cultural backgrounds, and speak more than 800 different languages.

A Diverse Continent

The land of Africa is characterized by vast diversity—from barren deserts to lush rain forests, snow-peaked mountain ranges to breathtaking waterfalls, uninhabited wastelands to bustling cities. Help students explore Africa's diverse landscape with a challenging learning center. At a center, place a world atlas that contains a variety of maps showing Africa's vegetation, rainfall, minerals distribution, population, physical geography, etc. Trace the Africa pattern on page 104; then duplicate the pattern on heavy paper to make a set of task cards. Write questions such as those that follow on the cards; then place the cards at the center. A student visiting the center chooses a card and uses the maps to answer its question.

Task Card Questions:

- Look at the population map. Why do you think Africa's population is concentrated in certain areas? (Hint: use the other Africa maps to help you.)
- What African cities are located in the most densely populated areas?
- Compare Africa's minerals distribution to its population distribution. What do you notice from this comparison?
- Compare Africa's population distribution to its vegetation. How do you think the vegetation affects where Africans live?
- How does the location of the equator seem to affect the types of vegetation found in certain areas of Africa?
- Compare a map showing Africa's rivers and mountain ranges to its population map. How does the location of the rivers and mountains relate to where Africans live?

African ABC Books

Africa's varied cultures are described in stunning fashion in the Caldecott Medal–winning picture book, *Ashanti To Zulu: African Traditions* by Margaret Musgrove (Dial Press). In the book, each letter of the alphabet is used to describe the ceremonies, celebrations, and day-to-day customs of a specific African ethnic group. Share this book with your class as an introduction to a fun bookmaking project. Have students (individually or in pairs) create their own African alphabet books on topics such as African Wildlife, Africa's Plants, African Landforms, Africa's Cities and Special Places, Africa's Natural Resources and Products, or Africa's Natural Wonders. Duplicate a large supply of the book page pattern on page 105 for each child or team. Have students research their topics and use the pages to create their own "_____ to _____" alphabet books. Display the finished books in your school's media center.

Compare Africa's population distribution to its vegetation. How do you think the vegetation affects where Africans live?

Dynamic African Dioramas

Many people mistakenly think that Africa is mostly deserts and rain forests. In fact, less than one-fifth of Africa is comprised of tropical rain forests. Two-fifths is desert, while more than two-fifths is characterized by grasslands known as *savannas*. Explore these vastly different physical areas with a cooperative group project. Divide students into six groups (two groups per area: desert, rain forest, savanna). Give each group a large cardboard box such as one used to package a television or other appliance. Trace the Africa pattern on page 104 onto a sheet of paper; then duplicate it onto light-colored construction paper (approximately ten copies per group). Give each group its patterns and a copy of page 104. Have groups follow the steps on the reproducible to create fabulous dioramas depicting the diversity of Africa's land. (For a picture of a completed diorama, see page 104.)

Africa And Current Events

Civil wars, national elections, famines, environmental issues—the continent of Africa is often a star of the nightly news. Post a list of Africa's countries and major cities (see below) near a map of Africa. Review the list with students so that they will be familiar with the names; then challenge them to bring in news articles or summaries of television newscast segments about Africa. After a student shares his article or summary, have him mount it around the map; then have him staple a piece of yarn from the clipping to the corresponding location on the map.

North Africa: Algeria, Chad, Djibouti, Egypt, Libya, Mali, Mauritania, Morocco, Niger, Somali Republic, Sudan, Tunisia, Western Sahara (occupied by Morocco)
West Africa: Benin, Burkina Faso, Cape Verde, Gambia, Ghana, Guinea, Guinea-Bissau, Ivory Coast, Liberia, Nigeria, Senegal, Sierra Leone, Togo
Central Africa: Angola, Burundi, Cameroon, Central African Republic, Congo, Equatorial Guinea, Gabon, Kenya, Rwanda, São Tomé and Principe, Tanzania, Uganda, Zaire
Southern Africa: Botswana, Comoros, Lesotho, Madagascar, Malawi, Mozambique, Namibia, South Africa, Swaziland, Zambia, Zimbabwe
Major Cities: Algiers, Tunis, Addis Ababa, Mogadishu, Khartoum, Cairo, Tripoli, Nairobi, Kampala, Lusaka, Pretoria, Cape Town, Johannesburg

A New South Africa

Apartheid—the oppressive system of racial separation instituted and sanctioned by the South African government—is no longer in place. Nelson Mandela became South Africa's first black president, leading the very country that imprisoned him for 27 years for his anti-apartheid activities. Introduce students to this courageous leader and the system that he helped dismantle with the reproducible on page 106.

To give students a perspective on apartheid, read aloud *Journey To Jo'Burg: A South African Story* by Beverly Naidoo (HarperCollins). When their baby sister becomes ill, 13-year-old Naledi and her younger brother journey to Johannesburg to bring their mother home. The trip brings them face-to-face with the cruelty of apartheid. After sharing the book with students, have them discuss apartheid and what Naledi and Tiro experienced on their trip. Ask, "What difference do you think the end of apartheid would have made in the lives of Naledi and Tiro?" Have students write personal reflections in their journals; or have them write poems that speculate about South Africa's apartheid-less future.

African Shadow Art

Add a touch of art to your Africa study with Marcia Brown's stunning picture book *Shadow* (Charles Scribner's Sons). Illustrated in collage, the book introduces students to a character often called forth by African storytellers and poets. Let students make their own shadow art using Brown's technique. Have each child use watercolors and a very wet brush to paint a piece of white paper. Instruct students that paint strokes should be made in the same direction and overlapped so that colors are blended. The student can add texture to the resulting "wash" by dabbing the surface with a tissue while the paint is still wet. Let the paintings dry overnight. The next day have students draw and cut out shapes of African designs, animals, dancers, or landscape elements from black paper (be sure to provide plenty of pictures of Africa for inspiration); then have them glue the paper cutouts onto the washes. Encourage students to make their paper cutouts detailed and intricate.

African Folktales

African folktales provide special insight into the cultures that created them. Share a few with your students (see the brief bibliography that follows); then divide your class into small groups to study the books. Have each group choose one story to share with the class. Allow groups to present their tales using a variety of methods: puppet shows, shadow plays, murals, reader's theaters, skits, flannelboard stories, etc.

The Village Of Round And Square Houses by Ann Grifalconi; published by Little, Brown & Company

Oh, Kojo! How Could You? by Verna Aardema; published by Dial Books For Young Readers

Brother To The Wind by Mildred Pitts Walter; published by Lothrop, Lee & Shepard Books

Sundiata: Lion King Of Mali by David Wisniewski; published by Clarion Books

Agassu: Legend Of The Leopard King retold by Rick Dupre; published by Carolrhoda Books, Inc.

Why The Sky Is Far Away: A Nigerian Folktale retold by Mary-Joan Gerson; published by Little, Brown & Company

When Hippo Was Hairy And Other Tales From Africa by Nick Greaves; published by Barron

Talk, Talk: An Ashanti Legend by Deborah M. Chocolate; published by Troll Associates

Spider And The Sky God: An Akan Legend by Deborah M. Chocolate; published by Troll Associates

African Proverbs

Proverbs are simple bits of wisdom which are commonly used in African conversations and are an important part of African oral tradition. Ask students to speculate about both the superficial meaning and the deeper meaning of each African proverb listed below. Then have each child write in his journal about a time when one of the proverbs rang true in his own life.

- If you do not respect a penny, a dollar will not respect you.
- He who throws a stone into a crowd doesn't know who will be hit.
- The giraffe knows that height is not reached in a hurry.
- An old stick cannot be straightened.
- The black ant may swallow the giraffe.
- A reflection does not see itself.
- Unless you call out, who will open the door?

Research Projects

Involve your students in a variety of exploratory, hands-on projects with these suggestions:

- Make a list of what you think are the 15 most significant events in Africa's history. Arrange the events on a timeline. Add illustrations to your timeline.
- Research endangered animals of Africa. Design a brochure to educate others about these animals and what can be done to save them.
- Illustrate several different types of homes found in Africa, including those in both rural and urban settings. Describe how each home is well suited for its environment.
- Draw a large map of Africa. Label each country with its name and the date it gained its independence. On a separate piece of paper, list the country that ruled each African nation before it gained independence.
- Research to find out the causes of food shortages suffered by many African countries. List the causes on a large chart; then list at least three suggestions for what African nations can do to provide enough food for their people.
- Study the government of one African country. In a diagram or chart, compare and contrast that government with the United States government.
- Find out more about African art. Make a mobile showing examples of African artwork.

The "Real" Africa: An Assessment Tool

When you're ready to assess your students' progress on their African studies, give them a chance to apply what they've learned to a real-life situation. Instead of (or in addition to) a standard test, pose the following challenge to students:

We have just finished studying Africa and are now experts on this fascinating continent! Now it's time to share our knowledge with others. How can our class educate the other students in our school about the real Africa? To answer that question, first list ten facts you think are the most important for people to know about Africa. Then describe how our class can teach other classes in our school about those facts. Be specific in your ideas. For example, don't just say, "Make posters." Describe what the posters should say and how they should be illustrated.

From reading over your students' ideas, you'll get a good picture of whether they grasped major concepts and have an accurate picture of the real Africa themselves.

Helpful Resources

Our Global Village: Africa
Written by Nancy Klepper
Illustrated by Larry Nolte
Published by Milliken

The Multicultural Game Book
Written by Louise Orlando
Published by Scholastic Inc.

African Crafts
Written by Judith Hoffman Corwin
Published by Franklin Watts

Pam Crane

Name _____   Completing a group project

Africa: A Diverse Continent

Like many people, you probably thought of Africa as mostly jungles and deserts. Wrong! The magnificent continent of Africa has a little bit of everything: snow-peaked mountains, grassy plains, barren deserts, tropical rain forests, breathtaking waterfalls, bustling cities—you name it!

Most of Africa can be classified as either grasslands (also called *savannas*), deserts, or tropical rain forests. Your group is going to study one of these physical areas in depth. After your teacher assigns an area to your group, follow the steps in the Africa pattern to make a dynamic diorama!

Area (circle one):
Desert   Savanna   Rain Forest

Steps:

1. Research your physical area of Africa to find out information about the topics listed below. Keep your notes in a group folder.

   climate   vegetation   landforms   wildlife
   population   natural resources   minerals   agriculture

2. Cover the outside of a large cardboard box with paper.

3. Inside the box, use art materials to create a scene showing your physical area. Include elements that will illustrate your area's wildlife, people, landforms, climate, natural resources, vegetation, agriculture, and mineral wealth.

4. Cut out the Africa patterns that your teacher will give you. Write your information in complete sentences on the cutouts; then glue them to the sides, back, and top of your box.

5. Add other African decorations to the outside of your box if desired.

6. Share your diorama with the rest of the class.

Diorama
Information on Africa patterns glued to top, back, and sides

scene inside box

©1999 The Education Center, Inc. • *The Best Of The Mailbox*® *Social Studies • Intermediate •* TEC1474

- -

Note To Teacher: Use this reproducible with "Dynamic African Dioramas" on page 101. Provide each group with a large box (such as one used to package a television or other appliance), scissors, glue or a stapler, colorful paper, art supplies, and a folder. Trace the Africa outline on a piece of paper; then duplicate it on construction paper for each group (approximately ten copies per group). Also use this reproducible with "A Diverse Continent" on page 100.

Name_____ Reading comprehension, critical thinking

A Long Road To Freedom

In April of 1994, a new era began in South Africa. Nelson Mandela was elected as the nation's first black president. The road that led to this amazing success story was a long and difficult one.

As a young man, Nelson Mandela joined the fight against his country's *apartheid* laws. Apartheid kept people of different races—whites, blacks, and coloreds (people of mixed descent)—separate in many ways. Even though blacks made up over 70 percent of South Africa's population, whites controlled the country. Blacks weren't allowed to vote in national elections. Other basic freedoms were denied. For example, most whites lived in towns and cities like those in the United States. Most blacks had to live in crowded *homelands.* These poor areas might not have had running water, electricity, or good farmland. There were also few jobs in the homelands. A nonwhite person had to have a work pass to even enter a white neighborhood. Nonwhites couldn't attend the same schools as whites. Most restaurants, sporting events, and theaters were also segregated.

Nelson Mandela fought hard to end apartheid. In the early 1960s, he was arrested and sentenced to life in prison. Mandela spent the next 27 years in jail. Much of that time was spent in a cell that was only six feet wide. Meals consisted of cornmeal cereal and a drink made from ground-up corn. Mandela and his fellow prisoners were often forced to work long hours with no breaks. Mandela was allowed to have only one visitor and to write and receive only one letter every six months.

While Mandela was in jail, the fight to end apartheid continued. In February 1990, Mandela was released from jail. He led negotiations between the South African government and anti-apartheid leaders. This resulted in the end of apartheid and the first free election in South Africa's history. Nelson Mandela was elected the nation's first black president. His courage and that of South Africans who worked with him proved that freedom for the oppressed can be achieved.

Directions: Pretend that you are a black South African student. You've faced the unfairness of apartheid all your life. Now apartheid is gone. How do you think your life in South Africa will be different? Complete the chart below. Use the back of this page if you need more space.

NOW THAT APARTHEID IS GONE	
EDUCATION	
HOME LIFE	
SOCIAL LIFE	
FUTURE	

Bonus Box: After getting out of prison, Mandela said, "I never thought that a life sentence truly meant life and that I would die behind bars." Why do you think Mandela believed he would one day get out of jail? Write your answer on the back of this page.

Note To Teacher: Use with "A New South Africa" on page 101.

The Power Of Peace
Thematic Activities Exploring Peace And Conflict

In our growing and changing world, children are confronted by a myriad of problems that are often difficult to understand. Civil wars, violence on television, riots in our major cities, families dissolving—all are issues that can confuse students and impact them in powerful ways. Today's teachers want to help their students learn to deal with the conflicts they face, both simple and serious. Give your class a chance to examine the power of peace and the challenges of conflict with the following thematic activities, reproducibles, and literature suggestions.

by Kimberly Bruck

People Of Peace

Throughout history, certain people have stood out as advocates for peace. Introduce students to these exceptional personalities with a research activity. To begin, ask your media specialist to gather a selection of reference materials pertaining to the "People Of Peace" listed below. Write the list on the chalkboard; then explain to students that these people dedicated their lives to preserving peace. Have each student choose a person from the list to research. Give each child a copy of the reproducible on page 110; then complete the following activities:

- **Activity 1:** Give students adequate time to research their peace advocates; then have them follow the directions on the reproducible to complete the peace symbol project. After completing Activity 2, punch a hole in the top of each project and string a piece of yarn through the hole. Hang the projects from your classroom ceiling for an eye-catching display.

- **Activity 2:** Allow time for each student to tell the class about his peace advocate. As a student shares, have each classmate list the advocate's name and one fact he learned from the presentation. Collect the lists at the end of the sharing time and use them to play a "People Of Peace" trivia game. Divide your class into two teams. Read a fact from a student's list to a player on Team 1. If the player correctly identifies the peace advocate being described, she earns a point for her team. If she gives an incorrect answer, play goes to the next team. The team with the most points at the end of the game wins.

People Of Peace

Bishop Desmond Tutu	Andrei D. Sakharov
Albert Schweitzer	Jimmy Carter
Dr. Martin Luther King, Jr.	Alfred B. Nobel
Mohandas K. Gandhi	Jane Addams
Woodrow Wilson	Ralph J. Bunche
Theodore Roosevelt	George C. Marshall
Elie Wiesel	Linus Pauling
Mother Teresa	Dag Hammarskjöld
Anwar el-Sadat	Lech Walesa
Menachem Begin	Mikhail S. Gorbachev
Henry A. Kissinger	

All In My Mind?

Admiral Arleigh Burke of the United States Navy once said, "The major deterrent [to war] is in a man's mind." Encourage students to begin thinking about the subject of peace by having them reflect on Burke's quote. After discussing the quote, share with students a quotation collection such as *Bartlett's Familiar Quotations* (published by Little, Brown and Company) or *Simpson's Contemporary Quotations* (published by Houghton Mifflin Company). Place the book and a blank journal at a center. Challenge each student to look up the subject of *peace* or *war* and select one quote; then have him write the quote and its author on a page in the journal. Below the notation, have the student write a sentence or two reflecting on the quote's meaning.

After each student has had an opportunity to add a quote to the journal, give each child an index card. On the card, have the student write his own quote about peace or war, adding a reflection on its meaning on the back of the card. Collect the quotes. At the beginning of each day, choose one to read aloud and discuss. Continue until each child's quote has been shared.

Conflict On Television

Violence and unresolved conflict—the seeds of war—are frequent topics on many of today's television programs. Use this medium to launch an investigation of conflict resolution. Videotape a portion of an appropriate television program; then show the program to your class. Have students recall the conflicts included in the program and brainstorm positive, nonviolent ways of resolving those disputes. As a follow-up to the discussion, give each student a copy of the reproducible on page 111. Have each child choose a 30-minute program (with a parent's approval) to watch. Point out that students can choose to watch a news broadcast, a prime-time show, or a sporting event. Have students complete the chart on their reproducibles; then have small groups discuss their findings in class the following day.

Read All About It!

Newspapers overflow with articles in which conflict is the central theme. Give students an opportunity to practice their critical-thinking skills with these newspaper activities:

- **Activity 1:** Cut apart a current newspaper. Give each student one page and a light-colored highlighter pen. Tell students to read their pages and select one article that includes a conflict with a negative resolution. Have each student highlight the conflict described in his article and its resolution. Remind students that some articles may contain more than one conflict, and ask them to highlight all conflicts they read about. After students have highlighted the information, have them rewrite the articles in their own words, offering a positive and peaceful resolution to each conflict. Be sure students include catchy headlines that will attract readers.

- **Activity 2:** To make an interesting display, have each student cut a sheet of white duplicating paper in half to make two long strips. Have the student tape the two strips end to end to make one long column on which to copy his rewritten article in Activity 1. Staple the completed articles on a bulletin board to resemble the columns of a newspaper. Add the title "Read All About It!" at the top of the display. Your display will be a unique reading experience for all onlookers—a newspaper with only good news!

Picturing Peace

The Big Book For Peace (published by Dutton Children's Books) is a collection of stories, pictures, poems, and a song about many kinds of peace. It was created by more than 30 of the most popular authors and illustrators of children's books. Use this unique volume in the following creative-thinking activity. Begin by sharing the picture stories "The Dream" by Steven Kellogg and "A Ruckus" by Thacher Hurd with your students. Discuss how Kellogg and Hurd used illustrations and sparse text to create picture stories on the theme of harmony or peace. Ask students to identify the images and phrases in the stories that represent peace to them. Next give each child a piece of construction paper that has been three-hole punched along one side. Divide students into two groups. Have one group write the sentence starter "War is..." at the top of their papers; have the other group label their papers with "Peace is...." Direct each student to finish the sentence on his paper, then illustrate his sentence with magazine pictures or original drawings. After students have shared their work, bind the pages together in a three-ring notebook to make a class book.

Thanks For Keeping The Peace

On the last Monday in May, our nation celebrates Memorial Day, an occasion to honor Americans who gave their lives to preserve peace in our world. In commemoration of this holiday, have students create special poems thanking area veterans for helping to keep the peace.

Begin by asking a local chapter of the Veterans of Foreign Wars, the American Legion, or the Veterans Administration to help you distribute the completed projects. Have students brainstorm a list of words or phrases that reflect peace (*harmony, love, togetherness, accord, cooperation,* etc.). Instruct each student to use the list to create a short poem about peace. Duplicate the medal pattern on page 111 onto construction paper. Give each student a copy of the pattern, a 10-inch length of red-white-and-blue ribbon, scissors, glue, and a small manila envelope. Have the student copy his poem onto the medal; then have him cut out the medal and glue two pieces of ribbon to the back as shown. Finally have the student decorate his envelope and place the medal inside. Distribute the special thank-yous to area veterans.

Honoring Peacemakers

Dynamite and peace—two things that seemingly don't go together, but do. In 1867, Swedish chemist Alfred B. Nobel invented dynamite. Hoping the explosive would be used for peaceful purposes, Nobel became dismayed at having created a substance that could be used in war. As a result of his guilt, Nobel established a fund to be used to award annual cash prizes, one of which was for the most effective work in promoting peace. So began the Nobel Prize for peace.

Ask students to brainstorm ways people can help others, work to solve conflicts, or keep the peace. Have each student think of one person who has promoted peace in his home, classroom, school, community, nation, etc. Give each student a copy of the medal pattern on page 111 that has been duplicated on white construction paper. Have the student cut out and label his medal with the name of his peacemaker; then have him add a few sentences telling how that person promoted peace. Instruct students to color their medals and attach colorful ribbon as shown above. Hold a Peace Prize ceremony during which each child shares his medal. After the ceremony, mount the medals on your classroom door for a thought-provoking display.

Dedicated To Peace

The following organizations are dedicated to the preservation of peace and the eradication of war. Contact them for information which may be helpful in planning your unit activities.

The Lion And The Lamb Peace Arts Center: provides an opportunity for the study and promotion of peace and international understanding through the arts and literature for children. The center has more than 4,000 children's books, 75 videos, and 800 reference books for adults on various peace themes. These materials can be borrowed for two to three weeks, provided shipping and handling costs are covered. For information about these items, the original art collection, and speakers' availability, contact by writing: Center Director, Bluffton College, Bluffton, OH 45817 or calling (419) 358-3207.

Peace Action: dedicated to developing a link between peace, the environment, and economic justice. Contact Peace Action, 1819 H Northwest, Suite 420, Washington, DC 20006.

Name _____ Research skills

A Person In Pursuit Of Peace

Follow these instructions to complete a research project on a famous peace advocate.

1. Glue this page to a sheet of white construction paper.
2. **In Section 1:** list your peace advocate's name, birthdate, death date (if applicable), and homeland.
3. **In Section 2:** describe one of your peace advocate's most important accomplishments in the area of world peace. Be sure to use complete sentences.
4. **In Sections 3 and 4:** give one or more interesting facts about your person.
5. Cut out the peace symbol.
6. On the back of the peace symbol, draw a picture of your peace advocate or illustrate his/her contribution to peace.

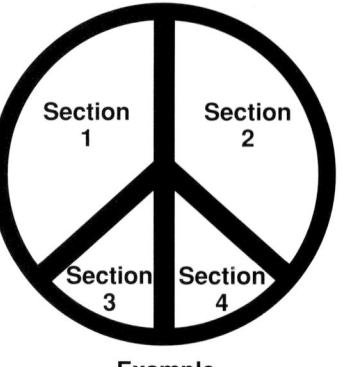

Example

©1999 The Education Center, Inc. • *The Best Of The Mailbox® Social Studies • Intermediate •* TEC1474

Note To Teacher: Use with "People Of Peace" on page 107. Provide each student with an 8 1/2" x 11" sheet of white construction paper, scissors, and glue.

Pattern

Use with "Thanks For Keeping The Peace" and "Honoring Peacemakers" on page 109.

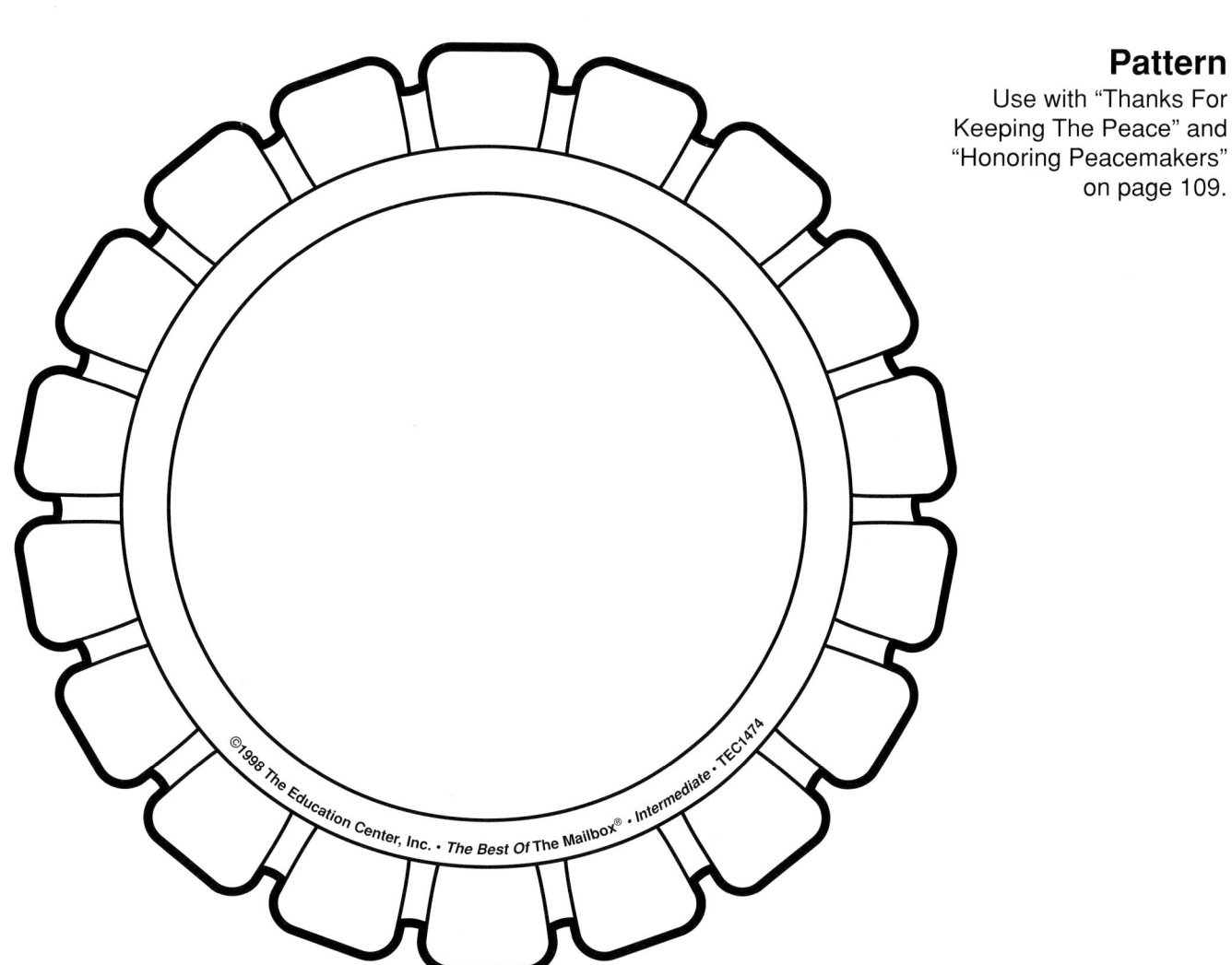

Name _____ Recalling/analyzing events

Conflict On Television

The nightly news, your family's favorite drama, the Monday night football game—all of these programs probably include at least one conflict. How easily can you identify the conflicts and solutions included in most shows? Watch a television program (with a parent's approval) for 30 minutes. Write a brief description of three conflicts you observe during the program. If the conflict was resolved, give the solution. If the conflict was left unresolved, suggest a peaceful solution of your own.

Name of program: _____ Time: _____

	CONFLICT	SOLUTION
1.		
2.		
3.		

©1999 The Education Center, Inc. • The Best Of The Mailbox® Social Studies • Intermediate • TEC1474

Note To Teacher: Use with "Conflict On Television" on page 108.

The Inuit

The Inuit are among the most adaptable people on Earth. For hundreds of years, they have made their homes in the harsh Arctic climate. Introduce students to the traditional culture of these native people with the following creative activities and reproducibles.

by Lisa Waller Rogers and Debra Liverman

About These Activities

Inuit (IHN-yoo-iht) are people who live in and near the Arctic. Today more than 100,000 Inuit live in Russia, Alaska, Canada, and Greenland. Because the Inuit have always lived in groups scattered over this huge region, it is virtually impossible to describe a general way of life for all Inuit. The activities in this unit focus on the traditional way of life, much of which most Inuit people no longer follow.

Season To Season

From season to season, the Inuit used whatever resources were available in their area. They learned the yearly migration patterns of Arctic birds and animals. And they understood signs of changes in weather conditions and ice and snow formations.

Get students thinking about the seasonal activities in the traditional Inuit culture with the activity on page 116. Have each child complete the reproducible; then go over the correct answers with the class. As a follow-up, have each student use six sheets of computer paper (still connected) and the steps below to create a booklet featuring a year in her life. Display the booklets on a bulletin board titled "Season To Season."

Figure 1

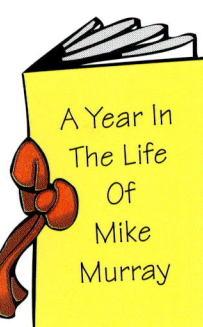

Figure 2

Steps:
1. Fold each page of computer paper in half lengthwise to create an accordion fold of the stack. This will create 12 pages (Figure 1).
2. Write "A Year In The Life Of [your name]" on the back of the first page.
3. Starting with page 2, label each page with a month, beginning with January.
4. Illustrate each page with something that you normally do during that month.
5. Fold the book back up. Punch a hole in the center of the left margin of the stack (Figure 2). Be sure that the hole is punched through all the sheets of paper.
6. Slip a piece of yarn or ribbon through the hole and tie it to hold the pages in place.

Lucky Charms

The Inuit are famous for their soapstone, animal bone, or ivory carvings. Inuit hunters often wore *amulets*, or charms, carved into the shapes of the animals that they hunted. The carvings were thought to help them in the hunt. Guide students through the steps below for carving their own amulets. Then have each student write a paragraph telling how he hopes his carving will bring him luck.

Materials for each student:
1 bar of soft bath soap
1 plastic knife
1 toothpick
1 pencil
permanent felt-tipped pens
1 damp paper towel

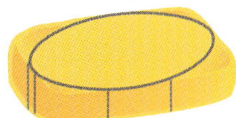 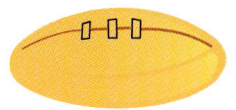

Steps:
1. Decide on an object to carve. Remember, it should represent an area in which you hope to be lucky. For example, carve a football for luck playing football.
2. Use the knife to scrape off any lettering from your bar of soap.
3. Use the pencil to draw the outline of your object on one side of the soap. Draw the object in reverse on the other side of the soap. Then draw the top, bottom, and sides of the object on the soap.
4. With the knife carve away the soap a little at a time until you have the object's basic shape. Continue to carve until the soap is in the desired shape.
5. Engrave and add fine details using the toothpick and felt-tipped pens.
6. When you are finished, rub a damp paper towel all over your carving to smooth it.

Land Of The Midnight Sun

Imagine trying to sleep on summer nights when it's bright as day! Or not seeing the sun for part of each winter! This is what it's like in the Arctic region. Every June 21, the sun never sets. Each following day has a little less light than the day before. By December 21 there is complete darkness and the sun never rises. Every autumn the Inuit played a string game called Cat's Cradle. By playing this game, they hoped to prevent the sun from falling below the horizon, signaling endless winter. The Inuit also made animals out of the string, which were sometimes used to help tell stories and legends.

Have each student tie the two ends of a three-foot length of yarn together to make a loop; then have him follow the steps shown for making a cat's cradle. Next challenge each student to devise his own string design. Have him write a paragraph explaining his design and telling a brief story about it. Then have students sit in a circle on the floor and share their tales just as the Inuit did during the winter months.

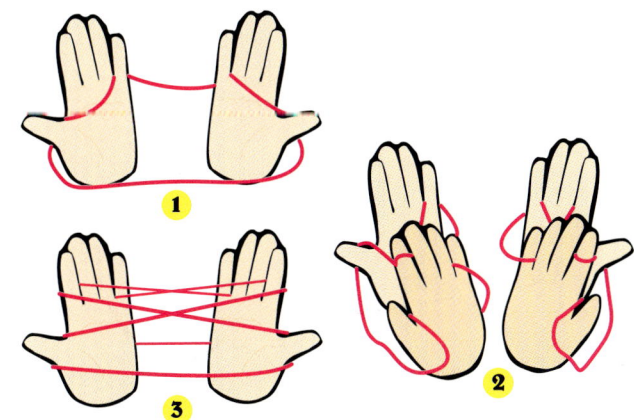

Cat's Cradle
1. Loop the string around your thumbs and little fingers.
2. Put your index finger through the loop across each palm.
3. Spread your hands apart to make the cat's cradle.

Snowy Shelters

Ask students to tell what they know about the Inuit and the word *igloo* will probably come up! To the Inuit an igloo is any house, but an *igluvigak* (eeg-LOO-vee-gack) is a snow house normally used as a temporary shelter when traveling. Because it is such an ingenious shelter, many survival kits give directions on how to make a snow house if you're caught in a blizzard.

Divide your class into small groups. Use the recipe below to make modeling dough for each group. Then give each group the dough, a copy of page 115, and the other materials listed on that page. Challenge the group to complete the model activity as instructed. Display the models in your classroom or school media center. For more information on how the Inuit built snow houses, read *Building An Igloo* by Ulli Steltzer (Henry Holt And Company, Inc.; 1995) and *Houses Of Snow, Skin And Bones* by Bonnie Shemie (Tundra Books Of Northern New York, 1993).

No-Cook Modeling Dough
(enough for one group)

Mix together 2 cups flour, 1 cup salt, and 1 cup of water.

Arctic Animals

The Inuit don't live in the Arctic completely by themselves. They share their harsh environment with many Arctic animals. Introduce students to some of these animals by reading *Mama, Do You Love Me?* by Barbara M. Joosse (Chronicle Books, 1991). Then have students create a large mural of Arctic animal life. Start by dividing students into three groups—*ocean, land,* and *sky*. Instruct each group to research the animals that live in its assigned environment during the summer months. Next hang a large sheet of butcher paper across a wall. Use a pencil to divide the paper into three sections: the top for the sky, the bottom left for the ocean, and the bottom right for the land. Finally have each group use a variety of art materials to design its portion of the mural to show the animals that live in its region during the summer. Afterward have each group share information about each animal in its design.

Novel Tie-In

Bring literature to your study of Inuit life with the help of the Newbery classic, *Julie Of The Wolves* by Jean Craighead George (HarperCollins Children's Books). This story follows the adventures of a 13-year-old Inuit girl lost on the treeless tundra. After reading the book, have each student complete the reproducible on page 117. Then, as a class, brainstorm ways that students today can "read nature" like Miyax did.

Name_____ Following directions

Building A Snow House

Ever try to build a house out of snow? If so, you probably didn't have much luck! The Inuit use a special process when building a snow house, or *igluvigak* (eeg-LOO-vee-gack). Read the paragraph that explains this process below. After you learn the secret to building a snow house, follow the directions at the bottom of this page to build your own igluvigak.

How To Build A Snow House

The first thing an Inuk does is mark a circle in the snow where he wants the house. It's important to find an area with the right kind of snow—not too hard, not too soft. Then he cuts blocks of snow using a *snow knife*. A snow knife is a long, straight knife made from whalebone. After all the blocks are cut, it's time to start building.

The Inuk places a layer of blocks around the circle in the snow. Then he uses his knife to cut diagonally into a few blocks to form a ramp (see Figure 1). This is the secret to building a snow house. Next he stacks the remaining blocks in a spiral to form a dome-shaped house. He fills in any spaces between the blocks with loose snow. Then he cuts a small opening near the top for air to escape. A block of ice could serve as a window. The Inuk would simply cut a hole in the side of the house and remove the ice block. Finally he cuts a hole for an entrance and adds a porch (see Figure 2). The porch keeps cold air from going inside the igluvigak. It also gives the Inuk extra space for storing things.

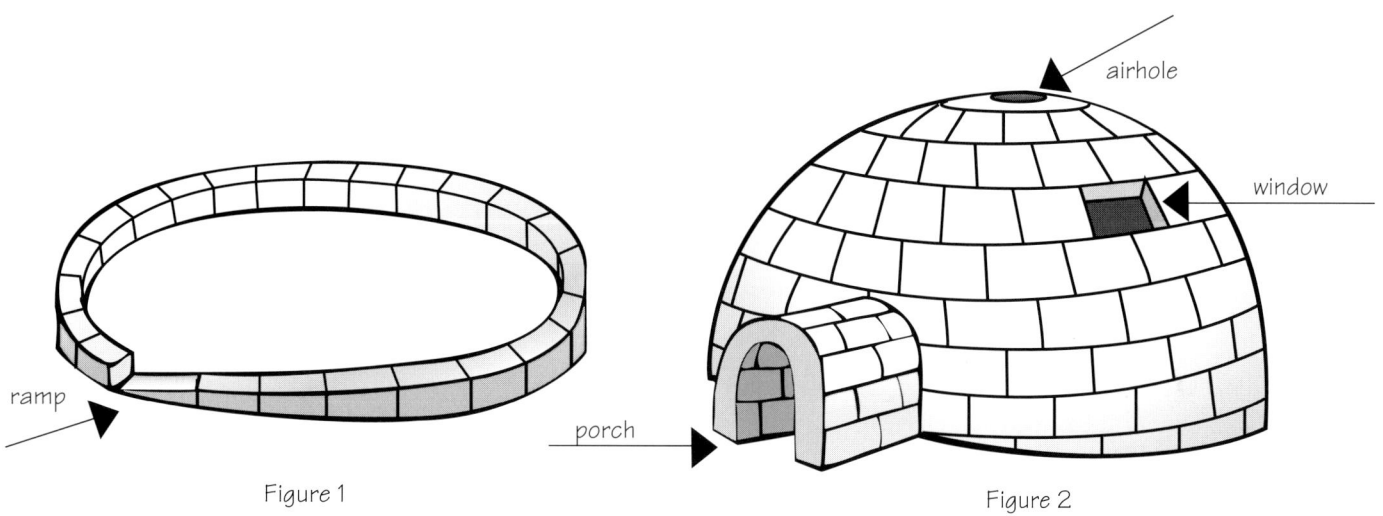

Figure 1 Figure 2

Materials for each group: modeling dough, a large Styrofoam® ball cut in half, plastic knives, pencil, ruler, white tempera paint, paintbrush, a piece of cardboard to serve as a base for the model

Steps:
1. Place the Styrofoam® on the cardboard.
2. Use a plastic knife to cut several rectangular blocks of dough (about 1" x 2").
3. Place a single layer of dough blocks on the cardboard around the perimeter of the Styrofoam® mold.
4. Cut a few of the blocks diagonally to create a ramp (see Figure 1).
5. Continue adding blocks in a spiral around the Styrofoam® mold until you've created a dome. Pinch the blocks together as you work.
6. Fill in any empty spaces between the blocks with small amounts of dough.
7. Cut a window in the side. Also make a small airhole at the top of your house.
8. Cut a hole for the entrance; then use more dough blocks to form a porch (see Figure 2).
9. Let your model dry overnight; then paint it white with tempera paint.
10. If desired, add model people and animals to your arctic scene.

©1999 The Education Center, Inc. • *The Best Of The Mailbox® Social Studies • Intermediate* • TEC1474

Note To The Teacher: Use with "Snowy Shelters" on page 114. Provide each group with the materials listed (see page 114 for the dough recipe). Explain to students that *Inuk* is the singular form of *Inuit*.

Name _____

Critical thinking

Season To Season

Snow Blocks

Imagine that you are an Inuk thinking about all you have done over the past year. Cut out each snow block. Then put each block on the month in which you may have completed that activity. When you are satisfied with your arrangement, wait for your teacher to go over the correct answers. Then glue each snow block in the correct month's box.

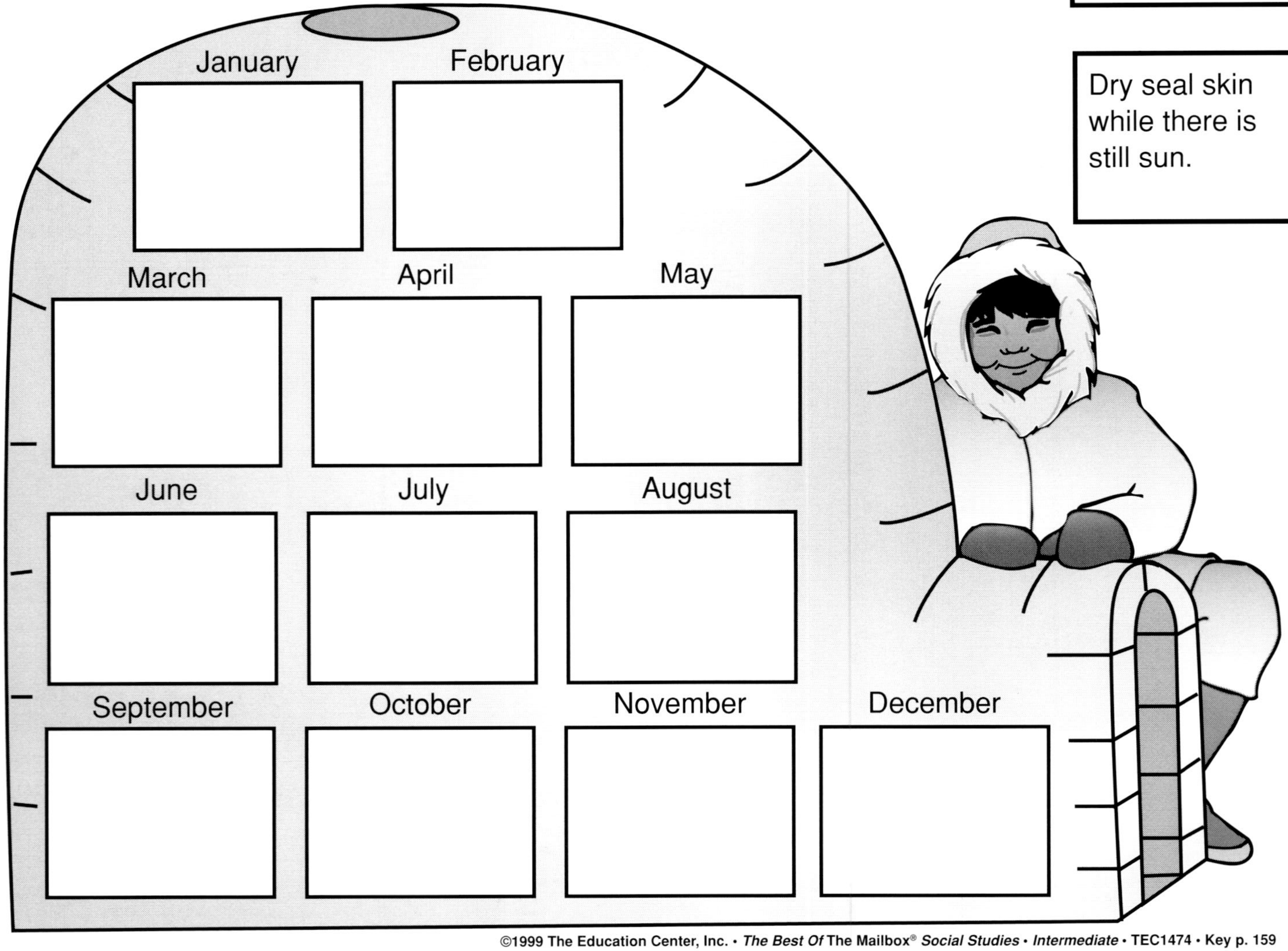

| Set up winter camp on sea ice. | Sea ice melting. Move family inland. | Start of whaling season. Get new set of clothing. | Get ready for constant darkness by end of month. | Hunt seal from kayak. | Hunt for seal as they come up through breathing holes. |

| Hunt whales that migrate north after sea ice melts. | Dry seal skin while there is still sun. | Hunt caribou while they are fat and furry. | Gather berries and roots to eat. | Midsummer sun. Wear underclothing with fur turned out. | Stay indoors and play games and tell stories. |

January February
March April May
June July August
September October November
December

Note To The Teacher: Use with "Season To Season" on page 112. Provide students with scissors and glue. See page 158 for the answer key. Explain to students that *Inuk* is the singular form of *Inuit*.

Name _____

Julie Of The Wolves
Reading comprehension

Reading Nature

In *Julie Of The Wolves,* the Inuit girl Miyax was able to read signs left by nature. She learned to find food and get around, and was accepted into the wolf pack. Read each sign below. On the line, write the letter of the meaning for that sign according to Miyax.

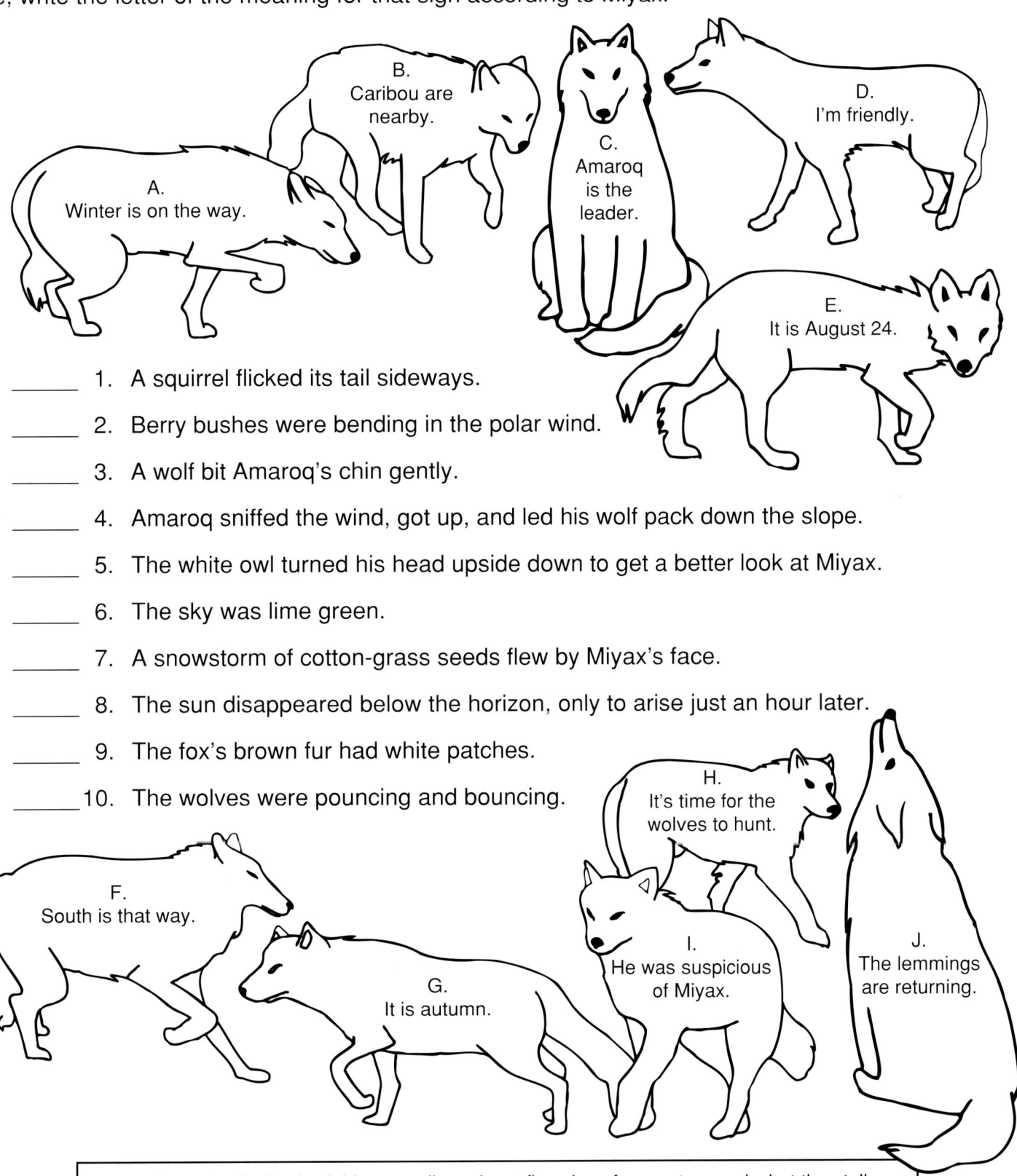

A. Winter is on the way.
B. Caribou are nearby.
C. Amaroq is the leader.
D. I'm friendly.
E. It is August 24.

_____ 1. A squirrel flicked its tail sideways.

_____ 2. Berry bushes were bending in the polar wind.

_____ 3. A wolf bit Amaroq's chin gently.

_____ 4. Amaroq sniffed the wind, got up, and led his wolf pack down the slope.

_____ 5. The white owl turned his head upside down to get a better look at Miyax.

_____ 6. The sky was lime green.

_____ 7. A snowstorm of cotton-grass seeds flew by Miyax's face.

_____ 8. The sun disappeared below the horizon, only to arise just an hour later.

_____ 9. The fox's brown fur had white patches.

_____ 10. The wolves were pouncing and bouncing.

F. South is that way.
G. It is autumn.
H. It's time for the wolves to hunt.
I. He was suspicious of Miyax.
J. The lemmings are returning.

Bonus Box: On the back of this page, list at least five signs from nature and what they tell you.

Note To The Teacher: Use with "Novel Tie-In" on page 114. Or use as part of a literature unit on *Julie Of The Wolves.*

World Map

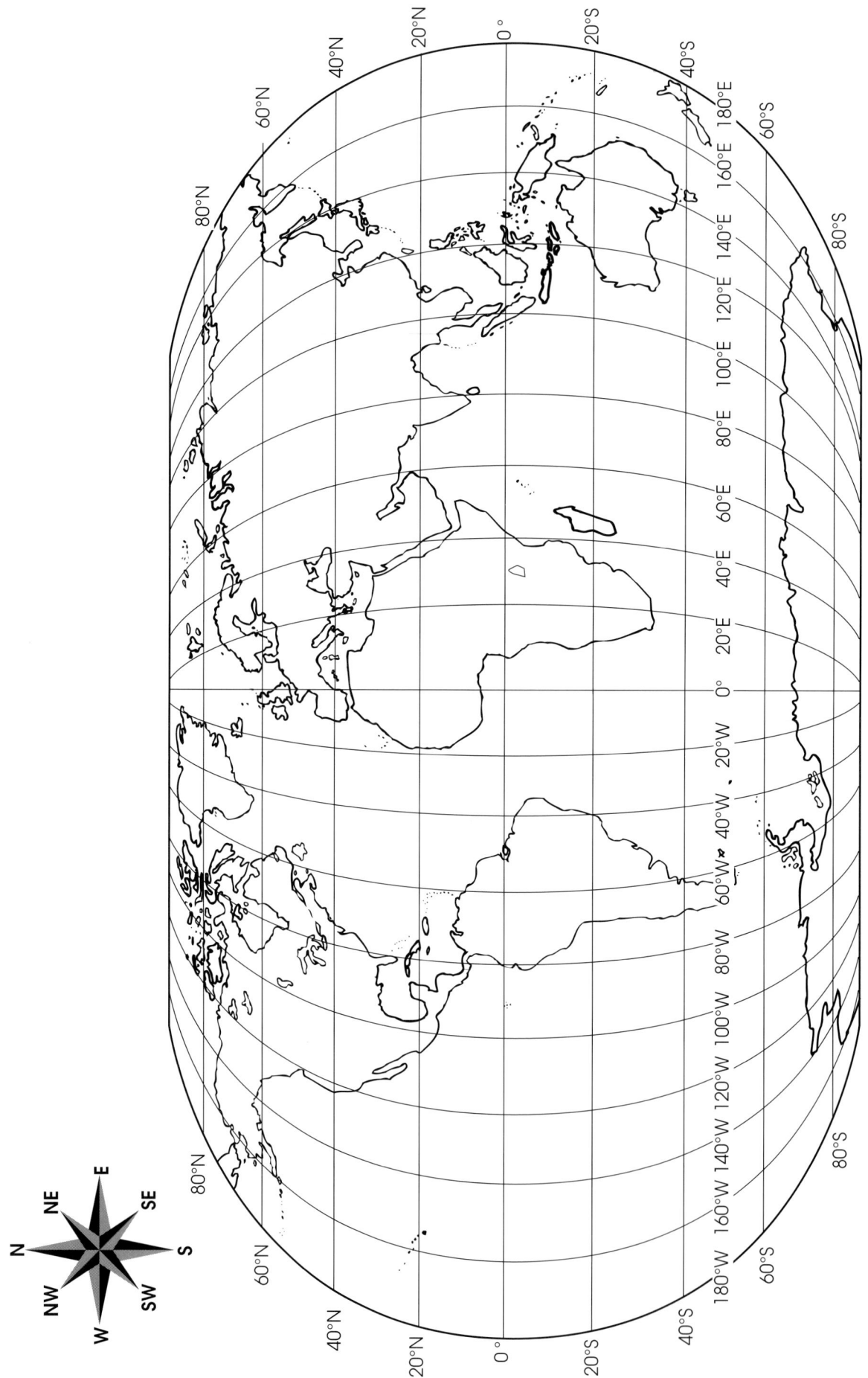

Getting A JUMP On Geography

A Collection Of Our Subscribers' Favorite Geography Activities

Use this classroom-proven collection any time of the school year to turn your students into globe-trotters who are just jumping to study geography!

Armchair Travelers

Set up a classroom travel agency to introduce students to a variety of world countries. A few weeks before the project, have students write to the embassies of the countries you wish to research. Once the information arrives, divide the class into cooperative groups and assign one country to each group. Instruct the group to use the embassy brochures and other resources to design an informational poster that will provide others with a glimpse of its country. After each group has presented its poster to the class, hang the posters near a world map. Attach a string to each poster and connect it to the country on the map to show its location. *Judith S. Baker—Gr. 4, Dean S. Luce Elementary, Canton, MA*

U.S. Regions Flip Chart

Your students will flip over this research idea! Gather several sheets of poster board—one for each U.S. region your class is studying plus an extra for a cover. Cut an inch off the bottom of one sheet; then cut each consecutive sheet one inch shorter than the previous one until you can arrange the sheets according to the illustration. Place the sheets on top of each other as shown. Punch two holes at the top through all the sheets.

Assign each group a U.S. region to research. Give each group one of the poster sheets (keep the smallest sheet to use later). Instruct the group to use its sheet to make an informational chart about its region. The chart should include a map that shows individual states, major cities, and landforms of the region. In addition, have the group summarize information about its region by including a table, a graph, and/or a report. Attach all the finished charts together with two metal rings as shown, using the smallest sheet as a cover. Label each sheet according to its region on the exposed bottom tab. *Faith Shiver and Hope Haire—Gr. 4, Mitchell County Middle School, Camilla, GA*

Geography For Your Sweet Tooth

Did you know that one way to a student's brain is through his stomach? To prove this point, place a simple cutout of the United States (use the map on page 128) on a lightly greased cookie sheet. Lightly dust the cookie sheet with flour; then remove the pattern to reveal a U.S. outline on the cookie sheet. Spread cookie dough on the sheet to fill in the map outline. Bake as instructed by the recipe. Spread frosting on the cooled cookie; then add decorations to highlight major landforms. For example, try M&M's® candies for the low, rounded Appalachian Mountains; pointy chocolate chips for the high, peaked Rocky Mountains and West Coast ranges; blue frosting from a tube for the Great Lakes and the Mississippi River; green frosting for the interior plains; and orange sugar sprinkles for the Great Basin. After completing this activity, encourage students to digest the information by eating their yummy map! *Adapted from an idea by Sally Dederich—Gr. 4, Peshtigo Elementary, Peshtigo, WI*

Where In The World?

Review basic knowledge of world or U.S. geography weekly with this simple game. Gather pictures of famous landforms or places in the United States or world. At the beginning of each week, post one picture on a bulletin board along with a thought-provoking research question. Instruct each student to write her name and the answer on a slip of paper and place it in a container. At the end of the week, draw names one by one from the container until you find a correct answer. Reward that student with a small, inexpensive prize. Use this idea to quiz students on famous people, too. *Melissa Miller Haase—Gr. 4, Bart-Colerain Elementary, Christiana, PA*

Travel Across The U.S.A.!

With your students' help, make a terrific geography game that's certain to become a class favorite! Assign each pair of students two or three states to research. After students have researched their states, give each pair five index cards for each state it researched. Instruct the pair to write a question about one of its states on each card, then write the answer on the back of the card. Collect the cards. To make the gameboard, glue a copy of the map on page 128 to a piece of poster board. Place the gameboard, question cards, and two game markers at a center. Allow two students to play the game according to these directions:

1. Stack the question cards faceup.
2. Each player puts his marker on an East Coast state. (More than one marker can be placed on a state.)
3. Player 1 draws a card and gives the answer. If correct, the student moves his marker to a bordering state. If incorrect, he returns the card to the bottom of the stack and doesn't move his marker.
4. The winner is the first player to move his marker all the way across the United States to a West Coast state.

Adapted from an idea by Caroline Jensen and Janice Holsteen, American School in Aberdeen, Aberdeen, Scotland

Color The State
Using an overhead projector, project a transparency of the U.S. map on page 128 onto a large sheet of paper. Call on a student to come to the paper map and name one state and its capital. If the student is correct, let him color in the state and label it on the paper map; then call on another child. If a student cannot correctly locate a state or its capital, he is eliminated from play. Winners are the students still playing when the map is completely colored and labeled. Draw names to see which of the winners gets to take the map home. *Neva J. Doerr—Gr. 4, Creighton Community School, Creighton, NE*

Which Way Do We Go?
Real globe-trotters know their directions! Give each child an 8 x 8 grid to number from 1 to 64 consecutively (see the illustration). Call out a starting square and a direction, such as, "Begin on square 54. Go west two squares. Then go north four squares. Where are you?" As students call out the answer, you can quickly determine which ones have mastered directions. *Patricia Blevins—Gr. 4, Avondale Elementary, Canton, OH*

Quickdraw!
Help students master the names of various landforms by playing a game of Quickdraw. Write the names of different landforms on separate cards. Divide the class into two to four teams. Choose one team to start the game. Have one of that team's members pull a card from the stack and draw a picture of that landform on the chalkboard. If his team correctly identifies the landform before time is up, the team earns a point. If the team does not correctly identify the landform, the card is returned to the stack and the next team gets to play. The team that correctly guesses the most landforms wins. *Carolyn M. Jones—Gr. 4, Weston Middle School, Weston, CT*

Which Way To Route 66?
Place a supply of state road maps at a geography center. With the maps, include 10 to 15 task cards that you've labeled with directions, such as "Start at Columbus and head north on Interstate 71 until it reaches a city that is famous for its baseball team. What is the name of the city?" During center time, instruct one student to read a question from a task card while another student finds the answer on the map. Have students take turns reading questions and checking each other's answers. *Lori Levings—Gr. 4, Cardington, OH*

The U.S.A. Is In Great Shape!

It's no puzzle to see why this eye-catching display is bound to be a class favorite! Purchase an inexpensive puzzle of the United States (one in which each state is a separate piece). Then follow these directions:

1. Cut out 25 white triangles and 25 red triangles from poster board.
2. Number the triangles as shown.
3. Glue each state puzzle piece to a numbered triangle according to the date on which that state was admitted to the Union (ask your librarian for a listing of these dates). For example, glue the Delaware puzzle piece to the number 1 triangle, the Pennsylvania puzzle piece to the number 2 triangle, and so on.
4. After the glue has dried, mount the triangles on a bulletin board as shown. Add an Uncle Sam character and the title "The U.S.A. Is In Great Shape!"

Carolyn Martin—Gr. 6, Bridge Creek School, Blanchard, OK

Name That State

Help students recognize the shape and location of each state with this quick-and-easy game. Create a set of flash cards that show the unlabeled outline of each state and a list of its bordering states. Have two students come to the front of the classroom. Flash a state card to the students and see which of them can correctly guess the name of the state. Leave the cards at a center for students to practice with during free time. *Jeffrey J. Kuntz—Gr. 4, West End Elementary, Punxsutawney, PA*

The World At Your Fingertips

Let your students' fingers do the walking to locate different countries of the world! Provide each pair of students with two 8 1/2" square sheets of lightweight paper, a copy of "Making A Finger Popper" on page 130, a blank world map, and a world map that is labeled with countries. Have each student follow the directions to create a finger popper. Then have pairs of students use their poppers to play this game:

1. Player 1: Choose a color from your partner's finger popper.
2. Player 2: Spell out the color using your finger popper. For the first letter of the color, open the popper in one direction. Open it in the other direction for the next letter. Keep opening the popper in a different direction for each letter.
3. Player 1: Choose a number from those showing after Player 2's last move.
4. Player 2: Count out the number. Open the popper back and forth as you count. Repeat steps 3 and 4.
5. Player 1: Choose a number that is showing after Player 2's last move.
6. Player 2: Lift the flap of the chosen number. Read the country that's written under that number.
7. Player 1: Locate that country on the blank map.
8. Player 2: Check your partner using the labeled world map. If correct, award your partner one point. If incorrect, show your partner the correct location of the country.
9. Switch roles and play again!

Simone Lepine—Gr. 5, Syracuse, NY

Product Pursuit
Where in the world do we get the products that we eat, wear, and use? Duplicate the form on the top of page 129 for each student. Write the names of different products on slips of paper and place them in a jar. Have each student draw one product from the jar. Instruct the student to use research skills to find the top producer (state or country) of that product. Then have the student use her findings to complete the form. Post the completed forms around a world or U.S. map on a bulletin board. Use yarn to connect each form to the country or state that is its product's top producer. *Karen Bryant—Gr. 4, Rosa Taylor Elementary, Macon, GA*

State Surprise Boxes
Culminate your study of states by having each student construct a state surprise box. To complete this activity, provide each student with the following materials: a lidded Styrofoam® box (used for take-out food in restaurants), brown modeling clay, several other colors of modeling clay, a copy of the patterns on the bottom of page 129, a marker or pencil, scissors, and glue. Have the student follow these steps to complete his surprise box:
1. Use brown clay to make a relief model of your state on the inside of your box.
2. Add landform details with different colored clays.
3. Fill in information on the map key pattern on page 129. Cut out the pattern and glue it inside the lid of your box.
4. Write three clues about the identity of your state on the "What's The State?" pattern on page 129. Cut out this pattern and glue it to the top of your box's lid.

Nicole Iacovazzi, Owego Elementary, Vestal, NY

From My Point Of View
Learn geography all year long with this easy idea. Each month feature a different part of the world, such as Asia, Canada, or the Great Plains states. Divide that month's part of the world into separate divisions (countries, states, provinces, and/or cities) so that each student has a specific place to research. After researching his place, have the student present his information orally by pretending to be that spot on the globe. Instruct the student to use phrases such as "I am the country of India," "I am located on the continent of Asia," and "The Indian Ocean borders me to the south." *Jeannette Freeman—Gr. 4, Baldwin School of Puerto Rico, Condado, Puerto Rico*

Pro Sports And Geography

During the fall, I type a list of all the professional football teams and give each student a copy. Students are challenged to locate each pro football city on a map and then write its latitude and longitude coordinates beside the city's name on the list. In the spring I repeat the activity as a review, using the names of professional basketball teams. What a great way to use a topic kids love to review map skills! *Dawn Carmack, Munford Middle School, Munford, TN*

Take Along A Travelmate!

All it took to get my students excited about geography was a collection of stuffed animals we called Travelmates. I placed each animal into a student-sized backpack, along with a supply of preprinted return labels and a logbook. Our Travelmates tag along with parents on business trips, students visiting Grandma's, and anywhere there is a traveler willing to let a Travelmate tag along. A Travelmate host is asked to complete a page in the logbook and send our class a postcard or photo showing where the Travelmate is vacationing. If a student is hosting a Travelmate, he gives an oral report about his trip when he returns. Our class keeps a Travelmates scrapbook that includes both world and U.S. maps. After receiving information about a Travelmate's trip, we color in the location on a map and add any souvenirs the stuffed critter brought back to the scrapbook. *Maxine Pincott—Gr. 4, Oliver Ellsworth School, Windsor, CT*

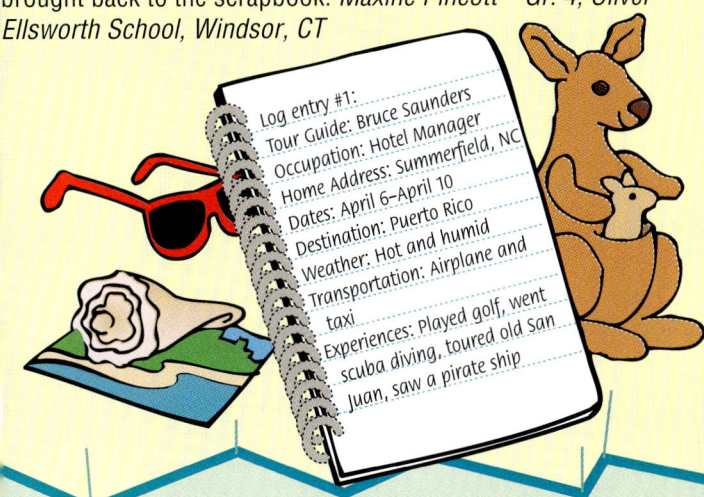

Cookie Elevation Maps

Bet your students will take more than one bite of this yummy geography project! Purchase a U.S.-shaped cookie cutter. After studying about elevation, give each student a portion of refrigerated sugar-cookie dough (the amount will depend on the size of your cookie cutter). Have the student use a rolling pin to roll out the dough on waxed paper. Next have her cut the shape with the cookie cutter, and then use extra dough to add mountain ranges such as the Rockies and the Great Smoky Mountains. Prepare yellow, green, and orange edible paint using the recipe that follows; then have each student paint her cookie to indicate areas of low, medium, and high elevations. Sprinkle the cookies with a light dusting of sugar before baking them. *Karen Brown—Gr. 4, Hamilton-Parsons Elementary, Romeo, MI*

Egg Yolk Paint

Combine one egg yolk with 1/4 tsp. of water. Add food coloring to make the desired color. Paint on with a paintbrush.

It's A Wonderful Day In The Neighborhood

To reinforce the concepts of cardinal directions, intermediate directions, and using a map key, draw a simple neighborhood map on a transparency or bulletin board. Mark the streets, stores, buildings, parks, and other elements on the map with labels that use the names of your students. Make sure each student is represented in this mythical neighborhood.

Once the map has been completed, create a set of question cards based on the map. For example: "Billy is going to Amy Walker Park to play basketball. If Billy leaves from Baxter's Shoe Store, in which direction will he travel to get to the park? Name the streets on which Billy will travel." Give each group several cards to answer. Or challenge students with a question anytime you have a few extra minutes to fill. *Jeffrey J. Kuntz—Gr. 4 Social Studies, West End Elementary, Punxsutawney, PA*

"Worldwise" Tic-Tac-Toe

Turn your students into able globe-trotters with this fun game. Tape a large, unlabeled world or U.S. map on your chalkboard. Beside the map, draw a 4 x 4 grid. Label the backs of 16 self-sticking notes with the names of continents, countries, oceans, or states (depending on which map you use). Stick a note inside each grid square so that its label is hidden.

To play, divide the class into an *X* team and an *O* team. In turn, have a player from each team remove a note from the grid, read its label, and place it correctly on the map. If he's correct, let the student draw an *X* or *O* in the square. If he's incorrect, have him return the note to the grid. The first team to get tic-tac-toe wins. *Christine Juozitis—Gr. 4, Thomas Jefferson School, Binghamton, NY*

Geography And Current Events

Several subscribers suggested terrific ways to combine current events with geography. Try these ideas:

Yearlong Current Events Maps

At the beginning of the year, I give each of my students a blank world map. Every Wednesday we meet in groups to discuss news articles. As one group member summarizes his article, each of his teammates uses a marker to draw a star on his map indicating where the event took place. At the beginning of a new marking period, we all change and use a different color of marker. By the end of the year, we've traveled the globe—and gained a new understanding of current events! *Karen Scro—Gr. 6, Washington Irving School, Garfield, NY*

Short Clips

Clip short (one- or two-paragraph) articles from the daily newspaper. Tape each article to a colorful index card; then give a card to each group. Direct the group to spend ten minutes reading the article, discussing it, and finding its location on a world map. After the ten minutes is up, have a representative from each group summarize the article for the class and point out its location on the map. Have each group label a sticky note with the name of the location, then place it on the map. *Beverly Sharpe—Gr. 5, Thornton Elementary, Littleton, CO*

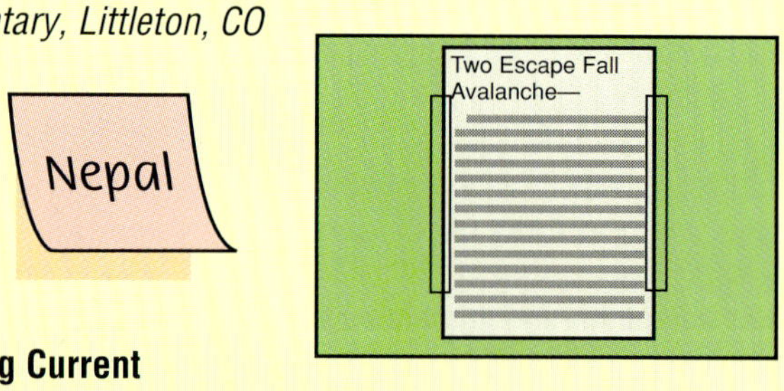

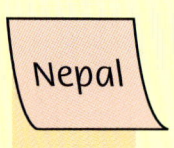

Where In The USA?

For a terrific interactive display, mount a U.S. map in the middle of a bulletin board. Periodically have each student bring a news article to class along with a summary written on a small index card. Have students staple their articles and summaries around the map; then have them connect the articles to the correct locations on the map using lengths of yarn. Change the theme of the board every six weeks to cover different maps (Europe, Asia, Latin America, etc.) or types of articles (football news, world capitals, etc.). Award ten extra-credit points to each student who contributes to the display. *Dawn Carmack, Munford Middle School, Munford, TN*

Keeping Current

For one week, have students collect and read newspaper articles on events happening outside the United States. Direct students to summarize each article and then write a new headline for it. Have students post their new headlines around a world map mounted on a bulletin board. Then have them use yarn to connect the articles to the correct locations on the map. *Mary Gates, New Milford, CT*

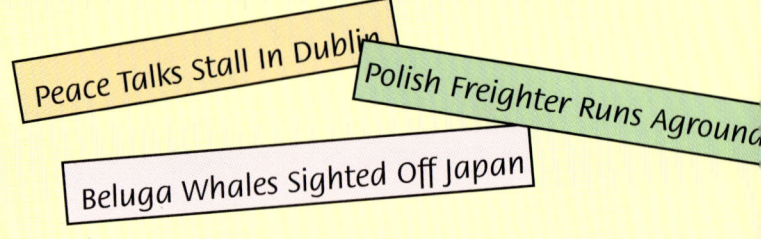

Consider The Source

Rivers have always been important; not only as sources of fresh water, but also for transportation and crop growth. Long ago the system of tributaries helped people travel more quickly from place to place. Using maps, examine with students the tributary systems of some large rivers like the Mississippi and the Amazon. Ask students, "What cities are on the river's banks? How far could someone travel from a tributary to the mouth of the river? How many tributaries are in the system?"

After this discussion, give each pair of students an atlas and a copy of the "Consider The Source!" reproducible below. Assign a major river to each pair (see the list on the right), reminding the students not to share the identity of their river with other classmates. When students have completed their reproducibles, have pairs swap their papers and try to identify each other's mystery river. *Mary Gates, New Milford, CT*

Major Rivers To Research:

Amazon	Colorado	Congo	Danube
Ganges	Huang Ho	Mekong	Mississippi
Missouri	Niger	Nile	Rio Grande
	Volga	Yangtze	

Names _____
Geography research

Consider The Source!

Long ago a river's *tributaries*—or branches—helped people travel more quickly from place to place. Now's your chance to do a little river research! Your teacher will assign you and a partner a famous river to research. DON'T let anyone know the name of your river and don't write its name anywhere on this sheet. Follow these steps:

1. Research your river; then fill in each tributary with the information needed.
2. Exchange papers with another pair of students.
3. Read the clues on the paper you received; then research to try to find the name of this mystery river. When you think you know the name of the mystery river, write it in the blank and return the paper to its owners for checking.

Name of the mystery river: _____

Tributaries:
- Name of a tributary
- A large city on my banks
- Country(s) I flow through
- Continent on which I'm found
- Location of my source
- My mouth empties into...
- A special clue

Pattern

Use this map with "Geography For Your Sweet Tooth" and "Travel Across The U.S.A.!" on page 121 and "Color The State" on page 122.

Patterns
Use with "Product Pursuit" on page 124.

_____
Name Of Product

_____
_____
Top Producer

_____
_____
_____
_____
Facts

Picture Of Product

Researched by _____

©1999 The Education Center, Inc. • *The Best Of* The Mailbox® *Social Studies* • *Intermediate* • TEC1474

Use these patterns with "State Surprise Boxes" on page 124.

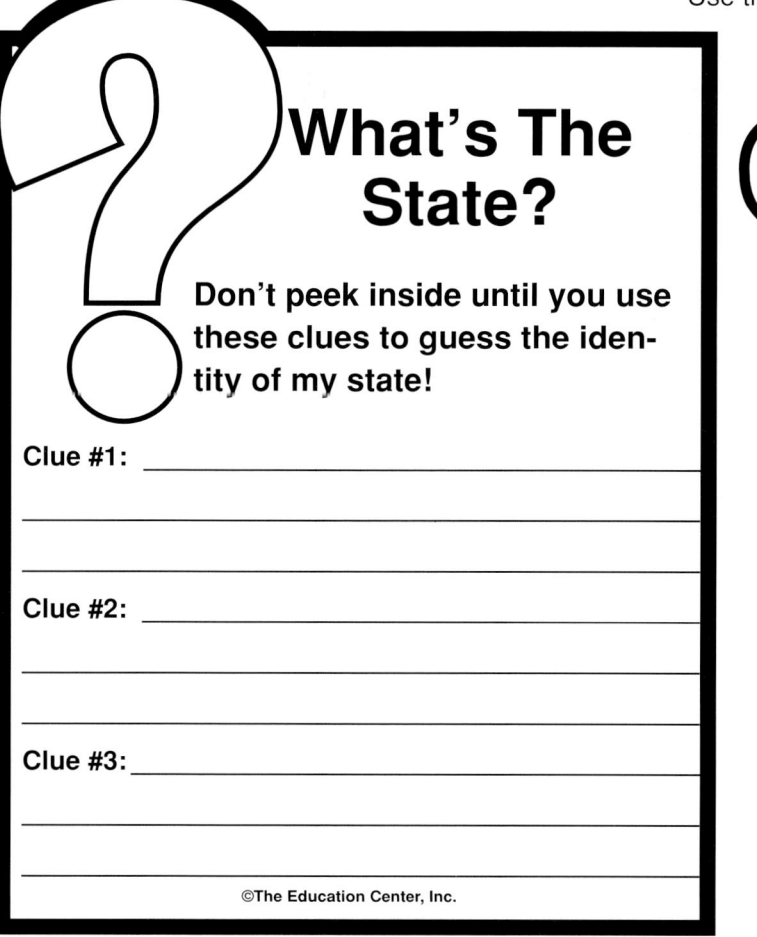

What's The State?

Don't peek inside until you use these clues to guess the identity of my state!

Clue #1: _____
_____

Clue #2: _____
_____

Clue #3: _____
_____

©The Education Center, Inc.

The Key To My State

Map Key

©The Education Center, Inc.

Name _____ Following directions

Making A Finger Popper

This folded-paper finger popper has been around for generations. Use the directions below and the piece of paper your teacher will give you to make your own. Then use your finger popper to play the geography game "The World At Your Fingertips."

How To Make A Finger Popper:

1. Fold the square of paper in half from top to bottom (see A). Unfold; then fold again from side to side. Unfold again. Both folds will form a cross (see B).

2. Take the top two corners and pull them together toward the center to create a roof shape (see C). Crease the folds.

3. Repeat step 2 with the bottom half of the paper to form a smaller square (see D).

4. Flip the square and repeat steps 1–3. This will form an even smaller square (see E).

5. Notice that the paper is now divided into eight triangles (see E). Pick any eight numbers between 1 and 15. Write one of these numbers on each triangle (see F).

6. Pull up each flap. Notice that there are two triangles on the underside of the flap. Write the name of a different country on each of these triangles (see G).

7. Close all the flaps so that only the numbers show. Turn the square over. Notice the four small squares. Write the name of a different color on each of these squares (see H).

8. Now it's time to turn this paper into a game. Fold the square in half so that the numbers are on the inside of the fold. Slip the thumb and forefinger of your right hand under the color flaps on the right side of the folded paper. Slip the thumb and forefinger of your left hand under the color flaps on the left side of the paper. In order to make the top, outer corners meet in the middle, place your chin in the center of the fold and pinch the corners around it.

9. Practice moving the points of your finger popper—opening and closing the two halves so that you can see the numbers inside.

10. Follow your teacher's instructions on how to play "The World At Your Fingertips."

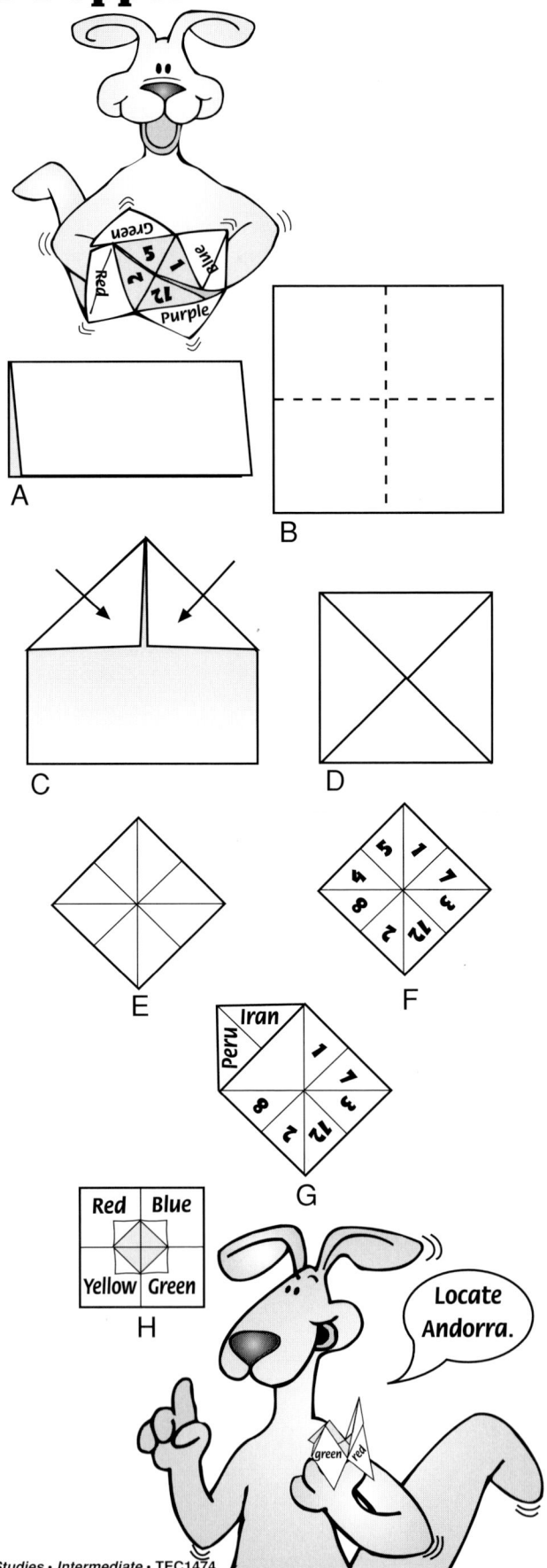

©1999 The Education Center, Inc. • *The Best Of The Mailbox® Social Studies • Intermediate •* TEC1474

Note To The Teacher: Provide each student with an 8 1/2" square sheet of paper. Use the completed finger poppers with the game described in "The World At Your Fingertips" on page 123.

Name(s) _____

World geography _____

What In The World Is Wrong With This Map?

This may look like a perfectly normal world map, but look again! There are 15 errors in this map. Draw a ★ on each error. On the back of this sheet, write a sentence to explain each error. Use an atlas or other world map to help you.

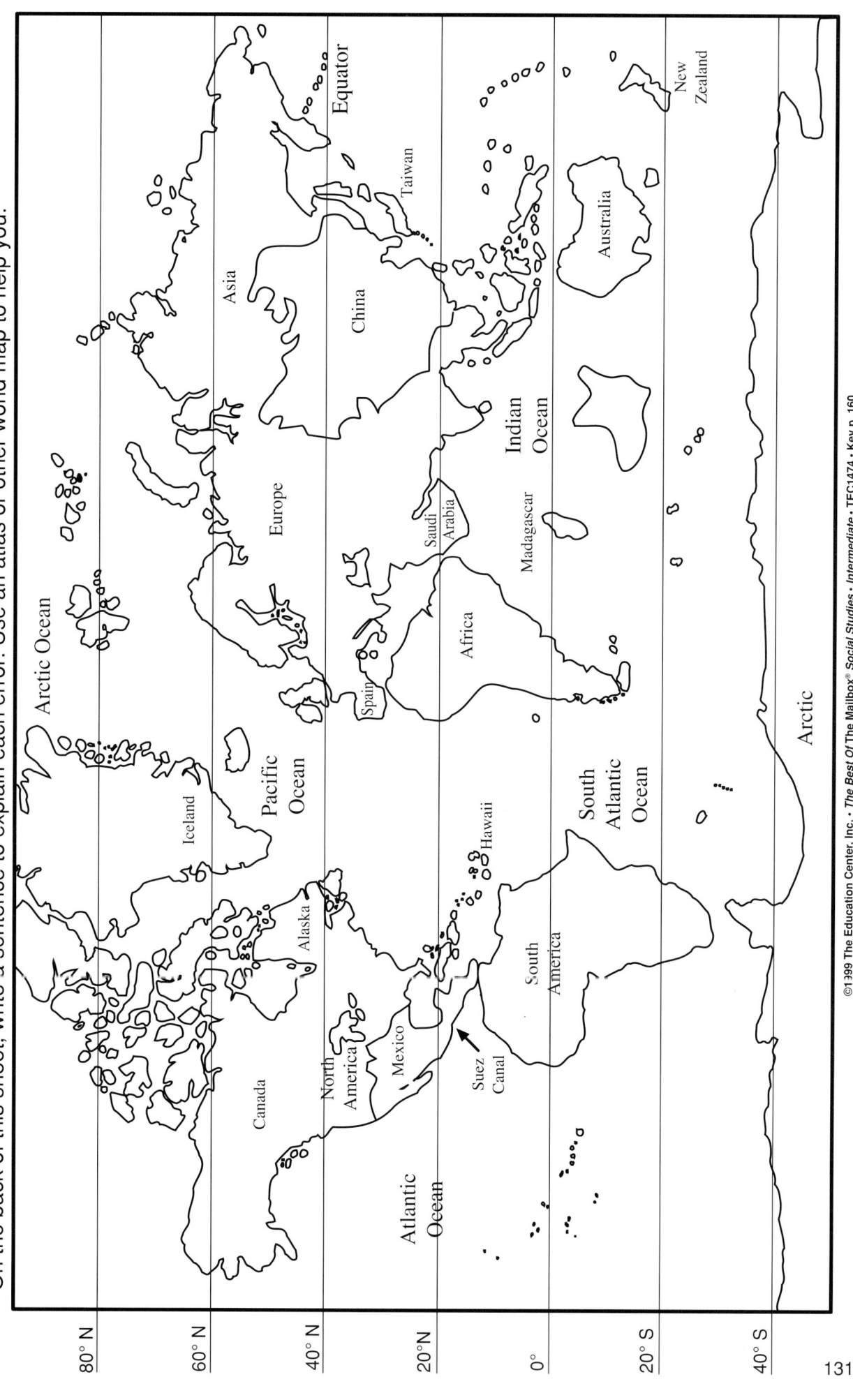

©1999 The Education Center, Inc. • The Best Of The Mailbox® Social Studies • Intermediate • TEC1474 • Key p. 160

131

Name(s)_____   Reading a road map, using a scale of miles

"Moooving" Across Your State

Use a road map of your state to answer the following questions. Write your answers in the blanks.

_____ 1. How many counties are in the state?
_____ 2. How many miles are represented by one inch on the map?
_____ 3. About how many miles is it from the eastern border to the western border of the state?
_____ 4. What is the state capital?
_____ 5. Name one interstate highway that is in your state.
_____ 6. How far is your hometown from the nearest state border?
_____ 7. In what direction would you travel from your hometown to reach the nearest state border?
_____ 8. In what county do you live?
_____ 9. Name a county that borders your county.
_____ 10. What county is directly east of your county?
_____ 11. How far is your hometown from the state capital?
_____ 12. In what county is the state capital located?
_____ 13. What are the letter and number coordinates of the state capital?
_____ 14. How many enlarged inset maps are on the road map?
_____ 15. What state park is nearest your hometown?
_____ 16. What highways would you take to get from the northeast corner of your state to the southwest corner?

In the boxes below, draw and color the map key symbol used for each item.
(If no symbol is given, create your own.)

state park	rest area	airport	railroad	college or university

state capital	city or town	interstate highway	forest area	compass rose

Bonus Box: Plan a trip to a state or national park that is in your state. Write travel directions explaining how to get there from your hometown. In your travel directions, include at least two places of interest at which to stop along the way.

Name(s)_____   Mapmaking project

Cartographer's Challenge

Follow the directions to create a map of your own imaginary country!

1. Read over the geographic terms below. With a partner or small group, discuss the terms to be sure that you understand them. Use a dictionary, textbook, or resource book if you need help.

2. On a scrap piece of paper, draw the outline of your imaginary nation.

3. Add the following items to your map:
   - title
   - compass rose
   - physical features map key
   - scale of miles
   - natural resources/products legend (showing at least six resources)

4. Circle 20 of the geographic terms listed below. Add labels on the map to identify those terms on your map.

5. Ask a partner to check your rough draft to make sure that you have labeled your map correctly and have included all required items.

6. Choose a theme for your map (cars, food, sports, famous people, music, cartoon characters, book titles and characters, games, etc.).

7. Use your theme to name all of your map's special features. For example, if you included a desert on your map and chose a games theme, you might call the desert "Dominoes Desert" or "Dice Desert." Be creative!

8. Once your rough draft is completed, use it to complete your final project. Be sure to make your map colorful with markers, crayons, fabric, etc.

Geographic Terms

archipelago	foothill	isthmus	peninsula	sound
bay	glacier	lowland	plain	source
canal	gulf	marsh	plateau	strait
canyon	harbor	mesa	port	swamp
cape	highland	mountain range	prairie	tributary
channel	hill	mouth	rain forest	tundra
delta	inlet	ocean	reservoir	valley
desert	island	peak	sea	volcano

The Great Shape Search

The shapes below represent five states, three continents, and eight countries. (Shapes are **not** drawn to scale.) Use an atlas or other resource book to help you identify each shape. On the back of this sheet, number 1–15; then write your answers.

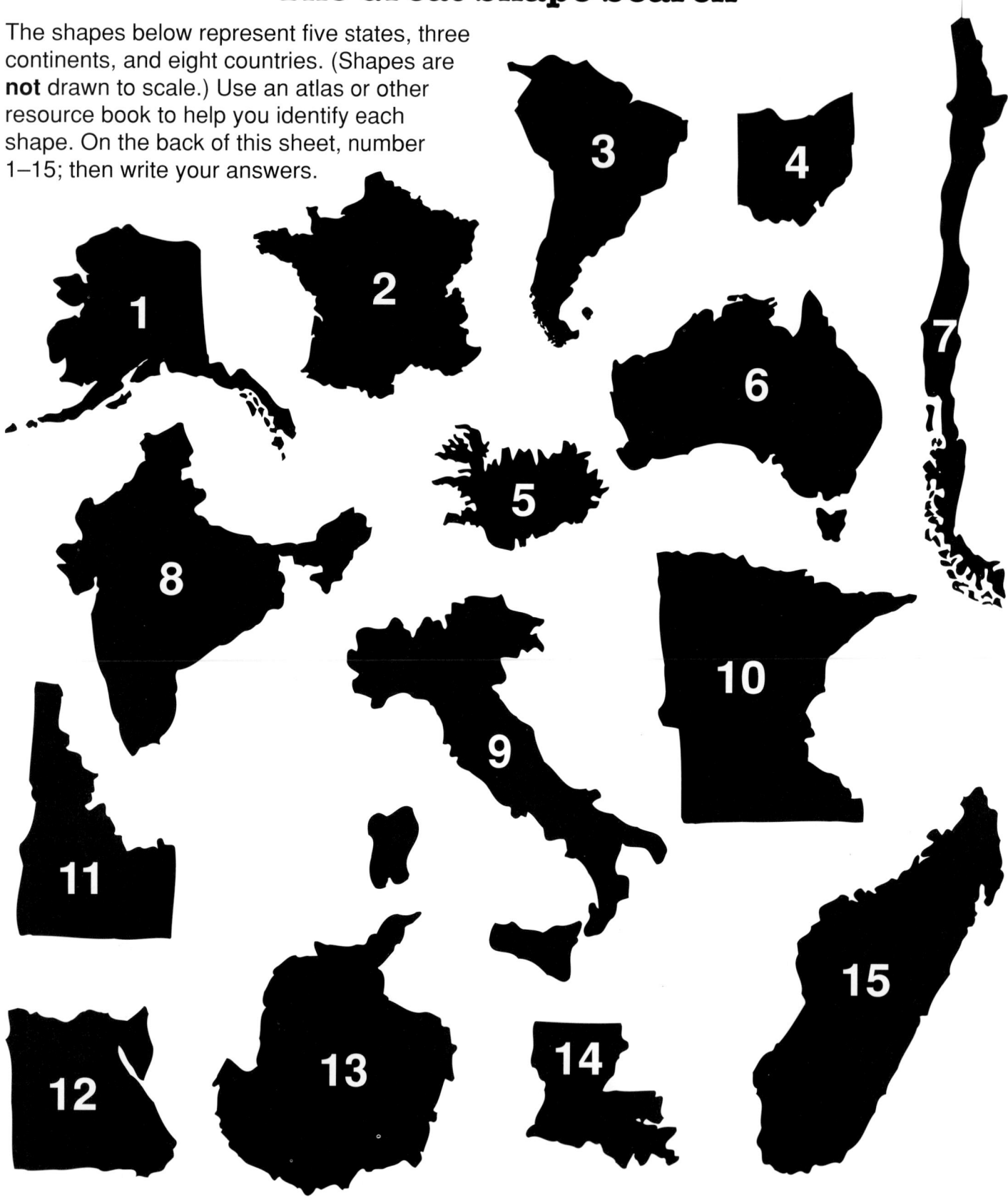

Bonus Box: Find three more distinctive shapes in an atlas. Trace the shapes on the back of this sheet. Challenge a friend to identify them using the atlas.

A Nose For News

Current-Events Activities To Keep Your Students In The Know

Spark your students' interest in current events with these newsworthy activities from our subscribers!

Extra, Extra, Read All About It!

Turn your class library into a bustling newsstand by placing several current periodicals and newspapers on display. If possible make an attractive newsstand using a cardboard or wire book holder. Update the stock of newspapers and periodicals regularly so students have a variety of fresh reading materials to choose from. You can bet that students will rush to check out the newsstand in their free time.

Kelly A. Wong, Berlyn School, Ontario, CA

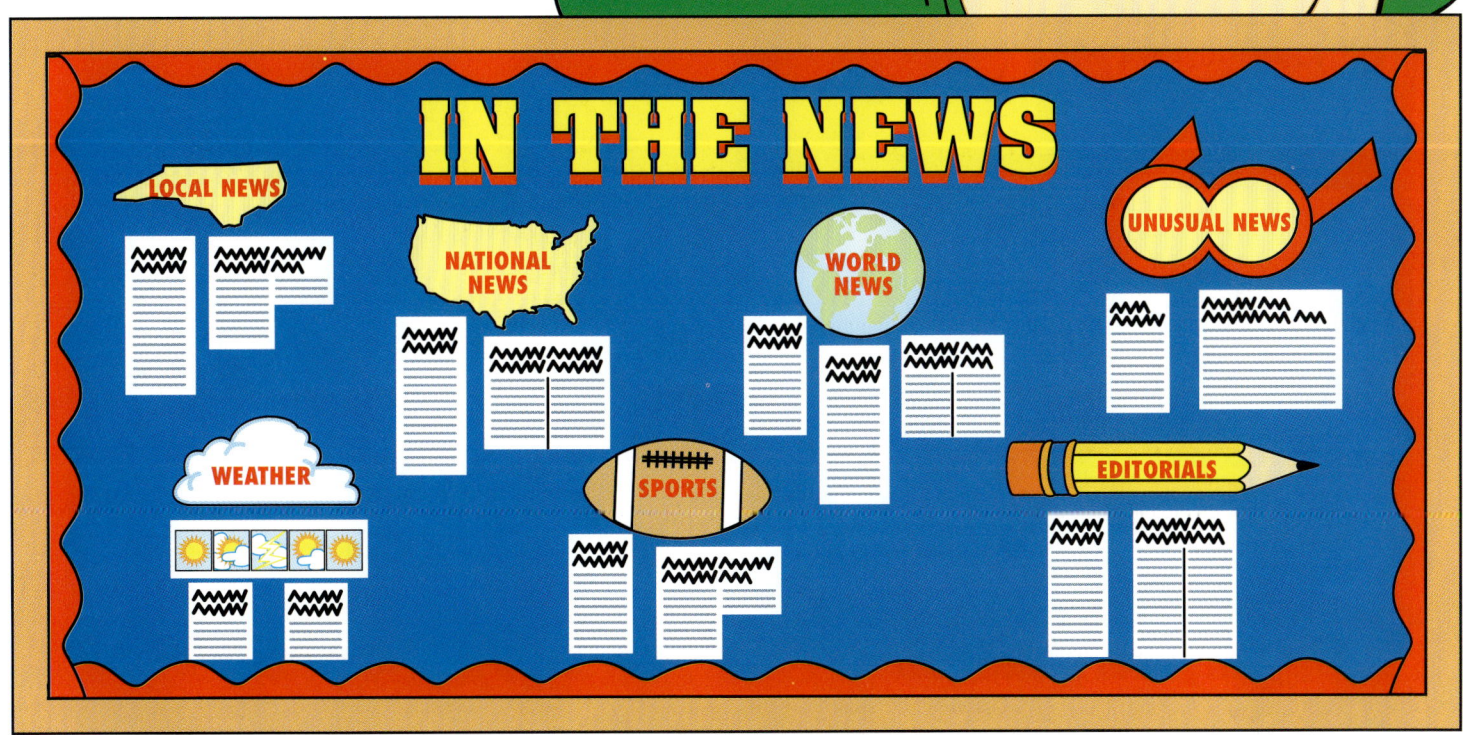

In The News

Keep your class in the know with this easy-to-make bulletin board. Divide a bulletin board into seven sections, labeling each with one of the following headings: *Local News, National News, World News, Unusual News, Weather, Sports,* and *Editorials.* Then divide your class into cooperative learning groups. On a rotating basis, assign each group a week in which it is responsible for filling the sections of the bulletin board with news articles on each topic. Instruct each group member to post her articles under the correct headings; then have her give a brief oral summary of the articles to the rest of the class.

Deborah Abrams—Gr. 5, Laguna Elementary, Albuquerque, NM

Games And Learning Centers

Centered On Current Events

Use this fun center to extend your study of current events into many different curriculum areas. Glue the front page of a newspaper on a large poster; then laminate the poster. Write the following activities on index cards:

- Write an ending for a story started on the front page.
- Create a new title for an article on the poster.
- Underline all the examples of [a specific part of speech] in an article.
- Find the main idea and supporting facts in an article.
- Practice reading an article aloud like a newscaster on the nightly news would.
- Determine where an article occurs and find the area on a map.

Place the poster, activity cards, and a wipe-off marker in a current-events center. Challenge students to come up with additional activities related to the curriculum to add to the center.

Jane Peege Sanders—Grs. 5–6, Lullwater School, Decatur, GA

Current-Events Jeopardy

Turn your study of current events into a challenging game with this fun activity. Divide your class into four cooperative groups. Assign each group one category—local, state, national, or world news. Instruct each group to collect newspaper articles relating to its assigned geographic area throughout the week. Invite groups to share details of the articles as they are brought in. Then collect each article and write a follow-up question on it. Play a Jeopardy®-style game using the questions on Friday for an exciting review of the week's current events.

Tammy Nelson—Gr. 5, St. Leo's School, Ridgway, PA

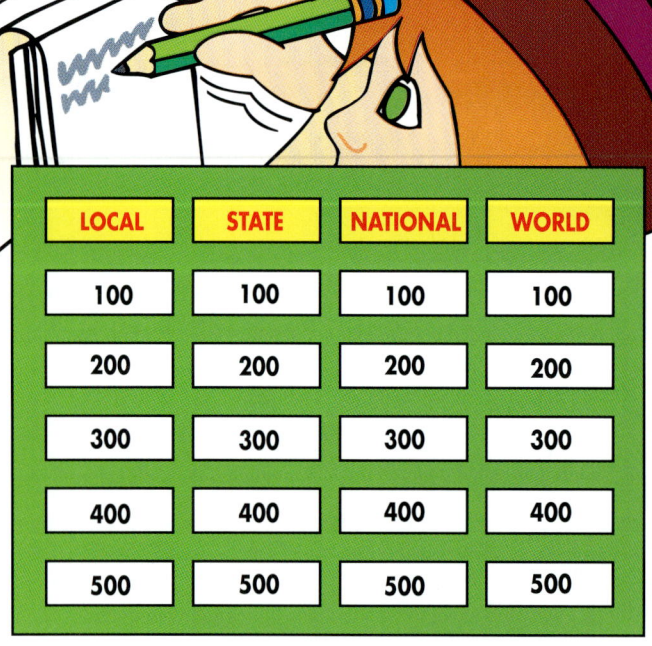

Mystery Person

Add a little mystery to your study of current events with this exciting game. Select an individual who has recently been featured in the news. Provide your students with a clue about the selected individual each day until students are able to guess the person's identity. When students have determined the identity of the individual, hold a discussion on the person and his or her newsworthy accomplishments. Students will soon realize that keeping up on current events will keep them informed while giving them an advantage in the game.

Liz Neufeld—Gr. 5, St. Elizabeth Seton School, Minneapolis, MN

Word Sleuths

Enlist the help of parents to teach your students new vocabulary using the newspaper. Instruct each student to read a short newspaper article of her choice with a parent. Then have her select one word with which she is unfamiliar. Tell the student to work with her parent to find out the following information about the word:
- definition
- base word
- prefix or suffix
- part of speech

Next ask the student to write the word in a sentence and illustrate it. Invite each student to share the work she did with her parent on a day set aside as Word Sleuth Day. Display the cooperative parent/child work on a bulletin board in your room.

Margaret Zogg—Substitute K–6, Liverpool School District, Liverpool, NY

Map Skills Activities

Where In The World?

Combine current events with the study of geography in this easy-to-make center. Glue a world map onto the outside of a manila folder; then laminate the folder. Instruct each student to choose an article from the world news section of the paper and write a four-sentence summary of it, including characters, setting, problem, and resolution. Then have the student use a wipe-off marker to circle the article's setting on the laminated map folder. Direct the student to place the completed summary and the article in the folder.

As a variation, give each student a laminated folder in which you've glued world, U.S., and state maps. Have students keep the folders in their desks to pull out as a quick reference during current-events discussions.

Jennifer Lee—Gr. 6, Van Buren Elementary, Hamilton, OH and Susan Phillips, Harwood Elementary, Harwood, ND

Linking News With Latitude And Longitude

Keep your students abreast of current events while providing practice with important mapping skills with this activity. Divide your class into cooperative groups of three students each. Provide each group with the latitude and longitude coordinates of a place in which a recent current event has taken place. Have each group use the coordinates to pinpoint the location of the news event on a world map. Then instruct the group to look through the newspaper and find a news article whose setting matches the provided coordinates. Invite each group to share a summary of the news event and its coordinate setting with the rest of the class.

Susan Sandman—Gr. 5, Parkview Middle School, Creve Coeur, IL

Writing Activities

Get To The Point

Teach your students about point of view with the help of current events. Begin by reading a current-events article to your students. Then have each student write an essay detailing his point of view on the issue. Display the students' viewpoints in the hall along with some blank paper. Attach a pencil to the blank paper; then post a sign to encourage other students to add their points of view about the issue to the display.

Michelle Discenza—Gr. 5, Morrisville Year-Round Elementary, Morrisville, NC
Debbie Brun—Special Needs, Silver Spring School, Rumford, RI

Figuring Out Figurative Language

Use the headlines of the newspaper to teach your students how to use figurative language. Select three headlines from the daily newspaper. Rewrite the headings using a form of figurative language such as rhyming or alliteration. Challenge your students to determine the news event each of the figurative headlines represents. For example, the alliterated headline "County Consents To Courthouse Cash" represents the news heading "Funds For New Courthouse Approved." Challenge students to use figurative language to rewrite additional news headings to share with the class.

Janice L. Roehr—Gr. 6, J. H. Gaudet Middle School, Middletown, RI

County Consents To Courthouse Cash

Lo And Behold—
It's Going To Get Cold!

Derelict Driver Demolishes Donut Delivery Truck

Rise And Shine With Current Events

Wake up your students in the morning with a daily dose of current events. Record a question about a recent current event on the board. Then instruct each student to read the question, write his answer on a piece of scrap paper, and turn in his response. Go over the answer to the question when all responses are turned in, or post the article for students to read at their leisure. Award students bonus points for correct responses.

Faye K. Wells, Marion County Elementary, Buena Vista, GA

Technology Ideas

Current Events On-Line

Surfing the Internet is a great way for your students to keep up on current events! Let students check out what's happening around the globe on the CNN website located at http://www.cnn.com (current as of September 1998). Challenge students to use the site to read up on current events; then have them complete the News Quiz for the day—a ten-question, multiple-choice quiz on the day's current events generated by CNN. If you do not have widespread Internet access in your school, print out the news articles and the News Quiz in advance and make copies for your students.

Nancy Thompson—Gr. 6, Randall School, Cortland, NY

Television And The News

What better way to keep up-to-date about current news events than by watching the nightly news! Tape segments of a national news program in the evening and bring the tape to school. Pick news features that are of interest to your students, such as stories on uniforms in school, dress codes, year-round schools, environmental issues, etc. Show your students the taped news segments and discuss them as a class. Then instruct each student to write a personal response to one news segment in his journal. Save the tapes and take them out in June to review all that has happened during the school year.

Amy Sain, Denmark Elementary, Jackson, TN

Logging In Current Events

Use your class computer to keep a running record of current events throughout the school year. Allow students to take turns being the reporter for a day. Record the month, date, year, day of week, and time on the chalkboard each morning. Then ask students to recall current news events, providing as many details as they can remember. Model proper writing techniques as you list the news information on the board. Instruct the reporter for the day to type the board's information and save it to a file labeled for that day; then have her print out a hard copy. Finally have the reporter place the hard copy in a three-ring binder labeled "Current Events Log." The result will be an up-to-date record of the year's current events.

Kimberley M. Kidd—Gr. 4, Acequia Elementary, Rupert, ID

Cooperative Activities

In The News
Staging a newscast is an excellent way to get students excited about current news events! Tape-record the musical score from a well-known news program. Then transform your room into a news set using pull-down maps, tables, chairs, a plastic microphone, and a pointer. Assign students to be field reporters and select one student to anchor the news program. Have each field reporter research a current news story and report on it during the newscast. Instruct the anchor to prepare the necessary commentary to introduce the field reporters. Practice the newscast and then videotape it. Treat parents to a viewing of the videotape at Open House.

Ann Scheiblin, Oak View School, Bloomfield, NJ

Current-Events Newsletter
Current events provide a great opportunity to get students writing. Instruct your students to gather news stories of interest to them throughout the week. Then on Thursday have students decide which news stories should be included in your class newspaper for that week. Allow students to take turns being the reporters, editors, and publishers of the paper. Direct students to prepare the final copy of the paper on the class computer. Then make copies of the week's newspaper and have students distribute them around your school. What a super way to stay informed and work on teamwork!

Tammy Nelson—Gr. 5, St. Leo's School, Ridgway, PA

Cooperative News-Reporting Teams
Help each student develop a nose for news with this exciting activity. Divide your class into cooperative groups of three. Have the groups take turns being responsible for a week's news. Within each group, assign one reporter each for local, national, and world news. Have the assigned reporter follow news stories in his category for the week. Then have him write a description of the one story he feels is the top one of the week. Finally have the student write a brief summary of his thoughts on the issue. Allow the three reporters to share their stories with the class on Friday.

Lori Brandman—Gr. 5, Shallowford Falls Elementary, Marietta, GA

A Map Skills Excursion

Get your students ready for an adventure into the charted world of map skills! Use this collection of ideas and activities to prepare your students for a yearlong journey with map skills.

ideas by Joy Kalfas

Pretravel Preparation

Demonstrate the significance of maps with this introductory activity. Direct each student to fold a sheet of paper in half. Instruct him to write explicit directions on how to get to school from his house on one half of the paper; then have him quickly sketch a map that includes street names and landmarks to show the same route on the other half. Direct each student to exchange maps with a classmate and determine which is easier to follow—the written directions or the map. Explain that maps provide a picture and are therefore easier for many people to follow. Reinforce this concept by having each student visualize the following location: "Laos is a country in Asia that is located south of China. It is just east of Thailand and directly west of Vietnam." Discuss why this task is difficult. Next display a world map and have a volunteer locate Laos on the map using the same set of directions. Point out that using a map often makes it easier to find a location.

Conclude this activity by dividing your class into groups of four or five students. Give each group a sheet of chart paper and a marker. Instruct each group to title its paper "Why We Use Maps"; then have the group brainstorm and list uses for maps and why they are important. Create a master list of "Why We Use Maps" on the chalkboard from the students' responses.

Tour Groups

No trip is complete without tour groups! Explain that tour groups travel together and often wear distinguishable colors so they can spot one another and prevent one member from being separated from the group. Divide your class into tour groups of four or five students. Then arrange each child's desk so that he is in a cluster with his assigned tour group. Give each group a few sheets of construction paper, one sheet of poster board, and markers. Challenge the students to select names and catchy slogans for their tour groups. Then instruct each group to use the construction paper to design name badges and the poster board to make a banner that represents its group. For example, a group that chooses the name and slogan "Cloud Riders—Our map skills are far above the rest!" might design blue nametags and a banner decorated with clouds.

For the first assignment, provide each tour group with a variety of maps and atlases. Allow the groups a few minutes to familiarize themselves with the maps. Then have each group create a list of items that most maps contain. Have each group share its list, avoiding repetitions, as you record the responses on chart paper titled "Items On A Map." Keep the chart posted in the classroom for reference throughout your map skills unit.

Cloud Riders

Our map skills are far above the rest!

Stephen
Katie
Leigh
David

Exploring Map Scales

Maps are never as large as the part of the earth that they show—and that's why knowing how to read a map scale is a must for young geographers! Introduce the concept of map scales by having each student fold a sheet of paper in half. Display a U.S. map; then instruct each student to quickly draw an outline map of the United States on the left side of his paper and an outline map of his state on the right side. Most likely students will draw the two maps relatively the same size. Explain that a state map can be just as large as a U.S. map. Then introduce the term *scale* and explain that cartographers use a scale to tell us the relationship between real distances and the distances on a map. Demonstrate the importance of scaling down each portion of the map proportionally by discussing a model airplane or car. Point out that if the wings were scaled down less than the rest of the plane, it would look funny and would not be an accurate model.

Next direct each student to a page that displays a map in his social studies text. Discuss where to look for the map's scale; then demonstrate how to measure a distance on a map using the scale and a sheet of paper (see the illustrations). For practice have each student find various distances on maps that are in his social studies text or on a wall map. Then duplicate a class set of page 144 and have each student complete the page as directed.

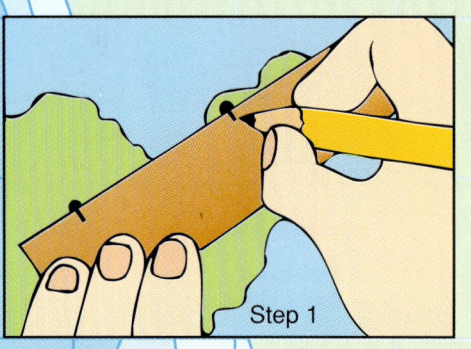 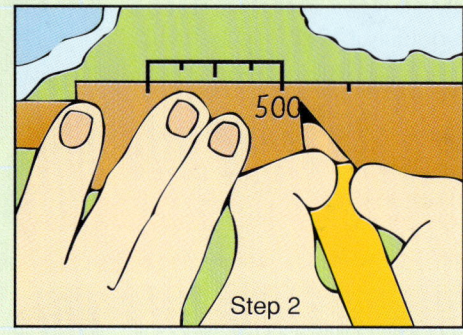 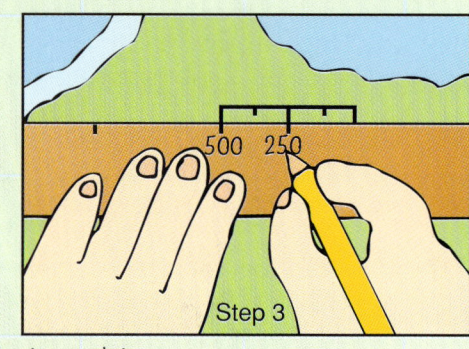

Step 1: Mark a piece of paper to show the distance between the two points.
Step 2: Place the paper along the map's scale. Line up the left mark with the zero on the scale. If the map scale is shorter than the distance, mark on the paper the endpoint of the scale and the distance it represents.
Step 3: Then line up that endpoint with the zero on the scale. Estimate the additional distance according to the scale. Add the two distances to find the total.

Battle Of The Brains

Pit your tour groups (see "Tour Groups" on page 21) against one another in this fast-paced challenge. Instruct each group to select a recorder; then announce one of the categories listed below. Give the groups two minutes to write down as many items that fit this category as possible on a sheet of paper. Encourage each tour group to whisper its responses to one another so that the other groups do not hear its answers. After two minutes call, "Pencils down" and have each group read aloud its written responses. Award each group one point for each correct response; then record the group's total points on the chalkboard. Continue the game by announcing a new category. The team with the most points at the end of the game is the winner.

Suggested categories: names of continents, names of oceans, states that begin with a specific letter, state capitals, foreign countries, foreign capitals, bodies of water, items found on a map

As The World Turns

When it's time to practice longitude and latitude, start spinning your classroom globe! Provide each student with a copy of a world map. Spin the globe; then stop it by placing your finger on a location. State the latitude and longitude of the location to which you are pointing. Then have each student find the called coordinates on her map and name the location of your secret vacation spot. For more latitude and longitude practice, duplicate one copy of page 145 for each student. Have each student fill in her bingo card as directed; then randomly call out the coordinates listed in the answer key on page 160 to play the game.

Visiting Various Symbols

Stars, dots, and lines—what would a map be without these symbols? Tell students that map *symbols* are pictures that stand for places that are too big to draw clearly on a map. Explain that a *legend* or *key* shows you what each symbol on the map means. Next have each tour group peruse a variety of atlases and maps in order to create a map legend for a town on a newly discovered planet. Have each group design a symbol for each of the following items: a mountain, a swamp, a river, a forest, a lake, an alien apartment building, a spaceship parking lot, a launchpad, and two other items of its choice. Give each group an 11" x 17" sheet of white construction paper on which to create its map legend. Instruct the group to use color on its legend and to be prepared to share each symbol with the class. As each group shares its legend, compare the different symbols used to show the same item. Display each group's legend on a wall. Or place each in a learning center; then challenge students to select a legend and use its symbols to draw a map of the imaginary town.

Venturing Across The Grid

Without a grid, finding a location on a map is like looking for a needle in a haystack! Relay this point to students by duplicating a section of a gridded street map for each child. Challenge each student to find a well-hidden road on the map. After students do some searching, explain how to find the location using the grid.

Next have students practice using grids by playing Cruise Ship. Label the vertical and the horizontal axes of a 10 x 10 grid as shown; then duplicate two copies per child. Have each student draw four cruise ships on one of his grids by coloring adjacent squares—two squares for his two-passenger cruise ship, three squares for his three-passenger cruise ship, four squares for his four-passenger cruise ship, and five squares for his five-passenger cruise ship. Divide your class into pairs. Instruct each pair to sit across from one another, but out of the view of one another's papers. In turn have each partner call out a grid location such as, "B7." Have his partner say, "Hit" if the student named a colored square and, "Miss" if he did not. Direct each partner to keep track of his called locations on the blank grid and the hits to his own ships on the colored grid. The first person to fill all four of his partner's ships (name each colored square) is the winner.

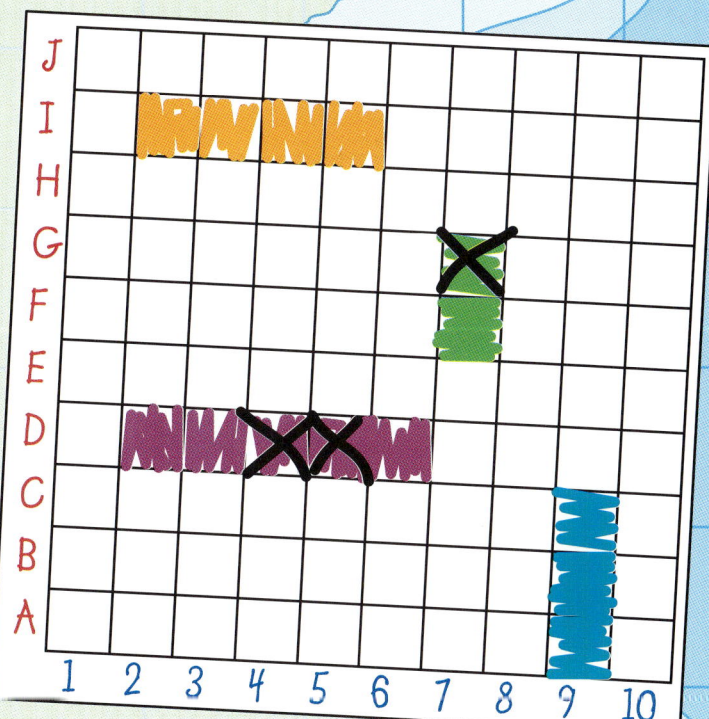

Final Destination

Wrap up your map skills adventure with a fun mapmaking project! Have each tour group apply its new map skills to create a map of a fictional city that is the perfect vacation spot for tourists. Provide each group with bulletin-board paper, rulers, pencils, several sheets of graph paper, and colored pencils or crayons; then write these steps on the chalkboard:

1. Name your vacation hot spot. Brainstorm at least seven tourist attractions in it.
2. Create a scale for your map. Use the scale to sketch the seven tourist attractions on a sheet of graph paper.
3. Draw a symbol for each attraction. Create a legend for your map.
4. Create and label a grid on your map.
5. Check your map for accuracy; then use the scale and your ruler to enlarge the map on to the bulletin-board paper.
6. Color your map and its legend.

Evaluate each group's map; then hang up each map for a classroom display.

Name _____ Map skills: using a scale

Scaling Around Orangestone Park

Put on your hiking boots, because your tour group is planning a hike through Orangestone Park! Your job is to determine the distance of a hike to the various locations on the map. Study the map of Orangestone Park; then use the scale along with a ruler or a sheet of notebook paper to measure the distances asked for in each of the questions below. Write your answers on the lines provided.

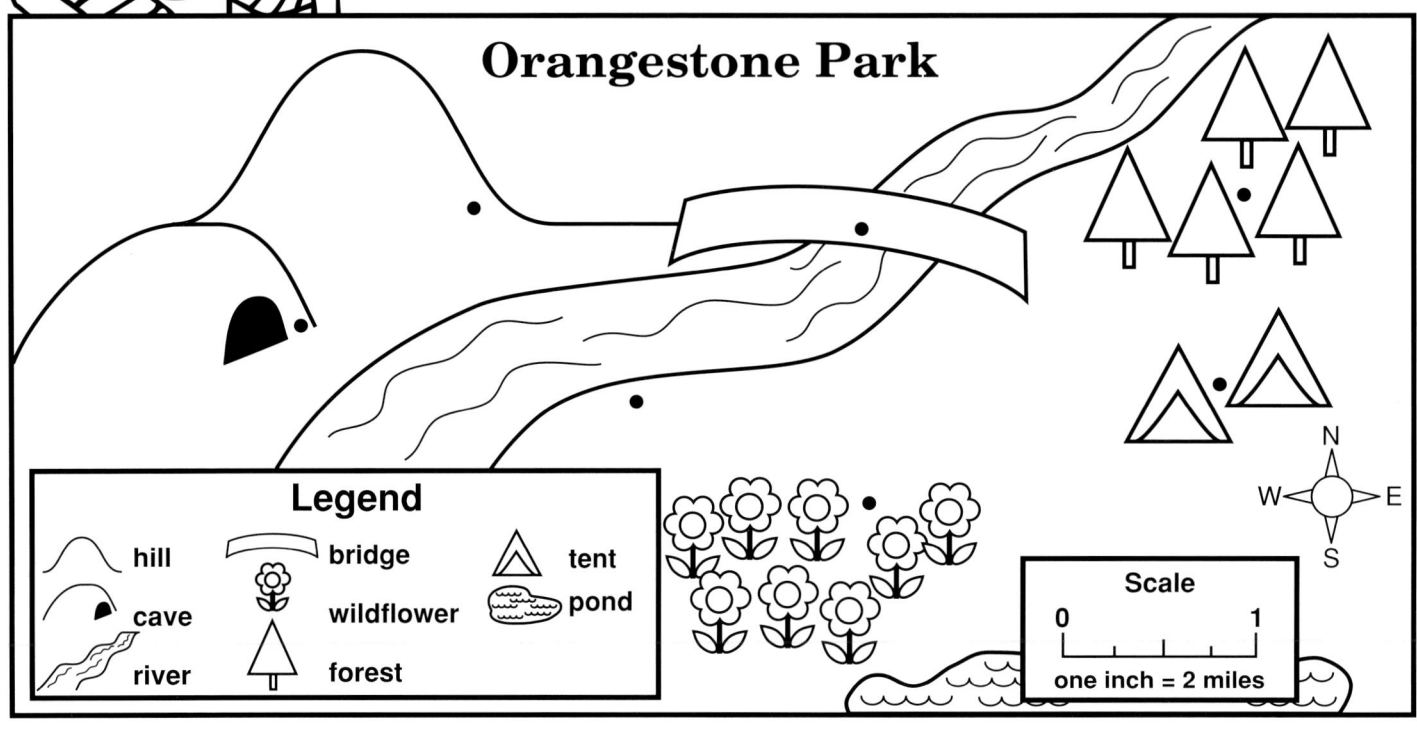

1. What distance does one inch equal on this map of Orangestone Park? _____
2. How far of a hike is it from the tents to the river? _____
3. How far will you have to hike to get to the hill from the tents? _____
4. If you hike from the wildflowers to the tents, then to the bridge, how many miles is your hike? ___
5. If you start at the bridge, is it shorter to hike to the hill or to the cave? _____ How much shorter? _____
6. If you start at the tents and hike across the bridge to the hill, then back across the bridge to the tents, how long is your hike? _____
7. How long is the hike from the hill to the cave? _____
8. If you hike from the tents to the forest, how many miles is your hike? _____
9. If you hike from the tents to the forest, then to the wildflowers, across the bridge, to the bottom of the hill, and finally to the cave, about how many miles will you hike? _____
10. One of your tour group members is lost in Orangestone Park. Follow these clues to find him.
    • From his tent, he hiked two miles north.
    • Then he hiked five miles southwest.
    • Finally he hiked about three miles northwest.
    Where is your friend? _____

Bonus Box: Pretend that you are lost somewhere in Orangestone Park. On the back of this paper, write clues to help your fellow hikers find you. Exchange your clues with a partner and see if he or she can rescue you.

©1999 The Education Center, Inc. • *The Best Of The Mailbox® Social Studies • Intermediate* • TEC1474 • Key p. 160

144   Note To The Teacher: Use this page with "Exploring Map Scales" on page 142.

Name_____   Map skills: latitude and longitude

Bingo With "L-attitude"

It's bingo time! Fill in each box of your bingo card with one of the cities listed below. Then listen for your teacher to call out a latitude and longitude coordinate. Look up each coordinate on your world map to find the city that is located there. If you have that city written on your bingo card, cover the square with a chip. Call out, "Bingo," if you cover five squares in a row vertically, horizontally, or diagonally.

LATITUDE

LONGITUDE

Amsterdam	Cairo	Helsinki	Milan	Rome
Athens	Calcutta	Johannesburg	Montreal	Santiago
Baghdad	Dublin	London	Moscow	Sydney
Beijing	Fairbanks	Madrid	Mumbai (Bombay)	Teheran
Brasília	Glasgow	Melbourne	Munich	Vienna
Buenos Aires	Harare	Mexico City	Oslo	

B I N G O

©1999 The Education Center, Inc. • *The Best Of* The Mailbox® *Social Studies* • *Intermediate* • TEC1474 • Key p. 160

Note To The Teacher: Use this page with "As the World Turns" on page 142. For a listing of the cities' latitude and longitude coordinates, see page 160. Give each student a handful of dried beans to use as bingo chips.

Sail Into Social Studies

Chart a course toward fun with these teacher-tested social studies ideas sent in by our subscribers!

"We The People..."

Introduce your students to the preamble of the U.S. Constitution by reading the book *We The People: The Constitution Of The United States Of America* (Doubleday & Company, Inc.; 1991) by Peter Spier. Then divide your class into small groups. Assign each group a phrase from the preamble such as "We the people," "establish justice," and "provide for the common defense." Direct each group to write its phrase on a large sheet of chart paper and then illustrate the phrase's meaning. After each group has illustrated its phrase, fasten the pages together in the correct order to make a big book outlining the preamble. Challenge your students to make similar books based on other historical documents or songs such as "America The Beautiful."

Elise Nash—Gr. 5, Delaware Academy, Delhi, NY

Westward Ho!

Put a new spin on your study of the westward expansion of the United States with this fun idea! Gather photos depicting families from the late 1800s—historical biographies are a great resource. Duplicate each photo and cut out the face of one of the figures. Tape a student's school photo underneath the empty space so that the child's face shows through; then make a copy and give it to the featured student. Repeat this procedure to make a personalized photo for each student. Challenge each student to design a frame for his family photo.

Extend this activity by having each student write several journal entries narrating his family's adventures as pioneers on the western frontier. Give the journal paper an aged appearance by painting brewed tea or coffee on unlined paper in advance of the writing activity. Display the finished photos and journal entries for others to enjoy!

Debbie Patrick—Gr. 5, Park Forest Elementary State College, PA

Mapping It Out

Having trouble finding a large map for a particular region your class is studying? Solve the problem by making a copy of a small map of the area. Draw evenly spaced grid lines on the map; then assign coordinates and make a copy for each student. Using a sheet of paper that is the desired size of your enlarged map, make a larger grid with the same coordinates as the small one. Cut apart the enlarged grid, giving each student one specific coordinate square. Direct each student to reproduce his assigned smaller grid square on his larger paper square with a pencil. Check each student's square against the original map grid for accuracy; then have the student revise as needed and trace over the pencil outline in black marker. Place the completed students' squares together to form a large map of your region of study.

Anna Coor—Gr. 5, Pendergast Elementary, Phoenix, AZ

Passport, Please!

Make studying other countries a real adventure with the help of personal passports. Begin by dividing the class into several small research groups. Assign each group a country to research. While groups are researching, duplicate one copy of the patterns below for each student. Make multiple copies of page 148 for each student (one copy for every two countries presented). Have each student follow the steps listed to the right to make a passport booklet.

Once passports are made, set aside a sharing day. Have each group teach the class about its country while classmates take notes on pages in their passports. For fun, provide a rubber stamp with which to stamp each child's passport after a group's presentation. By the end of the sharing session, each student will have a completed passport verifying the "trips" he took via his classmates. Adapt this idea to use when studying states or U.S. regions too.

Carrollyn Allen—Learning Disabilities
Western Middle School, Burlington, NC

Making a passport:

1. Fold a 9" x 7" sheet of construction paper in half to make a folded card.
2. Glue the passport cover pattern on the front of the card.
3. Fold your copies of the visa pages along the horizontal dotted line with the printed side facing out; then use a glue stick to glue the three edges of each folded paper together.
4. Stack the visa pages. Fold these pages together along the dotted vertical line in the center; then staple these pages inside the passport booklet as shown.
5. Glue the Passport Information Page atop the first page of the passport booklet as shown. Complete the information on this page.

Passport Cover Pattern

PASSPORT

United States of America

Passport Information Page

Passport Information

Name: _____

Address: _____

_____

Grade: _____ Homeroom: _____

Height: _____ Weight: _____

Eye color: _____

Hair color: _____

Date of birth: _____

Place of birth: _____

Date issued: _____

Date of expiration: _____

Draw or glue a picture of yourself in the box.

Signature: _____

©1999 The Education Center, Inc. • *The Best Of The Mailbox® Social Studies • Intermediate* • TEC1474

Visa

Country: _____
Capital: _____
Government: _____
Currency: _____
Major industry: _____
_____
Geography: _____
_____
Transportation: _____
_____
Language(s): _____
_____
Religion(s): _____
_____
Education: _____
_____

Illustrate the country's flag in this box.

Official Stamp

Date of entry: _____
Date of departure: _____
Notes (other interesting facts):
_____
_____
_____
_____
_____
_____
_____
_____
_____

Visa

Country: _____
Capital: _____
Government: _____
Currency: _____
Major industry: _____
_____
Geography: _____
_____
Transportation: _____
_____
Language(s): _____
_____
Religion(s): _____
_____
Education: _____
_____

Illustrate the country's flag in this box.

Official Stamp

Date of entry: _____
Date of departure: _____
Notes (other interesting facts):
_____
_____
_____
_____
_____
_____
_____
_____
_____

Note To The Teacher: Use with "Passport, Please!" on page 147.

TRAVELING TRAVELOGS

Take your class on a grand tour of the globe—without having to leave the classroom—with this exciting geography project!

by Patricia Altmann

What Is A Traveling Travelog?

In this project, each student will make a travelog consisting of a journal and a scrapbook. The *journal* is sent to an out-of-town friend, who is asked to complete information about his or her city, state, or country. This person is also asked to send the student a postcard from his or her city, then forward the journal to another friend. The journal will be returned to the student after it has traveled to six different locations. The *scrapbook* is kept in the classroom to display postcards and to record data on the locations the journal visits. After all the traveling journals are returned to your students, complete the activities below for some "geo-rific" practice with important skills.

Activities To Do After The Journals Are Returned

- Using a U.S. and/or world map and its mileage scale, estimate the distance your travelog traveled. Then find the latitude and longitude of each location in your travelog.
- Write a first-person narrative from the viewpoint of your journal about its journey.
- Choose one place your journal visited that you would like to visit one day. Write a short paragraph explaining your choice.
- Make a travel brochure about one of the places your journal visited.
- Create a mural, collage, or pop-up book showing all of the locations your journal visited.

Getting Ready

The first step is to have each student make his travelog journal and scrapbook.

Materials For Each Student:
1 copy of pages 150, 151, and 153; 2 copies of page 152; 4 sheets of construction paper in various colors; 1 recent student photograph; 1 envelope; stapler; glue; crayons

Making The Travelog Journal:
1. Have each student complete page 150.
2. Have the student color his copy of page 151 and glue his photograph where indicated.
3. Have the student staple together page 150, page 151, and the two copies of page 152 (in that order).
4. Have the student address an envelope with an out-of-town friend's address, write the school's return address on the envelope, and then place his travelog journal inside.
5. Mail each student's journal.

Making The Travelog Scrapbook:
1. Have the student staple the four sheets of construction paper together.
2. Instruct the student to glue the top half of page 153 to the first page of the scrapbook. Then have him glue the bottom half of page 153 onto the next page. Have the student glue the postcards he receives on both sides of the remaining pages.
3. When a student's travelog journal returns, instruct him to use the information in each entry to complete his Travelog Scrapbook Data Sheet.

Dear friend,

I am a student in the _____ grade at _____ in
(grade number)   (school's name)
_____, _____, USA. I am learning about U.S. and world geogra-
        (city)   (state)
phy. With your help I can learn more about many different places. Here's how you can help me:

1. Complete one journal entry in my attached Travelog Journal by writing about the city in which you live.
2. Send a postcard from your city addressed to me at the school address below.
3. Send my Travelog Journal on to a friend or relative who lives in a different region of the United States or another country.

I will be keeping track of my journal's journeys back here in the classroom. I've created a scrapbook for the postcards that I'll receive from around the country and the world. I will also record in my scrapbook data on each location my journal visits.

Thank you for helping me with this fun project. Don't forget to send me a postcard and forward my journal to a friend. If you are the last person to receive my journal or if it is close to the due date below, please return my Travelog Journal to the address below along with your postcard.

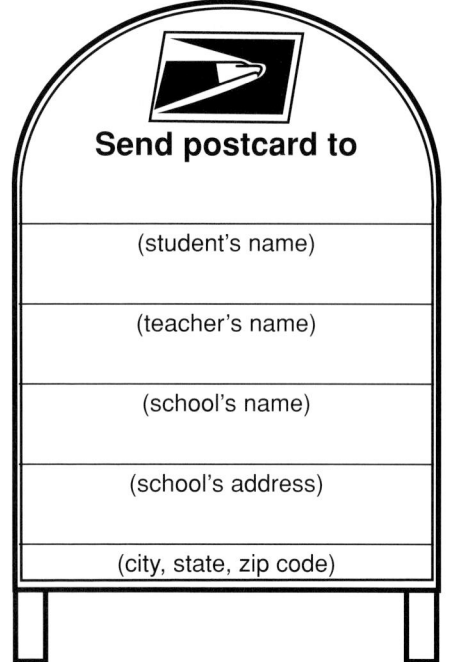

Send postcard to

(student's name)

(teacher's name)

(school's name)

(school's address)

(city, state, zip code)

Sincerely,

_____
(student's name)

VERY IMPORTANT

This Travelog Journal is due back to the address at the left by _____.
(date)

©1999 The Education Center, Inc. • *The Best Of* The Mailbox® *Social Studies • Intermediate* • TEC1474

150   **Note To The Teacher:** Use with "Getting Ready" on page 149.

Travelog Journal Entry

Date: _____

Name: _____ Location: _____
Climate: _____
_____
Landmarks: _____
_____
_____
Industries: _____
_____
_____
Other neat facts: _____
_____
_____

Travelog Journal Entry

Date: _____

Name: _____ Location: _____
Climate: _____
_____
Landmarks: _____
_____
_____
Industries: _____
_____
_____
Other neat facts: _____
_____
_____

Travelog Journal Entry

Date: _____

Name: _____ Location: _____
Climate: _____
_____
Landmarks: _____
_____
_____
Industries: _____
_____
_____
Other neat facts: _____
_____
_____

©1999 The Education Center, Inc. • *The Best Of* The Mailbox® *Social Studies • Intermediate* • TEC1474

Note To The Teacher: Use with "Getting Ready" on page 149.

MY TRAVELOG SCRAPBOOK

_____
(student's name)

TRAVELOG SCRAPBOOK DATA SHEET

	Location	Climate	Landmarks	Industries	Other Neat Facts
1					
2					
3					
4					
5					
6					

Note To The Teacher: Use the two forms above with "Getting Ready" on page 149.

Setting The Stage For Social Studies

Get ready to draw back the curtain on exciting, new ideas for teaching U.S. geography and government. They're sure to leave students yelling, "Encore!"

Living Geography

Liven up a lesson on physical geography by having students act out the topography of different U.S. regions. Divide students into six groups. Arrange the groups in a right-to-left (east-to-west) order; then assign each group a different region from the chart shown. Beginning with the coastal lowlands, direct each group to perform its assigned part. When all the actions have been completed, ask students to observe the diversity of the resulting landscape.

Cathy Ogg—Gr. 4
Happy Valley Elementary
Johnson City, TN

Coastal Lowlands—lie flat on floor
Appalachian Highlands/Ozark-Ouachita Highlands—stand upright with hands clasped together above heads
Interior Plains—lie flat on floor
Rocky Mountains—stand upright on chairs with hands clasped together above heads
Western Plateaus, Basins, And Ranges—some lie flat on floor; others lie on floor on their backs, holding legs and arms up to make a U-shape
Pacific Ranges And Lowlands—some mimic the Rocky Mountains group; others lie flat on floor

Welcome To Congress!

Help students appreciate the role lawmakers play in our government by transforming your classroom into a mock Congress. Announce that you will act as president for the next three days. Assign each student a role as a U.S. senator or member of the House of Representatives from a different state. Then follow this three-day plan:

Day One: Have each student make a nametag that designates his title. Direct the senators to sit on one side of the classroom and the representatives on the other. Have each student write a *bill*—a brief proposal he hopes will become a law (a new classroom rule).

Day Two: Have each student present his bill. Direct the House of Representatives and the Senate to vote on each bill; then have Congress send on any bills receiving unanimous consent in both houses to you for approval. Sign or veto the bills, reminding students that Congress can override your presidential veto with a 2/3 majority vote in both houses.

Day Three: During this day, observe the laws that were voted into effect. Follow up by having each student write a paragraph explaining how a bill becomes a law.

Leslie Davidson—Gr. 4
New Caney Elementary
New Caney, TX

Review Preview

Looking for a fun way for students to review U.S. states and capitals and important geography terms? Use the challenging puzzle on page 155 and the wordplay activity on page 156 to fill the bill!

Freddy's Capital Challenge

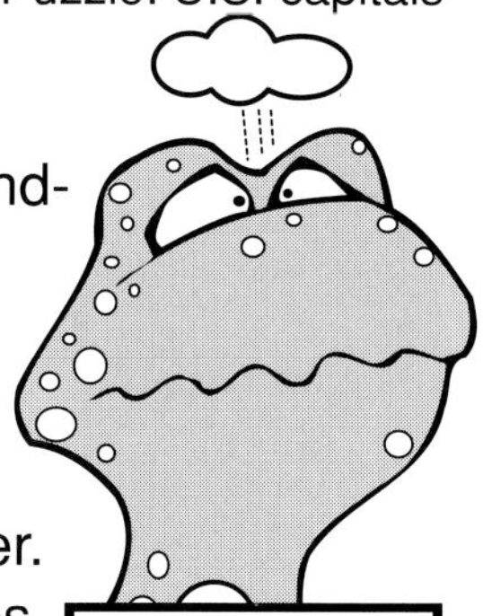

Freddy and his froggy friends are fried! They've been stumped by the states-and-capitals puzzle below. The states and capitals on the sides of the boxes do not match. To help Freddy and the gang, follow these steps:

1. Cut out the boxes and save the bottom portion of this page.
2. Arrange the boxes so that *all* their sides match a capital city with its state.
3. When you're finished, glue the boxes in place on a sheet of construction paper. Glue the bottom portion of this page to the construction paper below the boxes.
4. Look at the bold letter in the center of each box. Beginning with the box at the top right, copy the letters onto the blanks below the boxes in a left-to-right order. The resulting sentence will tell you one more thing to do.

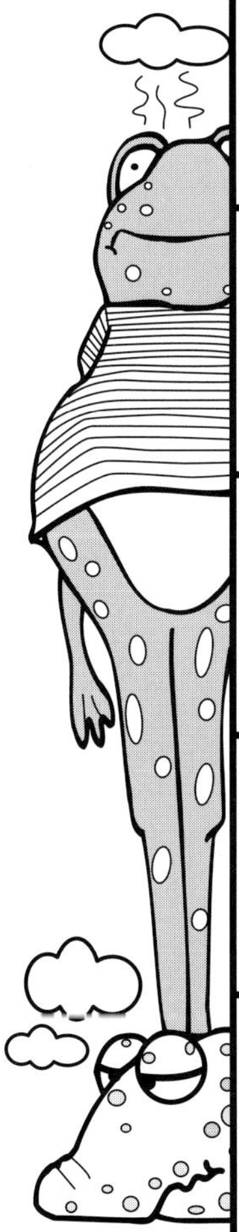

Puzzle: U.S. capitals

N — OK

MD / **A** / NV	WA / **E** / NH	Austin / **H** / NJ	Santa Fe / **T** / MO	Lansing / **M** / OR	Carson City / Olympia / Jackson	Frankfort / **A** / Phoenix
IN / **U** / MT	Dover / **T** / CO	CA / Montgomery / **A** / Salem / FL	Tallahassee / **P** / PA	Concord / Baton Rouge / **F** / DE	ND / Juneau / **D** / IA	
Lincoln	Columbia	Springfield	Bismarck	Providence	Boise	
Annapolis / **C** / AL	SC / **T** / HI	Honolulu / **E** / AK	Jefferson City / **I** / UT	Trenton / Salt Lake City / **T** / MS	Oklahoma City / NM / **E** / KY	
Raleigh	St. Paul	Albany	Sacramento	Hartford		
NC / **L** / MA	Columbus / **I** / AR	CT / Denver / **H** / TN	IL / Boston / **O** / LA	KS / Helena / **N** / OH	AZ / Nashville / **E**	
Indianapolis	Atlanta	Pierre	Topeka	Augusta	Des Moines	
NE / **S** / VA	NY / Cheyenne / **E** / WV	ME / Richmond / **T** / WI	MN / Montpelier / **T** / WY	GA / Madison / **A** / VT	ID / Charleston / **S**	

___ ___ ___ ___ ___ ___ ___

___ .

_____

Bonus Box: Name the two states that gave land for the site of our national capital.

Name _____   Reviewing geography terms; wordplay

You Must Be Hearing Things!

Freddy has been studying hard for a geography quiz. So hard that he's beginning to hear things. In fact, he's even hearing the words he studied in other people's conversations! Look at the bold words and letters in the sentences below to help you figure out the words Freddy's hearing. Write each word in the blank provided. Then write the letter of the matching definition below in the blank beside each word. The first one has been done for you.

1. **I** saw the sky diver **land** in the field.
2. Skiers flock to the **beaut**iful Rocky Mountains in winter.
3. Natalie's dog chewed on her dad's **golf** balls.
4. Stan got a **base** hit **in** the third inning.
5. The **sores** on the dog's paws were almost healed.
6. Ned's song was a **tribute** to his friend **Carrie.**
7. **Can Juan** identify the rock?
8. The **mound** of sand must have weighed a **ton.**
9. To**day's** game ended with no one getting **hurt.**
10. Todd walked **straight** over to the game booth.
11. Amy thought it was strange that the museum had a **plaque** of an elephant's **toe.**
12. My uncle's air**plane** arrived on time at the airport.
13. The **pens in** the box belonged to **Sue La** Grande.
14. The main character in the book had to **save** his sister **Anna** from the bear.
15. **His** bicycle **must** be brand-new.
16. **Val** and **Lee** signed up for the talent show.

	Word	Definition
1.	*island*	F
2.		
3.		
4.		
5.		
6.		
7.		
8.		
9.		
10.		
11.		
12.		
13.		
14.		
15.		
16.		

A. small, flat-topped hill with steep sides
B. large or small depression in the land or the ocean floor
C. very deep valley with steep sides
D. very dry place, with little rainfall and few plants
E. part of the ocean that extends into the land
F. body of land completely surrounded by water
G. narrow strip of land joining two larger bodies of land
H. land with a broad base that rises sharply into a peak from the land around it
I. piece of land extending into the water from a larger body of land
J. large, high, rather level area that is raised above the surrounding land
K. treeless grassland, or a grassland with a few trees and bushes
L. place where a stream or river begins
M. narrow body of water that connects two larger bodies of water
N. stream that empties into a larger stream or lake
O. long, low area, usually between hills or mountains or along a river
P. wide area of flat or gently rolling land

Am I hearing things?

Bonus Box: On the back of this sheet, write sentences like the ones above for the words *canal, channel, continent, harbor, delta,* and *oasis.* Then have a classmate try to guess the geography word in each sentence and tell its meaning.

Answer Keys

Answer Keys

Page 17
1. Philadelphia
2. Baltimore
3. Boston
4. Newport
5. Charleston
6. New York City

Page 18
Answers will vary.
1. Abigail Adams, the wife of John Adams, influenced her husband to consider the rights of women.
2. John Adams was one of the first to propose independence and helped write the Declaration of Independence.
3. Samuel Adams led Boston's resistance to the Tea Act.
4. Ethan Allen was a patriot of the American Revolution and leader of the Green Mountain Boys.
5. Crispus Attucks was the first man killed in the Boston Massacre.
6. George Rogers Clark was an American soldier who prevented the British from claiming what later became the Northwest Territory.
7. Margaret Corbin took her husband's place when he was killed during battle and continued to fight until she was seriously wounded.
8. William Dawes rode with Paul Revere and Samuel Prescott to warn colonists that the British were coming.
9. James Forten was captured in the war at the age of 15 and spent seven months on a British prison ship.
10. Benjamin Franklin persuaded the French to help the colonists during the war.
11. Nathanael Greene was a revolutionary soldier who was responsible for victories in the South.
12. Nathan Hale became a hero when he volunteered to spy on the British for George Washington.
13. John Hancock was the first to sign the Declaration of Independence.
14. Mary "Molly Pitcher" Hays carried pitchers of water to her husband and other soldiers during the Battle of Monmouth.
15. Patrick Henry spoke the words, "give me liberty or give me death!"
16. Thomas Jefferson wrote the Declaration of Independence.
17. John Paul Jones was an American naval captain who captured 16 ships on his first cruise aboard the *Providence* in 1776.
18. Marquis de Lafayette was a French military leader who served as a major general in the Continental Army.
19. Richard Henry Lee was a leader of the American Revolution who proposed a resolution restricting the importation of slaves.
20. Francis Marion, nicknamed "swamp fox," commanded the capture of British forts in Charleston, South Carolina.
21. Thomas Paine wrote *Common Sense,* a document that helped persuade colonists to push for independence.
22. Samuel Prescott warned the colonists of Lincoln and Concord that the British were coming after Revere was captured and Dawes was forced to retreat.
23. Paul Revere rode with Prescott and Dawes to warn Concord colonists that the British were coming.
24. Deborah Sampson disguised herself as a man and fought in the American Revolution.
25. Roger Sherman was appointed to the committee to write the Declaration of Independence.
26. Friedrich von Steuben was a Prussian-American general who reformed the army to make it more disciplined and efficient.
27. George Washington led Americans in their fight for independence.
28. Phillis Wheatley was a slave who wrote a poem about America's struggle for freedom.

Page 24
1. May was the best time to start if pioneers were leaving from Independence, Missouri. If pioneers started too early, the rainy spring left mud that would trap wagon wheels. Also the grass wouldn't be tall or thick enough to feed the cattle on the trip. If they started too late, the winter snowfall could trap them in the mountains.
2. *Scows,* large flat boats, took wagons across the Missouri River at the start of the trip. Once into Indian territory, some Indians would use rafts to help the pioneers cross if they paid them. Some pioneers would work together to build rafts from willow branches and long grasses to get the wagons across. Other times pioneers took the wheels off their wagons and floated them across after their boards had been sealed watertight with tar or wax mixed with ashes. It could take a large wagon train five days to get everyone across the river.
3. Some pioneers put the eggs in the flour barrel.
4. The pioneers learned from the Indians how to dry the meat through a process called *jerking.* These dried meat strips kept for a long time.
5. The pioneers burned dried buffalo droppings—called *buffalo chips*—for their fires. In the Rocky Mountains, the pioneers burned sagebrush branches and roots.
6. There were a few forts and trading posts along the trail where wagon trains could stop. Here the pioneers could buy or trade for items, such as sugar, flour, coffee, and leather. However these supplies were not always available.
7. Sometimes pioneers had to borrow a neighbor's oxen to help get a wagon up a high mountain. Once at the top, the pioneers would send the oxen back down the mountain to bring up the next wagon. Some people left large items and boxes along the trail because they just couldn't get them over the mountains.
8. The pioneers put poles between the wheel spokes to prevent the wheels from turning too fast. Also they tied one end of a rope to a large tree at the top of the mountain and the other end to the back of the wagon. This allowed the pioneers to loosen the rope slowly and ease the wagon down the mountain.

Bonus Box: Many westward travelers—including children—kept diaries while on the trails.

Page 29
Answers will vary. Possible answers include:
1. Railroads were needed to transport supplies, soldiers, and weapons during the war. They were also needed to ship raw materials to factories.
2. Southern cotton growers needed the northern factories to process their cotton. During the war, the cotton could not be shipped to the North for processing.
3. Lack of adequate railroad track, wealth produced, farms, and bank deposits would all affect the South's ability to feed its soldiers and citizens.
4. Money was needed to finance all aspects of the war: salaries, uniforms, weapons, food, medical supplies, etc.
5. Because almost the entire war was fought in the South, the North was forced to invade the South. The Union army had to ship supplies across enemy lines and camp in unfamiliar and unfriendly territory.

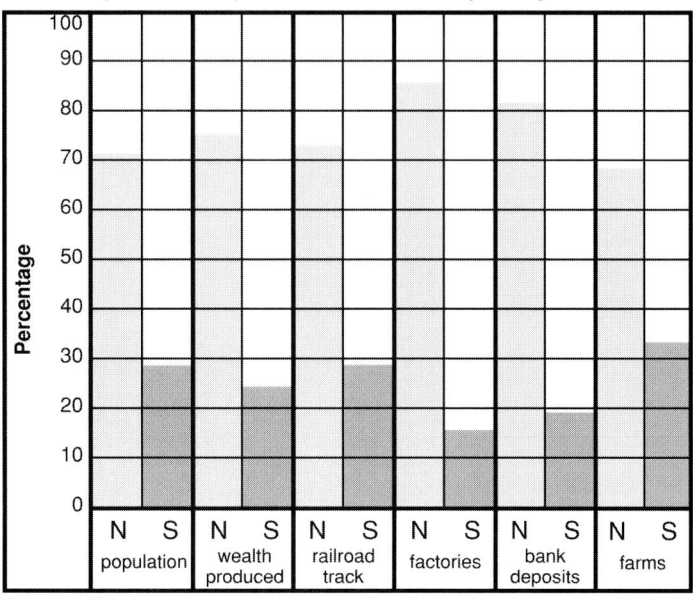

Page 38
1. France
2. Belgium
3. The Netherlands
4. Denmark
5. Norway
6. Finland
7. Estonia
8. Latvia
9. Lithuania
10. Czechoslovakia
11. Poland
12. Austria
13. Hungary
14. Romania
15. Yugoslavia
16. Albania
17. Greece
18. Bulgaria
19. Russia

Page 45
1. National Leader
2. Head Of State
3. Legislative Leader
4. Commander In Chief
5. Head Of State
6. Party Leader
7. Commander In Chief
8. National Leader
9. Chief Diplomat
10. Chief Executive
11. Legislative Leader
12. Chief Diplomat

Page 73
1. The <u>Etruscans</u> lived in Italy before the rise of the Roman Empire.
2. <u>Romulus</u> and <u>Remus</u> founded Rome in 753 B.C.
3. The city-state of <u>Carthage</u> was located on the continent of Africa.
4. The <u>Roman Empire</u> surrounded the Mediterranean Sea.
5. The <u>Forum</u> was used for business, government, religious, and social activities.
6. The <u>Roman Empire</u> included England.
7. <u>Julius Caesar</u> was assassinated on March 15 in 44 B.C.
8. The main <u>road</u> that led out of Rome was called the Appian Way.
9. Roman <u>public bathhouses</u> were heated by hot air from furnaces channeled beneath the floors.
10. The volcano that buried <u>Pompeii</u> was Mount Vesuvius.
11. <u>Aqueducts</u> were used to carry water from the mountains to homes and other buildings.
12. <u>Gladiators</u> were slaves or warriors who fought to the death for the entertainment of the Romans.
13. A <u>Centurion</u> was a Roman soldier who was in charge of a group of soldiers in the Roman army.
14. The animal used to pull a <u>chariot</u> was a horse.
15. <u>Trajan's Column</u> is a famous stone monument illustrating the history of the emperor Trajan's military conquests.

Answer Keys

Page 74
1. Answers will vary.
2. Answer will vary: I–XXXI
3. Answer will vary: XXVIII, XXIX, XXX, or XXXI
4. XXII
5. CCCLXV
6. L
7. XXIII
8. IX
9. DCLVI
10. MCCCXLVII
11. Answers will vary.
12. Answer will vary.
13. MMMMCCLXXX
14. Answer will vary.
15. M̄M̄

Page 77
Answer Key for "Thanks For The Words"
Dutch: cruise, schooner, waffle
Spanish: chili, cocoa, machete, mustang, rodeo, stampede
French: beret, cadet, camouflage, champagne, chef, garage
German: delicatessen, Fahrenheit, hamburger, kindergarten, loafer, waltz
Greek: circus, dialect, genesis, nausea, phobia, psyche
Italian: balcony, balloon, broccoli, studio, trombone, violin
From The Netherlands: skate, sleigh

Page 80

See a world map in a current almanac for the boundaries and capitals of specific countries for Parts 3 and 4.

Page 81
Answer Key for "Buy Why?: An Introductory Activity"
- Money was rarely used in medieval times except by merchants. In the system of feudalism, nobles called *lords* ruled over sections of land granted to them by a king, in exchange for the promise of loyalty and the provision of fighting men. In turn, each lord granted smaller parcels of land to his knights and people who served under him, named *vassals*. A lord and his vassals had certain rights and duties toward each other. Poor peasants usually bartered or swapped goods.

- Stone made the castles better able to withstand attack. Stone walls could also be built several feet thick, which made it almost impossible for enemies to batter holes in them.

- Medieval towns were usually quite crowded and extremely dirty. The buildings were made of wattle and daub and timber. Because thoro woro no otrootlighto, people carried torches at night, which made fire a great risk. Human waste and garbage were thrown out in the streets, making disease a real risk too.

- In general, knights came from the upper level of society. It was expensive to be a knight; he needed a horse and expensive weaponry. Also it was a general rule—except in England—that only sons of knights could become knights.

- Education was not considered essential for either men or women in the Middle Ages. Most women had never attended school.

- By the 1000s, there were capable lords who provided some strong governments. Europe experienced more stability and peace during this period, which gave people time to explore new ideas and activities. Many peasants began to leave the manors in search of better jobs. More people became merchants and craftspersons. Medieval towns also grew due to the increase in trade.

- A deadly and highly contagious disease called the Black Death—which was carried by black rats and was also known as the bubonic plague—swept through Europe from 1347–1350. No cure was ever found.

- Because the few wars that were fought were waged in large-scale battles, kings and nobles no longer needed fortresses as homes. Castles were also deemed too old-fashioned, as more modern structures were now being built. And with the invention of gunpowder, castles were no longer invincible to attack.

Page 92

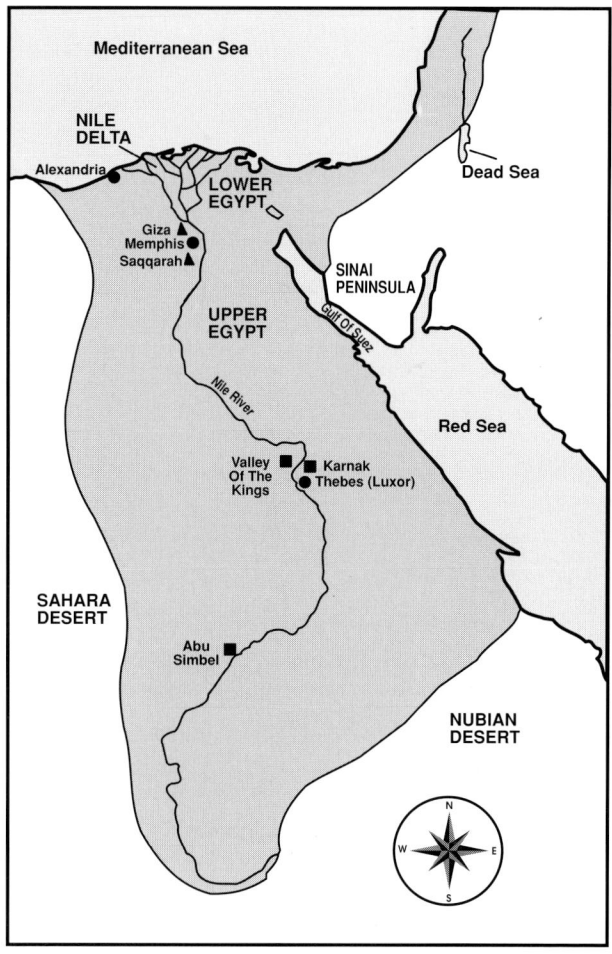

Page 98
1. Al
2. Sears Tower; 1,454 feet; 110 stories
3. 1866; Nobel
4. 168 gallons
5. South Africa, France, Gabon, Australia
6. 130,119 square miles
7. Roger Staubach
8. Hurricane Camille; 256 deaths
9. c. 610—c. 580 B.C.
10. James Buchanan
11. Death of a close family member
12. 200 Constitution Ave., NW, Washington, DC 20210

Page 100
Location: 1, 7, 16, 20
Place: 3, 4, 12, 18
Relationships Within Places: 6, 9, 13, 15
Movement: 2, 10, 17, 19
Regions: 5, 8, 11, 14

Accept any reasonable variations of these answers.

Page 117
The following is one way that the snow blocks can correctly be arranged. Italicized information indicates other months during which this information could be correct.

January: Stay indoors and play games and tell stories. *(February)*
February: Hunt for seal as they come up through breathing holes. *(January)*
March: Start of whaling season. Get new set of clothing.
April: Hunt seal from kayak. *(March, May)*
May: Sea ice melting. Move family inland. *(June)*
June: Gather berries and roots to eat. *(July, August)*
July: Midsummer sun. Wear underclothing with fur turned out.
August: Hunt whales that migrate north after sea ice melts. *(March, April, May, June, July)*
September: Dry seal skin while there is still sun. *(June, July, August)*
October: Hunt caribou while they are fat and furry. *(September, November)*
November: Set up winter camp on sea ice. *(October)*
December: Get ready for constant darkness by end of month.

Answer Keys

Page 118
1. D (I'm friendly.)
2. F (South is that way.)
3. C (Amaroq is the leader.)
4. B (Caribou are nearby.)
5. I (He was suspicious of Miyax.)
6. H (It's time for the wolves to hunt.)
7. G (It is autumn.)
8. E (It is August 24.)
9. A (Winter is on the way.)
10. J (The lemmings are returning.)

Page 131
The 15 mistakes are:
- Africa and South America have been switched.
- The equator is labeled on the wrong latitude line.
- The border of Mexico is too far north.
- The Pacific Ocean and Atlantic Ocean labels are reversed.
- Australia is shown upside down.
- Antarctica is incorrectly labeled Arctic.
- China is too large.
- Japan is incorrectly labeled Taiwan.
- The Great Lakes are located too far west.
- Florida is shaped like Italy.
- Hawaii is incorrectly located in the Caribbean Sea.
- Greenland is incorrectly labeled Iceland.
- An imaginary island is shown in the Indian Ocean.
- Alaska is incorrectly located in eastern Canada.
- The Suez Canal is incorrectly shown in Central America.

Page 134
1. Alaska (state)
2. France (country)
3. South America (continent)
4. Ohio (state)
5. Iceland (country)
6. Australia (country and continent)
7. Chile (country)
8. India (country)
9. Italy (country)
10. Minnesota (state)
11. Idaho (state)
12. Egypt (country)
13. Antarctica (continent)
14. Louisiana (state)
15. Madagascar (country)

Page 144
1. 2 miles
2. 6 miles
3. 8 miles
4. about 8 miles
5. It is shorter to hike to the hill.; about 2 miles
6. about 16 miles
7. 2 miles
8. 2 miles
9. about 16 miles
10. Your friend is at the river.

Page 145
Also use with "As The World Turns" on page 142.

52°N	4.5°E	Amsterdam, Netherlands
37.5°N	23°E	Athens, Greece
33°N	44°E	Baghdad, Iraq
39.5°N	116°E	Beijing, China
15.5°S	47.5°W	Brasília, Brazil
34°S	58°W	Buenos Aires, Argentina
30°N	31°E	Cairo, Egypt
22°N	88°E	Calcutta, India
53°N	6°W	Dublin, Ireland
64.5°N	147.5°W	Fairbanks, Alaska, USA
55.5°N	4°W	Glasgow, Scotland
17°S	31°E	Harare, Zimbabwe
60°N	25°E	Helsinki, Finland
26°S	28°E	Johannesburg, South Africa
51°N	0.1°W	London, England
40°N	3°W	Madrid, Spain
37°S	144.5°E	Melbourne, Australia
19°N	99°W	Mexico City, Mexico
45°N	9°E	Milan, Italy
45°N	73°W	Montreal, Quebec, Canada
55°N	37°E	Moscow, Russia
18.5°N	72.5°E	Mumbai (Bombay), India
48°N	11°E	Munich, Germany
59.5°N	10°E	Oslo, Norway
41.5°N	12°E	Rome, Italy
33°S	70°W	Santiago, Chile
33.5°S	151°E	Sydney, Australia
35°N	51°E	Teheran, Iran
48°N	16°E	Vienna, Austria

Page 155

Spelled-out sentence: NAME THE CAPITAL OF THE UNITED STATES.
Answer: Washington, D.C.
Bonus Box: Maryland *and* Virginia

Page 156
1. island; F
2. butte; A
3. gulf; E
4. basin; B
5. source; L
6. tributary; N
7. canyon; C
8. mountain; H
9. desert; D
10. strait; M
11. plateau; J
12. plain; P
13. peninsula; I
14. savanna; K
15. isthmus; G
16. valley; O